Lecture Notes in Computer Scienc

Edited by G. Goos and J. Hartmanis

Advisory Board: W. Brauer   D. Gries   J. Stoer

G. Vosselman

Relational Matching

Springer-Verlag
Berlin Heidelberg New York
London Paris Tokyo
Hong Kong Barcelona
Budapest

Series Editors

Gerhard Goos
Universität Karlsruhe
Postfach 69 80
Vincenz-Priessnitz-Straße 1
W-7500 Karlsruhe, FRG

Juris Hartmanis
Department of Computer Science
Cornell University
5149 Upson Hall
Ithaca, NY 14853, USA

Author

George Vosselman
Institute of Photogrammetry, University of Stuttgart
Keplerstr. 11, W-7000 Stuttgart 1, FRG

Dissertation der Landwirtschaftlichen Fakultät der
Rheinischen Friedrich-Wilhelms-Universität Bonn
D 98

CR Subject Classification (1991): I.2.8, I.5.4, H.1.1

ISBN 3-540-55798-9 Springer-Verlag Berlin Heidelberg New York
ISBN 0-387-55798-9 Springer-Verlag New York Berlin Heidelberg

This work is subject to copyright. All rights are reserved, whether the whole or part of
the material is concerned, specifically the rights of translation, reprinting, re-use of
illustrations, recitation, broadcasting, reproduction on microfilms or in any other way,
and storage in data banks. Duplication of this publication or parts thereof is permitted
only under the provisions of the German Copyright Law of September 9, 1965, in its
current version, and permission for use must always be obtained from Springer-Verlag.
Violations are liable for prosecution under the German Copyright Law.

© Springer-Verlag Berlin Heidelberg 1992
Printed in Germany

Typesetting: Camera ready by author/editor
45/3140-543210 - Printed on acid-free paper

Preface

This book is the result of an elementary study on relational matching. Relational matching is a method for finding the best correspondences between structural descriptions. In computer vision it is widely used for the recognition and location of objects in digital images. For this purpose, the digital images and the object models are represented by structural descriptions. The matching algorithm then has to determine which image elements and object model parts correspond.

This study particularly focuses on the evaluation of the correspondences. In order to find the best match, one needs a measure to evaluate the quality of a match. This measure usually quantifies the similarity between the image and the model elements. This strategy is based on the assumption that corresponding elements will have similar characteristics (like size, shape, etc.). This study reviews the evaluation measures that have been suggested over the past few decades and presents a new measure that is based on information theory. This new measure is integrated into tree search methods that are utilized to find the best match.

The resulting relational matching theory hence combines matching strategies, information theory, and tree search methods. Because the reader may not be familiar with all aspects, comprehensive introductions are given to these topics.

I would like to thank my supervisor, Prof. Wolfgang Förstner, for the pleasant cooperation and the many interesting discussions we had. I would also like to thank the German Research Society, which financed the Special Research Program "High Precision Navigation" (SFB 228) at the University of Stuttgart. The research for this thesis was performed within the image processing project of this research program.

Stuttgart, June 1992   George Vosselman

Contents

II Theory of relational matching

III   Object location by relational matching

Part I

Introduction to relational matching

1   Computer Vision and Matching

Computer Vision is the kind of image processing that results in information about the spatial and physical properties of the objects that have been recorded in digital images [Rosenfeld and Kak 1976, Ballard and Brown 1982]. It has outgrown all other areas within digital image processing and is the dominating theme on most conferences on image processing.

Traditionally Computer Vision research was done by electrotechnical engineers and physicists, but quite soon many other disciplines like medicine, mathematics, computer science, psychology, photogrammetry and other engineering disciplines joined in. This resulted in a very broad domain for applications of Computer Vision. Although the fields of applications often are very different, the image processing techniques that are used and the problems that have to be solved have very much in common. One of these common problems is the *correspondence problem*, or *matching problem*.

1.1   Correspondence problems

The correspondence problem is the problem of finding the corresponding features out of two or more data descriptions. It is one of the central and most difficult problems in Computer Vision: surface reconstruction from stereo images requires corresponding points from two images, recorded objects can only be recognized by matching image descriptions with object models and automatic navigation systems have to match images to digital maps.

The data of these images, object models, or maps can be described at different levels of abstraction.

At the lowest level images are described by their grey values. Algorithms matching small patches of grey value images have been developed to determine parallaxes [Helava 1976, Förstner and Pertl 1986] or to measure coordinates of signalized points by matching the image with an artificial mask.

At the next level features like points, lines and regions that can be extracted from the images are used for the matching. Surface reconstruction of recorded objects or terrains can be performed by matching the features of stereo images [Marr and Poggio 1979, Barnard and Thompson 1980, Hahn 1989]. Tracking features through sequences of images is used for the calculation of paths covered by vehicles. Image sequences can also be used for building up a three dimensional scene description [Gennery 1977, Moravec 1977]. Comparison of image features with features of digital maps is applied to automated map revision, and computer guided cartography makes use of general models to interpret image features [Nagao *et al.* 1979, McKeown *et al.* 1985, Fua and Hanson 1988].

At the highest level the data descriptions that are matched not only contain features but also the interrelationships between the features. Problems like three-dimensional object recognition and location [Binford 1982], navigation (mapping an image to a map) [Faugeras and Price 1981, Nevatia and Price 1982] can only be solved when the global context of the features is known. The topological and geometrical relations between features contain important information that is needed to constrain the large space of possible mappings between the features.

Because of these constraints, such *relational descriptions* can be matched without having a priori knowledge about the spatial relationship between them. Matching methods applied to lower level data descriptions need such knowledge, e.g. the relative orientation between two images resulting in the epipolar constraint. If such information is not available or not good enough only high level data descriptions can be matched. Reflecting the recent interest in robust methods, the computer vision literature of the last few years shows an increased number of publications dealing with high level representations (e.g. [Mohan and Nevatia 1989, Straforini *et al.* 1990]).

This thesis is an investigation into the *relational matching method*. Apart from *relaxation labeling* this method is the only method that can match relational descriptions. In contrast to the relaxation labeling, the relational matching method always finds the best mapping between the features of the descriptions. This thesis discusses and further develops the theories related to the relational matching method.

1.2   Relational matching theory

Theories, that state a problem, define the optimal solution and allow the derivation of an algorithm to find it, are sparse in computer vision. Many algorithms are designed on an ad hoc basis and have lots of tuning parameters (e.g. weight factors) which are hard to interpret and which optimal values often depend on the data the algorithms are to process. Many algorithms work, often only tested on a few images, without really understanding why they do work. A sound theory behind the algorithms is missing. Already several authors have complained about this situation and have urged the necessity of theory development, despite the complexity of computer vision problems [Haralick 1985, Price 1985].

Maybe due to their complaints, there is an increase in the number of papers founding new algorithms on the probability theory and the information theory. The information theory thereby gives an interesting alternative view on probabilities. Using principles from these well established theories, solutions could be derived to quite some fundamental problems in computer vision. Leclerc [1988], e.g., presented a new approach to image segmentation based upon the "minimum description length" principle of the information theory. Using the same principle, Fua and Hanson [1988] evaluate the detection and location of houses and roads in aerial images which are defined by generic models. Boyer and Kak [1986] defined an information-theoretic measure for comparing relational descriptions and Wallace and Kanade [1989] reported on a new clustering scheme which could be used for object recognition or perceptual grouping of features in a data set.

In this thesis, an attempt is made to describe and further develop the relational matching method using the information theory. Relational matching compares two relational descriptions. It has to find the best mapping from features in one description to the features of the other description. In order to find the best mapping, it has to measure the similarity between the features which are mapped to each other. This requires an evaluation function, a measure for comparing relational descriptions. We will discuss the evaluation function of Boyer and Kak [1986] and show that, although this function already is much better than previously published measures, it still has some drawbacks. Optimizing this function may lead to non-optimal mappings. Based on this analysis we will suggest a new evaluation function that eliminates these drawbacks.

Having an evaluation function, we can now look for the best mapping. Relational matching problems are solved with *tree search methods* that have been developed in the domain of the artificial intelligence. The tree search methods utilize the evaluation function together with heuristics to efficiently select the best mapping from the large space of possible mappings. As the value of the new function has to be maximized, whereas the values of usual functions have to be minimized, the tree search methods will be slightly adapted for the purpose of the new evaluation function.

The extraction of relational descriptions from the raw data (e.g. grey value or range images) of course is important to the matching method, because good descriptions, i.e. abstract descriptions without segmentation errors, are easier to match than bad ones. The description extraction will, however, not be a primary topic of this thesis. The stress will be laid upon the evaluation function and the search method of relational matching.

1.3   Organization of the thesis

Before going into the aspects of relational matching, chapter 2 first gives an overview and classification of the matching methods used in computer vision in order to have a better view on the characteristics of relational matching and to be able to recognize the advantages and disadvantages of relational matching. After that, chapter 3 gives a more formal definition of the relational matching problem and reviews the early development of relational matching in literature. Chapters 2 and 3 prepare for chapter 4 that outlines several problems in matching relational descriptions and that presents the contributions of this thesis in solving them. Chapter 4 concludes the introductory part of this thesis. The reader familiar with the matching literature may skip chapters 2 and 3, or have a short look at the notation introduced in chapter 3, and continue with the specific topics of this thesis that will be discussed in chapter 4.

The second part of this thesis contains old and new theories about relational matching. The method is described in general terms as a method that matches two relational descriptions. This description applies to all kinds of matching problems, e.g. image to image matching, image to model matching, etc. Because the information theory will play an important role in the chapter on the evaluation function, chapter 5 deals with the basic elements of the information theory. We will also derive some useful properties of information that will be used in the subsequent chapters. In chapter 6 we will review existing functions for comparing relational descriptions and develop the new evaluation function. Chapter 7 describes the tree search methods and shows how the new evaluation function can be combined with these methods.

In the third and last part of this thesis we show how the developed theories can be applied to the problem of locating three-dimensional objects in digital images. This problem is just one of the many problems that can be solved by relational matching and serves to show the new theories into some more detail. In chapter 8 we will describe the method that has been used to extract the relational descriptions from grey value images. In chapter 9 we specify the evaluation function for the object location problem into more detail and describe methods by which the components of this function can be calculated. The employed search method and heuristics and their performance are discussed in chapter 10.

Chapter 11 finally gives a summary of the results achieved in this thesis and an outlook to further improvements of the relational matching method.

2   A classification of matching methods

Matching algorithms may be analyzed by posing three fundamental questions:

- **"What kind of data is matched?"** As sketched in the previous chapter the data which is to be matched can be described at several levels of abstraction. This level of representation strongly influences the definition and performance of the matching algorithm.

- **"What is the best match?"** All matching procedures define the best match to be the one which optimizes the value of some evaluation function.

- **"How to find the best match?"** The central part of a matching algorithm describes how to find the match with the optimal value of the evaluation function.

After working out these questions, we will describe the use of multi-level descriptions in matching. This increasing popular technique speeds up the search and affects both the data description and the search method. Finally, we describe a number of well known matching methods along the lines defined above and discuss the advantages and disadvantages of the different algorithms.

2.1   Data description

A matching method matches two data descriptions, or, more precisely, it tries to find the best mapping between the basic elements of the descriptions. The data descriptions range from matrices of pixel grey values to relational descriptions.

2.1.1   Primitives

The basic elements are called the primitives of the descriptions. There are many types of primitives. In case of an image, the most obvious primitive type is the pixel. For many matching methods, however, a description by pixels is much to large to perform a search for the best match within a reasonable time limit. Such methods then use descriptions with other, more compact, types of primitives by which the essential information of the image can be stored in a smaller amount of primitives. These are primitives like points, lines or regions[1]. At this level one can also compose descriptions of object models or maps, using the same types of primitives. For describing three dimensional models or range images one can also use volumetric primitives like generalized cylinders.

---

[1] Such primitives can be extracted by a large number of image segmentation methods. An example is given in chapter 8.

The primitives are described by their characteristics. These are called attributes. Similarity in attribute values is the major guide to find the best primitive to primitive mapping. A primitive can be described by the names and the values of its attributes. Thus, as an example of the simplest primitive, one could describe a pixel no. 83 with row coordinate 119, column coordinate 34 and intensity 75 by primitive p_{83}

$$p_{83} = \{ \text{ (row 119) (column 34) (intensity 75) } \}$$

and region no. 5 defined by the centroid coordinates, its surface size and border length by primitive p_5

$$p_5 = \{ \text{ (centre-row 203) (centre-column 138) (surface 3892) (border 294) } \}$$

The attributes used in the descriptions above are all numerical, but, clearly, they can also have a symbolic nature, like for instance the polygon primitive below

$$p_2 = \{ \text{ (length 32.4) (closed true) (shape circular) } \}$$

describing a closed polygon representing a circle with circumference 32.4.

A description may use different types of primitives (e.g. primitives describing polygons and primitives describing regions). In such cases, the primitive type may also be considered a symbolic attribute to the primitive:

$$
\begin{aligned}
p_2 &= \{ \text{ (type polygon) (length 32.4) (closed true) (shape circular) } \} \\
p_5 &= \{ \text{ (type region) (centre-row 203) (centre-column 138)} \\
&\qquad \text{(surface 3892) (border 294) } \}
\end{aligned}
$$

Data descriptions, that merely are lists of primitives described by their attribute names and values, are called *feature based descriptions*.

2.1.2 Relations

Each primitive in a feature based description is a description of a small part of the image, map or model. All parts are considered to be completely independent of each other. Clearly, such descriptions lack all contextual information, whereas this kind of information may be very useful to a matching algorithm.

Consider, for example, the above descriptions with polygons and regions. If, in addition to the attributes of the primitives, it would be known that polygon p_2 is (a part of) the contour of region p_5 and one would like to find the corresponding polygon and region in another description, one can restrict the search to those pairs of a polygon and a region which not only have attributes similar to those of p_2 and p_5, but which also share the relationship that the polygon is (a part of) the contour of the region.

Thus, it is useful to extend the description of the primitives by a description of the interrelationships among the primitives. Such a description of primitives and their interrelationships is called a *structural* or a *relational description.*

The relationships can be represented in relation tuples. The relation "contour" e.g. is a binary relation between a polygon primitive and a region primitive. Thus, the "contour"-relation tuple of polygon p_2 and region p_5 would be

$$\{ p_2 \ p_5 \}$$

Collecting all pairs of polygons and regions for which the contour relation holds, the set of these binary tuples could look like

$$(\{ p_2 \ p_5 \} \{ p_2 \ p_4 \} \cdots \{ p_1 \ p_7 \})$$

Finally, one has to mark that this tuple list concerns the relation contour, which is just one relation out of many possible relations. This is usually done by making a pair of the relation name (e.g. contour) and the relation tuple list. E.g.

$$(\text{contour} \ (\{ p_2 \ p_5 \} \{ p_2 \ p_4 \} \cdots \{ p_1 \ p_7 \}))$$

Just like the primitives are described by their attributes, the relation tuples may also have attributes. In case of the contour relation, for instance, one may want to know the percentage of the region contour that is covered by the polygon, or the minimum distance between the polygon and the centre of the region. Storing both, the relation pair would be

$$(\text{contour} \ (\quad \{ p_2 \ p_5 \ (\text{coverage } 100) \ (\text{distance } 10.3) \}$$
$$\{ p_2 \ p_4 \ (\text{coverage } 34) \ (\text{distance } 5.7) \}$$
$$\cdots$$
$$\{ p_1 \ p_7 \ (\text{coverage } 100) \ (\text{distance } 25.4) \}))$$

Such relational descriptions tell a lot more about the data than the feature based descriptions do. They are needed for those matching problems that can not be solved without contextual information.

2.1.3   The image as a function of coordinates

Although it is possible to specify a grey value image by a set of pixels, with every pixel having a row coordinate, a column coordinate and a grey value attribute, the grey value is often looked upon as a function of the row and column coordinates:

$$g(r, c) \qquad r = 1, 2, \ldots, N_r \qquad c = 1, 2, \ldots, N_c \qquad (2\text{-}1)$$

When extending this description with an interpolation rule, the grey value can be considered a function over a continuous space of row and column coordinates. This interpretation is essential to some image to image matching methods, namely the area based matching methods.

2.2 The match evaluation function

The match evaluation function is a function on two data descriptions which has to guide the search method in finding the best match. The best match between two descriptions is the mapping for which the corresponding primitives of the descriptions show the best similarity in their attributes and, in case of relational descriptions, their relations.

The problem is with the definition of similarity. If we would only have one type of attribute with a numerical value, e.g. the grey value of a pixel primitive, this is still easy: one may say that two pixels are similar if the absolute difference of the grey values is small. However, in the case of two numerical attributes, e.g. the average grey value and the size of a region, this already becomes less trivial. What is more important: similar grey values or similar sizes? One may solve this problem by weighting the attribute values according to their standard deviations. But the similarity definition becomes even more complicated if one wants to combine these numerical attributes with symbolical attributes, like a predicate indicating whether a polygon is open or closed or a polygon shape classificator with categories "straight", "sinoidal" and "polynomial".

Looking for the mapping with the best similarity value (however this value may be defined) often results in a very time consuming search. Therefore, the space of possible mappings needs to be reduced. This can be achieved by imposing constraints. Two types of constraints have to be discerned: hard constraints and soft constraints. Hard constraints define the limits of the search space. In case the similarity function is a cost function, mappings outside these limits have infinitely high costs. Soft constraints, on the contrary, do not define which mappings are possible and which are not, but define a relative preference over the space of possible mappings. Soft constraints are used to implement heuristics in the evaluation function, which tell the search method where it will be more likely to find the best mapping.

2.2.1 Similarity measures

Similarity of two descriptions is usually defined as a cost function or a distance function. These costs are to be minimized and are zero only if both descriptions are identical. The costs of the mapping are defined by the similarity of the attribute values of the primitives (and relations tuples) that are mapped to each other. Usually, all attributes of all primitives and relations tuples are considered independent. Then, having defined the costs of a difference in attribute values, the costs of one primitive (or relation tuple) correspondence can be defined as the sum of the attribute costs, summed over all attributes of that primitive (or the relation tuple). Similarly the costs of a mapping is the sum of the costs of all primitive (and relation tuples) correspondences.

Thus suppose we have two feature based descriptions P and Q where both descriptions are sets of primitives $\{p_1, p_2, \ldots, p_N\}$ resp. $\{q_1, q_2, \ldots, q_N\}$. Further suppose that all primitives are described by N_a attributes a_k with values v_k and that a mapping h is given which maps the primitives of P to the primitives of Q, such that, when $h(p_i) = q_j$, primitive q_j of description Q is considered to be the corresponding primitive of primitive p_i of description P. Then the costs of the instantiation of p_i with q_j are defined as the sum of the attribute correspondence costs over all attributes.

$$\text{costs}(p_i, q_j) = \sum_{k=1}^{N_a} \text{costs}(v_k(p_i), v_k(q_j)) \tag{2-2}$$

where $v_k(p_i)$ denote the value of the kth attribute of the ith primitive of description P. The costs of the mapping h can be defined by:

$$\text{costs}(h) = \sum_{i=1}^{N} \text{costs}(p_i, h(p_i)) \tag{2-3}$$

What is left is the definition of the costs which are imposed if the attribute values of two corresponding primitives are not the same. Let us first consider numeric values. If there is only one attribute, the absolute or the square of the difference between the two values is often taken as the distance measure. This results in the L_1 resp. the L_2 norm. Problems arise if there are several different attributes. For instance, two feature based image descriptions exist of regions. All region primitives are ellipses which are described by two attributes: a roundness attribute which is the quotient of the shorter and the longer semi-axis and a size attribute which is the number of pixels within the region. All values of the roundness attribute are somewhere between 0 and 1, whereas the sizes of the regions may vary from a few pixels (say 10) to the number of pixels in the image. Clearly the values of the latter attribute are much larger and the difference between two region size attribute values will usually also be much larger than the difference between the values of two roundness attributes. Thus, when taking the costs of an instantiation of two region primitives to be the sum of the absolute or square values of the differences of the roundness and size values, the influence of the roundness attribute will be marginal and the best mapping will be the mapping with the best similarity in region sizes.

To get a more balanced measure, frequent use is made of attribute value transformations so that the range of the attribute values is about the same for all attributes. This may be achieved by scaling the values v into the interval $[0,1]$ (a) or in case of Gaussian distributed attributes by normalizing the distribution (b)

$$(a) \quad v' = \frac{v - v_{\min}}{v_{\max} - v_{\min}} \qquad\qquad (b) \quad v' = \frac{v - \mu_v}{\sigma_v} \qquad (2\text{-}4)$$

An even more sophisticated transformation is used by the Mahalonobis distance which builds a square sum which also corrects for dependencies between the attributes.

These linear transformations are to assure that all attributes are treated as equally important, i.e. on the average contribute a same amount to the evaluation function. However, this may not be the optimum. For example, suppose that two colour images are represented by regions which are described by their size and their average hue value. If we want to match two such descriptions of images taken from different positions, it is clear that the values of the size attribute are not invariant against a change in the position of the camera whereas the colours of the recorded objects, and thus the hue attribute values, will be constant. Hence, similar hue values contain more information about the correctness of a mapping than similar region sizes and, thus, the hue attribute should have a greater contribution to the overall similarity value than the size attribute. Many researchers therefore choose a weighting factor for each type of attribute to indicate the importance of similarity of this attribute. Assuming that the attributes of corresponding features will have the same values, the weights are functions of the correctness of this assumption. The costs of an instantiation of two primitives then becomes the weighted sum of the attribute costs:

$$\text{costs}(p_i, q_j) = \sum_{k=1}^{N_a} w_k \cdot \text{costs}(v_k(p_i), v_k(q_j)) \qquad (2\text{-}5)$$

where w_k is the weight of the kth attribute. The new evaluation function that will be developed in this thesis does not require such weights. The contributions of the attributes to the overall measure will already reflect their importance for the matching.

Beside the absolute or the square of the attribute value difference, there is a third approach for defining the costs of an attribute correspondence. This approach uses the probability theory and requires that the conditional probability (density) functions are known for all attributes. A conditional probability function $P_a(v_2|v_1)$ of attribute a defines how likely it is that the attribute of a primitive will take the value v_2 when it is known that the attribute of the corresponding primitive has value v_1. This conditional probability can be converted to a cost measure by taking the negation of the logarithm:

$$\text{costs}(v_1, v_2) = -\log P(v_2|v_1) \qquad (2\text{-}6)$$

This cost definition is also called the conditional information of v_2 by v_1. Summing up these costs means multiplying of probabilities under the logarithm and minimizing the costs is equivalent to maximizing the product of all probabilities. Under the assumption that all attributes of all primitives are independent, the mapping with the fewest costs is the mapping with the highest likelihood: the maximum likelihood mapping.

If there is only one attribute which is Gaussian distributed and it is expected that the attribute values of corresponding primitives are the same, the minimization of the square sum of the value differences is also known to give the maximum likelihood estimate. Thus, in this case, the square sum may be regarded a special case of the conditional information, which uses a more general probabilistic approach. Similarly, the maximum likelihood estimation of Laplacian distributed variables is found by minimizing the sum of the absolute value differences.

Attributes of a description do not have to be numerical. They also may have symbolic values. The similarity between two symbolic values, of course, can not be determined by a difference between the values. The simplest approach is to test if the two values are the same and to add a penalty to the total costs if they are not. This is a rather crude method. The costs of a correspondence of a symbol "a" with a symbol "b" are the same as the correspondence of symbol "a" with a symbol "c". Both correspondences are penalized by the same amount since the values are different. It may, however, well be that e.g. correspondence ("a","b") is more likely than correspondence ("a","c"). This brings us to another method which can be used for judging correspondences of symbolic attributes. If one can determine the conditional probabilities for all attributes (e.g. $P($"b"$|$"a"$)$ and $P($"c"$|$"a"$)$), one will be able to differentiate between the likely and the less likely correspondences of attributes with symbolic values.

For descriptions which use both numeric and symbolic attributes, it thus can be concluded that the only sound way to measure similarity between two descriptions is a probabilistic approach. In chapter 6 we will further explore the advantages and problems of the conditional information and present a new probabilistic measure.

2.2.2 Constraints

Usually a priori knowledge is available to the matching process in the form that certain combinations of attribute values are considered completely incompatible. E.g. when attribute value v is considered completely incompatible with attribute value v', all primitives $q_j \in Q$ having attribute value v' will be discarded when looking for the corresponding primitive of primitive $p_i \in P$ having attribute value v. This may be called a hard constraint: under no condition p_i with attribute value v will be mapped to q_j with attribute value v'. If the evaluation function is a cost function, the costs of such a mapping would be indefinitely high.

Soft constraints, on the contrary, are rules of thumb which are usually true for a good mapping, but are sometimes violated. They are to guide the search so that the best mapping can be found faster and are useful to define the best mapping among a group of mappings which all have about the same similarity values. This heuristic can be included into the evaluation function. A well known example for this is the so-called smoothness constraint used in image to image matching [Marr and Poggio 1979]. Since the recorded objects generally have piecewise smooth surfaces, it may be expected that two points that are adjacent in one image will also be adjacent in the other image. This heuristic is only violated at object boundaries. To improve the search characteristics, the curvature of the disparity map can therefore be added to an evaluation function which is to be minimized.

2.3   Search methods

The attributes of the descriptions often are geometrical measures. They are related to the coordinate system in which the data has been described. The two descriptions that are to be matched are described in two different coordinate systems (e.g. two images of different orientation, or an image and a 3D model). Thus, before one can calculate a similarity measure of two geometric attribute values, one needs to know the geometrical relationship between the two coordinates systems. In fact, finding the transformation parameters is often considered more important than finding the primitive to primitive mapping.

The mapping function and the transformation parameters clearly constrain one another. Assuming a (partial) mapping reduces the space of possible parameters. E.g. three point correspondences in case of image to 3D-model matching determine the parameters of the spatial resection. Vice versa, by fixing transformation parameters one limits the space of the possible mappings. E.g. a given relative orientation in case of an image to image matching problem, reduces the search to primitives on the corresponding epipolar lines. Due to this interaction between the space of mappings and the space of transformation parameters, some matching approaches try to find the best evaluation function value by optimizing over all possible mappings, whereas other methods optimize over the transformation parameters.

There are many search methods used in solving the correspondence problem. In the next paragraphs most of them will be briefly described. These methods are: tree search, simulated annealing, least squares, relaxation labeling and generalized Hough transform. They give a good impression of the variety of matching methods. We will review these methods and will especially consider their suitability for solving high level matching problems.

2.3.1 Tree search

Graphs and trees (graphs without cycles) are widely used in representing search spaces. Starting at some node (the initial problem state), the edges of the graph are traversed until a node is found which represents the solution to the problem. Applications have been reported of language understanding, scene interpretation, expert systems, theorem proving, operations research (the traveling salesman problem) and other problem domains [Barr and Feigenbaum 1981, Nilsson 1982]. The relational matching method also uses tree search methods to solve the correspondence problem.

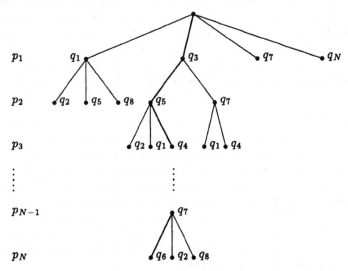

Figure 2.1: Search space representation in a tree. Each path from the root node to the bottom leaf nodes is a possible mapping.

The search space of the correspondence problem can be represented in a tree (see figure 2.1). The root node of the tree represents the initial problem state, where the mapping is undefined. At each level i a primitive $p_i \in P$, called a *unit*, is assigned to a primitive $q_j \in Q$, called a *label*. Going down from the node where label primitive q_j was assigned to unit primitive p_i, the next unit p_{i+1} has to be labeled, i.e. the assignment of a label to unit p_{i+1} is to be added to the partial mapping of the first i unit primitives. Only those M labels are considered for unit p_{i+1} that are compatible with this partial mapping, resulting in M branches in the tree leading down from the node where the unit p_i was labeled.

The depth of the tree is equal to the number of unit primitives in P, N. Each path from the root node to a leaf node has the same length N and represents a unique mapping $h : P \to Q$ that maps unit primitives p_i to label primitives q_j. All paths together, i.e. the tree, represent the search space for the best mapping.

The search is started at the root level. At this level all label primitives are selected that could be the corresponding primitive of the first unit primitive p_1. The selection is done on the basis of comparable attributes. One of the selected labels is picked at random (q_3 in the figure) and is assigned to unit p_1 at the first level in the tree. At the node where p_1 is instantiated with that label, the labels are selected that could correspond to the next unit primitive p_2. This selection again uses the attributes of the primitives but also uses the relations that exist between unit primitives p_1 and p_2. One will require that the labels selected for p_2 will have similar relations with the label assigned to p_1. If there is such a label for p_2, it is instantiated at level 2 and the search continues with the next unit. This is repeated until the last unit p_N has been assigned to a label or there is some unit p_i for which no admissible labels can be found. In that case, the current node can not be expanded. Therefore the search moves up one level to the parent node in the tree and moves down again along one of the other branches of that node. This strategy, called *backtracking*, is repeated until all nodes in the tree have been visited, while remembering the best path found so far, or until an admissible mapping has been found.

A mapping is evaluated by values (usually costs) which are assigned to the edges of the tree. In the example of figure 2.1, the evaluation function value of the instantiation of unit p_1 with label q_3 is a similarity measure, derived from the corresponding attribute values, which is assigned to the edge from the root node to node (p_1, q_3). The value assigned to the edge from node (p_1, q_3) to node (p_2, q_5) reflects the attribute similarity of primitives p_2 and q_5 and of the relation tuples (p_1, p_2) and (q_3, q_5). So, the sum of the values assigned to the edges of a path from the root node to a leaf node contains the evaluation values of all corresponding primitives and relations and thus is the evaluation measure for the mapping represented by that path.

Because this search method first tries the nodes below the current node, this method is called a depth first search method. The efficiency of the depth first tree search is fairly poor. It can be improved by changing the order in which the unit primitives are selected and the order in which the nodes are traversed. Several heuristics have been suggested to optimize the tree search. Because the tree search is the search method employed by relational matching, we will come back to these heuristics in a later chapter.

Due to the exponential complexity of tree searches this method can only be applied to sparse data sets, like high level descriptions. Since all possible combination of unit and label primitives can be tested it requires no a priori knowledge about the spatial transformation between the descriptions. This makes the tree search methods suitable for tasks like object location and recognition, i.e. tasks where no such information is available.

Examples of tree search methods are given in paragraph 2.5.1 (stereo matching) and paragraph 2.5.2 (object recognition).

2.3.2 Simulated annealing

Simulated annealing is (cf. [Geman and Geman 1984, Carnevali *et al.* 1985, Barnard 1986]) "an undirected Monte Carlo search that simulates the physical process of annealing in which a physical system composed of a large number of coupled elements is reduced to its lowest energy configuration by slowly reducing the temperature while maintaining the system in thermal equilibrium." The "coupled elements" are the primitives of a description (e.g. pixels), the "configuration" is the mapping and the "energy" of a configuration is the value of the match evaluation function. The energy is minimized by a stochastic optimization technique, like e.g. the Metropolis algorithm [Barnard 1986]. This algorithm randomly suggests changes in the configuration. A change is accepted if it results in a reduction of the energy. If it causes an increase of the energy of the system, it is accepted with a certain probability. This probability depends on the energy increase and the current temperature of the system.

The temperature should be decreased slowly to avoid that the algorithm ends up in a local minimum. The computational effort is quite large, but the algorithm can be implemented as a parallel operation on all primitives if the change in energy caused by a changed assignment for one primitive is a function of only a few adjacent primitives.

Starting at some mapping the stochastical optimization has to gradually change this mapping to the mapping with the lowest energy state. Small obstacles in the "energy landscape" can be overcome because the algorithm sometimes accepts a mapping with a higher energy state. When the energy landscape is very rough, i.e. far from being convex, a simulated annealing algorithm only has a small probability that the current mapping is in the right energy valley when the temperature is decreased. For a task like object recognition, which has a highly non-convex energy landscape, simulated annealing is not suitable. It can, however, be applied to stereo matching if the relative orientation of the images is roughly known [Barnard 1987].

Simulated annealing is used for stereo matching in the example of paragraph 2.5.3.

2.3.3 Generalized Hough transformation

The generalized Hough transformation is a robust method to locate objects which shape can be described by parameters [Hough 1962]. The Hough transform is very popular for the detection of straight lines in digital images. A straight line can be described by a rotation parameter ϕ and a parameter d for the distance between the line and the origin of the coordinate system:

$$r \cos \phi + c \sin \phi - d = 0 \qquad (2\text{-}7)$$

All image points (r, c) on a line with parameters ϕ and d will obey the above equation. One can also say that all lines through (r, c) have parameters (ϕ, d) that obey this equation. Thus a point (r, c) is associated with a curve in a parameter space with a ϕ and a d axis, representing all lines through (r, c). A second point (r', c') also has a curve in the parameter space. This curve intersects the curve of the first point at point (ϕ, d) in the parameter space, which represents the line through the two points (r, c) and (r', c'). Furthermore, the curves of all points on a straight image line will intersect at that (ϕ, d) point which specifies the line parameters. The location of this intersection point can be found by counting frequencies in an accumulator array.

This method can easily be extended for matching two feature based data descriptions. Suppose feature based descriptions P and Q are known to be related by a transformation T_X and the task is to determine the parameter vector $X = \{x_1, x_2, \ldots, x_N\}$. The parameter space, also called the Hough space, has an axis for each parameter x_i. The generalized Hough transform may be defined as follows.

Generalized Hough transform

1. Quantize the parameter space between appropriate minimum and maximum values for x_i, $i = 1, 2, \ldots, N$.

2. Form an accumulator array $A(x_1, x_2, \ldots, x_N)$ whose elements are initially zero.

3. For each combination of primitive $p_i \in P$ and $q_j \in Q$ calculate the range of parameters X that could be possible if p_i and q_j indeed are the corresponding primitives and increment the accumulator array for that range of parameters

$$A(x_1, x_2, \ldots, x_N) = A(x_1, x_2, \ldots, x_N) + 1 \qquad (2\text{-}8)$$

4. The maximum in the accumulator array will correspond to the transformation parameters which transform primitives p_i into primitives q_j.

The last statement becomes plausible if one considers that the correct combinations of p_i and q_j will vote for the same transformation parameters, whereas the votes of the incorrect combinations will be more or less randomly distributed over the Hough space.

Some matching definitions only have to solve for the transformation parameters between two coordinate systems, but if one also wants to know the primitive correspondences, the knowledge of the transformation parameters usually unambiguously implies the mapping. If it is still ambiguous, it certainly strongly reduces the search space of the possible mappings [Grimson 1988].

The computational effort of the Hough transformation exponentially increases with the dimension of the Hough space. Its use is therefore primarily restricted to matching problems with a small number of unknown transformation parameters, e.g. two shift parameters. Apart from the computational effort, a large number of parameters will be difficult to determine in a multi-dimensional Hough space since the peaks in the Hough space will be flattened out in all dimensions if the image features are a little noisy (which they usually are). Transformation parameters between features of high level descriptions are even harder to determine as high level descriptions only contain a small number of primitives.

The generalized Hough transformation is used for the location of houses in aerial photographs in the example of paragraph 2.5.4.

2.3.4 Least squares

The least squares method can be applied to the matching problem if there exists a functional relation between the attributes of the corresponding primitives and the parameters of the transformation between the coordinate systems of the two descriptions. If these functional relations are expressed in equations that are non-linear in the transformation parameters, they have to be linearized and approximate values are needed for the transformation parameters.

In the linear case, the vector of transformation parameters $x = (x_1 \; x_2 \; \cdots \; x_n)^T$ is expected to obey the equation

$$(a_{k1} \; a_{k2} \; \cdots \; kn) \; (x_1 \; x_2 \; \cdots \; x_n)^T = l_k' \tag{2-9}$$

and in the linearized case, we have

$$(a_{k1} \; a_{k2} \; \cdots \; kn) \; (x_1^0 + \Delta x_1 \; x_2^0 + \Delta x_2 \; \cdots \; x_n^0 + \Delta x_n)^T = l_k' \tag{2-10}$$

or

$$(a_{k1} \; a_{k2} \; \cdots \; kn) \; (\Delta x_1 \; \Delta x_2 \; \cdots \; \Delta x_n)^T = l_k \tag{2-11}$$

where a_{ki} and l_k are functions of the attributes of the k_{th} pair of approximately corresponding primitives p_k and q_k and of the approximate values of the transformation parameters. The equations of all approximately corresponding primitives build the linear system

$$A \; \Delta x = l \tag{2-12}$$

When the number of equations exceeds the number of transformation parameters, the corrections to the approximate values x^0 can be estimated by

$$\hat{\Delta x} = (A^T A)^{-1} A^T l \tag{2-13}$$

Under the assumption that all *observations* l_k are events of Gaussian distributed variables with the same standard deviation and are uncorrelated, the above equation gives the maximum likelihood estimation of Δx. The maximum likelihood estimation of the transformation parameters x is obtained by iteratively improving the approximate values x^0 $(x^0 + \Delta x \rightarrow x^0)$.

An advantage of the least squares method is that it also estimates the precision of the estimated parameters and the corrections to the observations. The feature based least squares matching [Barnard and Thompson 1980, Förstner 1986] uses this to cancel out incorrect primitive correspondences with a statistical test. Initially, a primitive p_i may have several corresponding primitives q_j. In the robust estimation the weights of the correspondences having a large correction of the observation value are gradually decreased and finally set to zero. I.e., the equations of such correspondences are removed, which means that those correspondences are considered incorrect and are not being used in the estimation of the transformation parameters.

The least squares method, like simulated annealing, modifies the initial mapping such that the value of an evaluation function (here the square sum of the residuals) is optimized. Whereas the simulated annealing can handle small deteriorations of mappings between the initial mapping and the best mapping, the least squares method needs a continuous decline of the square sum of the residuals. If the initial mapping is not close enough to the correct one the least squares method will fail. Therefore it can not be used for tasks like object recognition or location.

Least squares methods are used in the examples of paragraphs 2.5.5 (area based descriptions) and 2.5.6 (feature based descriptions).

2.3.5 Relaxation labeling

Relaxation labeling is an iterative process which tries to find an unambiguous mapping using the local constraints between the units $p_i \in P$ and the labels $q_j \in Q$ [Hummel and Zucker 1983]. A neighbour relation has to be defined over the units. The labelings of the units within the neighbourhood P_i of unit p_i are supposed to have an impact on the labeling of p_i. Furthermore, a constraint relation over labels at pairs (or n-tuples) of the neighbouring units defines the compatibility of the assignments. Initially, a set of possible labels Q_i is assigned to each unit p_i by comparing the attributes. There are two types of relaxation labeling methods: the discrete and the continuous relaxation labeling.

The discrete relaxation labeling method uses the label discarding rule to remove those labels from Q_i that are incompatible with all possible assignments $Q_{i'}$ of a neighbouring unit $p_{i'}$. After a successful relaxation each Q_i should hold one single label for unit p_i. The discarding rule states that a label $q_j \in Q_i$ is to be discarded if there exists a unit $p_{i'} \in P_i$ such that every label $q_{j'} \in Q_{i'}$ is incompatible with the assignment of q_j to p_i. This rule is applied to all labels of all units until no more labels can be discarded. Having n_P units and n_Q labels, this will take at most $n_P \times n_Q$ iterations.

The discrete relaxation labeling uses a compatibility function which marks a combination of label assignments either compatible or completely incompatible. The continuous relaxation labeling method, however, uses a function $r(p_i, q_j, p_{i'}, q_{j'})$ which gives real valued compatibility measures. These values are positive in case the assignments support each other and negative if they contradict each other. If it is zero, the assignments do not interact with each other. The continuous relaxation labeling method also uses weights for the assignments of the labels to a unit, thus expressing a relative preference for the labels. Each weight is a non-negative value and the sum of the weights of the labels of one unit is required to be one.

$$0 \leq w_{p_i}(q_j) \leq 1 \qquad (2\text{-}14)$$

$$\sum_{q_j \in Q_i} w_{p_i}(q_j) = 1 \quad \forall \ p_i \qquad (2\text{-}15)$$

Using these weights and the compatibility function, a function $S_{p_i}(q_j)$ can be defined. This function measures the support that the assignments in the neighbourhood of p_i give to the assignment of q_j to p_i. Rosenfeld *et al.* [1976] define this function as:

$$S_{p_i}(q_j) = \sum_{p_{i'} \in P_i} \sum_{q_{j'} \in Q_{i'}} r(p_i, q_j, p_{i'}, q_{j'}) \cdot w_{p_{i'}}(q_{j'}) \qquad (2\text{-}16)$$

They then define the new weights of the label assignments by the update formula:

$$w_{p_i}(q_j) = \frac{w_{p_i}(q_j)[1 + S_{p_i}(q_j)]}{\sum_{q_{j'} \in Q_i} w_{p_i}(q_{j'})[1 + S_{p_i}(q_{j'})]} \qquad (2\text{-}17)$$

Other support and updating formulas have been proposed by Peleg [1980], Faugeras and Price [1981] and Hummel and Zucker [1983]. Price [1985] gives a comparison of these relaxation labeling techniques. The continuous relaxation method has to be iterated until the weights of the assignments remain constant.

Discrete nor continuous relaxation are guaranteed to converge to a single unambiguous labeling [Waltz 1972]. Tree search strategies can be used to further disambiguate the labelings. Especially discrete relaxation can be a useful tool to reduce the search space of problems tackled with tree search methods. Like the tree search methods, the relaxation methods need relational descriptions, since the elimination of impossible mappings depends on the relations between the primitives. The main advantage of the relaxation labeling methods is that they can be implemented in parallel.

Relaxation labeling methods are used for scene interpretation in the example of paragraph 2.5.7.

2.4   Hierarchy

A common problem for most search methods applied to image to image matching is the initial value problem combined with the large amount of primitives to be matched. Because the evaluation function can be highly non-convex [Witkin *et al.* 1987], the search method either needs good approximate values for the best mapping or needs to try out many different starting values in order to find the global optimum.

Many of these problems can be solved by the use of hierarchical descriptions. Two different approaches should be discerned.

- The first and mostly used one derives series of increasingly smoothed images from the original images and uses these images or features detected in them for the matching. The smoothing is performed on the iconical level, i.e. the grey values. For a smooth description (low resolution) it will be relatively easy to find the optimal match, because the evaluation function is a function of the data and thus will also be smooth. The match of two smooth descriptions then supplies the initial values for the match of two descriptions on the next level of resolution. This process is applied recursively to the series of image descriptions until, finally, the original unsmoothed (highly resolved) descriptions can be matched using very good approximate values.

  The lower the resolution of an image, the less data is necessary for the description. In case of a feature based description this is clear: the smoother the image, the less features can be extracted. The details have been filtered away. Grimson [1985] pointed out that the use of several smoothness levels having little data at the highest, smoothest level and the use of hierarchy in his matching procedure, i.e. constraining the search on the lower levels by the results of the higher levels, reduces the complexity of the search to $O(n^2)$ for images of size $n \times n$, whereas it was $O(n^3)$ without the use of hierarchical image descriptions and matching.

  The smooth images usually are also compressed, e.g. by taking four pixels together to a new macro pixel. A pile of such increasingly smoothed and compressed images is called a pyramidal image description or an image pyramid (figure 2.2).

- The second approach is used for describing models in different levels of abstraction. Starting from a detailed model description more abstract descriptions are obtained by generalization. This more qualitative technique may use different kinds of primitives at each description level, whereas the smoothing technique uses the same kind of primitives at each level. Bobick and Bolles [1989] used the qualitative technique to represent objects in different scales. When a robot with some sensor approaches a thistle bush, it will first only see a blob, then may discover a few branches and only recognize it as a thistle bush when it is nearby. The models used for recognizing objects should reflect the resolution of the sensor data. This resolution of course varies with the distance of the sensor to the object and thus a series of object descriptions is needed to describe the appearances the object may have.

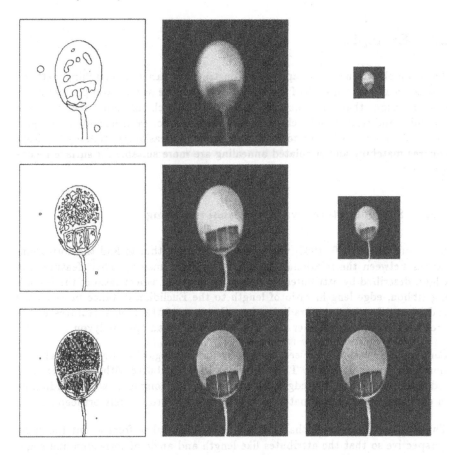

Figure 2.2: Pyramidal feature (first column) and image (third column) descriptions derived from increasingly smoothed images (second column).

The use of hierarchy solves many initial value problems, but it doesn't solve them all. For instance, if the approximate value of the rotation between two images is 90° off the actual rotation, the space of the evaluation function is still not convex enough to find the optimum by a simple optimization method. This is one of the reasons why hierarchy is hardly used for object recognition. The transformation between the image and the object model coordinate space is usually completely unknown. Another reason is that one would have to generate models for the different smoothness levels. But how should one estimate the corresponding model smoothness level if one doesn't even know the object(s) in the image and the distance at which they were recorded? The fact that stereo matching algorithms match images smoothed by the same filter solely depends on the assumption that the distances from the two camera positions to the recorded scene are approximately the same.

2.5 Examples

The examples in this paragraph are to illustrate the variety of matching methods and applications. For each of the search methods, one or two examples are given of applications that are typical for that type of search. Methods like relational matching and relaxation labeling are primarily used for tasks like object recognition and navigation (image-to-map matching), whereas other methods like least squares matching and simulated annealing are more suitable for surface reconstruction.

2.5.1 Symbolic stereo with relational matching

Boyer and Kak [1986, 1988] use a tree search algorithm to find the correspondences between the relational descriptions of two images. Their features are edges, described by attributes like mean orientation, aspect ratio of the bounding ribbon, edge length, ratio of length to the Euclidian distance between the endpoints, the dominant radial value, the area of the binary features and a predicate indicating whether the edge is a closed or an open polygon.

Four binary relations are used to express the topological and geometrical relationships among the edges. These relations were attributed with a predicate and indicated whether the two edges had one endpoint in common, had two endpoints in common, were approximately parallel or were approximately orthogonal.

The assumption is made that the two images are taken from about the same perspective so that the attributes like length and angle of corresponding edges should be comparable. To measure the similarity between attribute values, Boyer and Kak use the conditional probability $p(v_R|v_L)$ which is the probability that an edge in the left image with an attribute with value v_L will correspond to an edge in the right image with attribute value v_R. The probability tables, which should be known before the matching, are composed by evaluating numerous training matches, which were made by hand. Considering all attributes independent, the match evaluation function is the product of all conditional probabilities of the attributes of the matched edges and their relations.

The backtracking tree search algorithm, as described in paragraph 2.3.1, is used to find the best mapping. The left image edges, which do not have corresponding edges in the right image, are assigned to a wildcard. No penalty is needed for such an assignment, because the wildcard is only tried as a last resort, i.e. after all possible edges have been tried. The search efficiency heavily relies on the power of the attributes of the edges. By comparing these attributes of the edges in the left and the right image, for each edge of the left image, only a few edges of the right image are considered as a matching candidate. This, of course, strongly reduces the search space. After finding a mapping with N_W wildcards, it is assumed that any future mapping with a higher probability will have no more than N_W wildcards, thereby further constraining the search space. Thus, the best mapping, which also was the correct mapping, could be found in a reasonable time.

Boyer and Kak need the approximate values of the relative orientation to get a strong constraint from comparisons of attributes like angle and length. However, it is also possible to solve image matching problems without a priori knowledge about the orientation parameters. Even without this knowledge the attributes angle and length contain information, although the constraints they can put onto the search space are weaker. Consequently, the complexity of the search tree will be higher if the knowledge isn't available, but it is still possible to solve the matching problem.

2.5.2   3-Dimensional object recognition with relational matching

Recognition or location of 3-dimensional object models in digital images is usually performed by a tree search algorithm which has to find the best mapping between two relational descriptions.

Gmur and Bunke [1988a, 1988b] derive the relational description of the 3D model from CAD models and the image description by edge extraction with the Laplacian of Gaussian operator [Huertas and Medioni 1986]. Both descriptions use the line junctions as primitives and the lines as binary relations between the primitives. The line type (concave, convex) is used as an attribute to the relation. Assuming a parallel projection, the transformation of the model into the image can be calculated when four primitive correspondences have been found. Thus the search in the tree is mainly restricted to the first four levels. The transformation parameters are used to determine the vertices and the edges of the model which should be visible in the image. The evaluation function is a costs measure with three parts: a geometric part which is calculated from the differences between the coordinates of the vertices of the image graph and the vertices of the projected model graph and two parts which are proportional to the number of vertices which have to be inserted in resp. removed from the projected model graph in order to obtain the image graph. The evaluation of a hypothesized transformation (i.e. a set of four corresponding vertices) is done in linear time. The matching method shows fast results in recognizing objects in images that can be easily segmented.

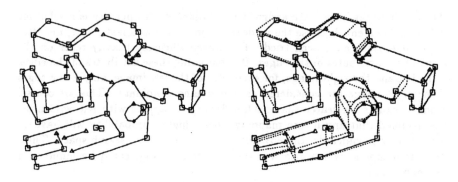

Figure 2.3: Image features and recognized object models (adopted from [Gmür and Bunke 1988a]).

Ben-Arie and Meiri [1987] recognize complex objects using points and planar faces as primitives. In a relaxation labeling process preceding the tree search, they calculate the label probability vectors (i.e. normalized weight vectors) using the primitive attributes and the non-geometrical relations between the primitives. Their evaluation function has two parts: a probabilistic part and a geometrical part. The probabilistic cost of a mapping is one minus the probability of the worst assignment of a model primitive to an image primitive as calculated by the relaxation labeling process. A geometric invariant can be calculated with three planar faces (which may also be imaginary planes defined by three points). The geometric part of the cost function reflects the changes in this invariant when calculated with different triples of planar faces. The best mapping is found by searching the tree with the A^* algorithm[2]. The object recognition with this matching method is fairly slow, but this may well be due to the poor image segmentation results.

Brooks [1981, 1983] describes the ACRONYM system which recognizes 3-dimensional objects and object classes (generic descriptions) in 2-dimensional grey value images using symbolic and geometric reasoning. The objects are described by generalized cylinders (cones in 3D, ribbons and ellipses in 2D) and relations like collinear, coincident, angle and distance. The viewing direction of the camera and the distance of the camera to the recorded objects are assumed to be approximately known. Based on similarity between a part of an object and a feature in the image object interpretations are predicted. These are verified by a backward chaining mechanism which checks whether the parameters of the geometric and relational description of the other image features lie within the bounds propagated by a constraint manipulation system. The constraints are given by the assumed correspondence of one or a few object parts.

---

[2]This algorithm will be described in chapter 7.

2.5.3   Stereo matching with simulated annealing

Barnard [1986, 1987] applied the simulated annealing algorithm to the stereo matching problem. He directly works on two grey value images and assumes that the relative orientation between the images is known. The disparity map, which maps the pixels of the left image to the corresponding pixels of the right image, is to be determined by minimizing the energy of the mapping. This energy function (i.e. the evaluation function) consists of two parts: a similarity term measuring the absolute grey value differences between the corresponding pixels and a smoothness term for each pixel in the left image which is the sum of the absolute differences between the disparity of the pixel and the disparities of its eight neighbours.

The simulated annealing starts with a random disparity map and a high temperature. In scanline order, for each pixel another random disparity is considered and possibly accepted (paragraph 2.3.2). After ten iterations, the temperature is reduced by ten percent and another ten scans are performed. This is repeated until the temperature falls below a certain value.

Although the simulated annealing algorithm described in [Barnard 1987] takes advantage of hierarchy by operating on pyramidal image descriptions and uses the efficient Creutz algorithm, it still suffers from a very large computational burden. It took about 12 hours on a Symbolics 3600 to match two images of 512x512 pixels with 50 levels of disparity. However, maybe future computers using massive parallel hardware or neural networks will make this algorithm, which is very suitable for implementations on parallel machines, attractive again. At the moment, however, hierarchical organized area based matching methods give much faster results.

2.5.4   Object location using the generalized Hough transformation

The generalized Hough transformation can be used for object location if only a few position parameters are unknown. In [Sester and Förstner 1989] it is used for finding a specified house roof in a digitized aerial photograph. Both the model and the image are represented by a set of straight lines (figure 2.4). The task is to find the shift parameters between the coordinate systems of the model and the image.

Since the rotation and the scale are approximately known, only a limited number of model line - image line correspondences have to be considered. For each combination the range of row- and column shifts is computed which could map the image line to (a part of) the model line. The values of the points in the Hough space that lie within this range are incremented proportionally to the value of a probability density function depending on the length of the image line, the

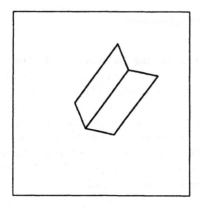 

Figure 2.4: Location of model lines (left) among image lines (right) (from [Sester and Förstner 1989])

uncertainty of its endpoints, the distance between the image line and the model reference point projected into the image and the variance of this distance. These last two terms are motivated by the uncertainty in the scale and the rotation parameter and the uncertainty in the model definition.

The generalized Hough transform proved to be very robust. Despite the large number of image lines and the small number of model lines, the shift parameters are easily identified by their peak value in the Hough space, but models with even less lines will probably give no significant peak in the Hough space.

The Hough transformation is very suited for tasks like the house location. For this problem the computational complexity is only of second order. A tree search algorithm matching the model lines on the average would take more time to find the solution.

2.5.5 Least squares area based matching

Least squares matching applied to area based image descriptions has become a popular method in photogrammetry in the last decade. The principle of this method is fairly simple. It says that the difference between the grey values of two corresponding points is expected to be zero when the coordinates of these points have been corrected for a small error in the assumed geometric transformation and the grey values have been corrected for a small error in the radiometric transformation.

If one can assume that the recorded object has a smooth surface which can be approximated by a tilted plane, the geometric transformation between two corresponding image points (r_1, c_1) and (r_2, c_2) can be described by an affine transformation and a shift.

$$\begin{pmatrix} r_2 \\ c_2 \end{pmatrix} = \begin{pmatrix} a_{11} & a_{12} \\ a_{21} & a_{22} \end{pmatrix} \begin{pmatrix} r_1 \\ c_1 \end{pmatrix} + \begin{pmatrix} a_1 \\ a_2 \end{pmatrix} \qquad (2\text{-}18)$$

A linear radiometric transformation is usually sufficient to correct for differences in brightness and contrast.

$$g_1 = b_1 \cdot g_2 + b_2 \qquad (2\text{-}19)$$

Having approximate values for these eight transformation parameters (denoted a_{ij}^0, a_i^0 and b_i^0) the observation equation can be derived. The observation becomes

$$\Delta g(r,c) = g_1(r,c) - b_1^0 \cdot g_2(a_{11}^0 r + a_{12}^0 c + a_1^0, a_{21}^0 r + a_{22}^0 c + a_2^0) - b_2^0 \qquad (2\text{-}20)$$

which is the difference between the grey values of the approximate corresponding points, corrected for differences in brightness and contrast. After linearizing, the coefficients of the unknown parameters are simple functions of the coordinates, the first grey value derivatives in row and column direction and the approximate values of the unknowns [Pertl 1985, Vosselman 1986]. This linear equation can be derived for each corresponding pixel pair. The least squares method then estimates the corrections to the eight transformation parameters. The approximate values needed for the transformation parameters, have to be quite accurate (e.g. 2-3 pixels for the shift parameters). This constraint can be relaxed by smoothing the images and using a hierarchy.

The least squares area based method has been used for reconstructing car surfaces matching small image patches [Schewe and Förstner 1986] and point transfer [Förstner and Pertl 1986]. Grün [1985] extended this approach to matching multiple images. He also uses the epipolar constraint to reduce the number of transformation parameters.

Larger object surfaces can not be described by a tilted plane. Rosenholm [1987] therefore divided the left image into small rectangular patches and assumed a bilinear transformation model for each patch. He required that the parallax field at the patch boundaries is continuous and uses a smooth constraint on the curvature of the parallax map to be able to determine the transformation parameters in patches with little texture.

Wrobel [1987a, 1987b] and, independently, Helava [1988] and Ebner et al. [1987] defined similar finite elements in the object space, thus directly determining the parameters of the object surface. This approach elegantly can match multiple images and can include more complex models describing e.g. surface reflectance properties [Wrobel 1989].

The area based matching can also be used for location of signalized points. [Fraser and Brown 1986]. Instead of matching two images, one matches an image with an artificial image or a functional description of the grey values of the signal. Having signals with good contrast, precisions of up to 0.03 pixels can be obtained [Vosselman and Förstner 1988]

Compared to other matching techniques, the area based least squares matching is very precise, but for surface reconstruction as well as for point mensuration it requires good approximate values for the transformation parameters.

2.5.6 Least squares feature based matching

In [Paderes *et al.* 1984, Förstner 1986] a least squares matching algorithm is presented which uses point features to find the parameters which describe the transformation between two image coordinate systems. Similar to the above area based approach, it is assumed that the surface of the recorded object is a tilted plane, thus yielding an affine transformation between the images.

The points are selected by an interest operator, which looks for points which can be measured precisely. In fact, it searches those areas which give the highest expected precision for the above area based approach. The gradient weighted centres of gravity within such areas define the subpixel coordinates of the points [Förstner and Gülch 1987].

After the point selection, a list of possibly corresponding points is made. Two points are considered a matching candidate if the cross correlation coefficient between the grey values of the areas surrounding the points is high enough (Förstner uses 0.5 as a threshold). For each point pair (i) we have the following two equations:

$$\begin{pmatrix} x_R^i - x_L^i + v_x^i \\ y_R^i - y_L^i + v_y^i \end{pmatrix} = \begin{pmatrix} a_{11} & a_{12} \\ a_{21} & a_{22} \end{pmatrix} \begin{pmatrix} x_L^i \\ y_L^i \end{pmatrix} + \begin{pmatrix} a_1 \\ a_2 \end{pmatrix} \tag{2-21}$$

The initial weights of the point pairs are computed from the cross correlation coefficients and the expected location precisions of both point areas. Using several weight functions, the weights of the point pairs are adapted after each least squares iteration. If a weight falls below 10% of the average weight, the point correspondence is considered to be incorrect. The algorithm stops if the transformation parameters are determined precise enough, if there are not enough point pairs left (<6) or if a maximum number of iteration has been performed. Remaining ambiguities (one point in the left image can still have several points in the right image) are resolved by taking the correspondence with the smallest residual value.

Although the least squares algorithm does not require approximate value, since, in this case, the observation equations are linear in the transformation parameters, this matching algorithm will not work without certain approximations. The overlap between the two images should be at least 70%. Otherwise, the number of false correspondences in the initial list of point pairs becomes to large to extract the correct ones. Also the rotation, shear and scale parameters should be known within 30%, because the cross correlation coefficient, used for the determination of the initial weights, is not invariant against changes in these parameters. Assuming a wrong rotation, e.g., would give low weights to the correct point pairs.

Obeying these restrictions, the least squares feature based method has proven to be a very powerful matching method. Even with up to 80% of the initial point pairs being wrong, it is capable of finding the correct mappings. Like all least squares methods it is, however, limited to problems where approximate values can be provided.

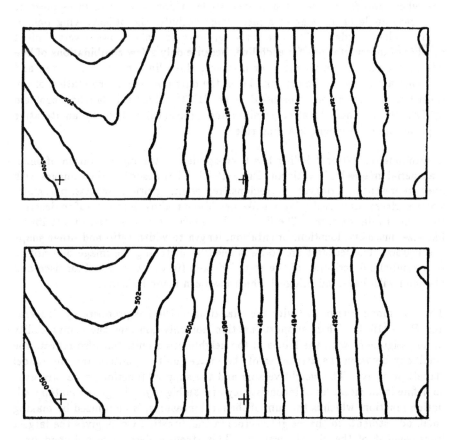

Figure 2.5: Isocontour map derived from operator measurements (upper map) and from matched point features (lower map).

Hahn [1989] used this matching algorithm to extract digital terrain models from digitized aerial photographs (figure 2.5). The accuracy of the matching algorithm approaches the accuracy of a human operator. Ackermann and Krzystek [1991] developed a hierarchical implementation, using the tilted plane model at the top level of the image pyramid and increasingly refined patches, similar to the finite element approach of Rosenholm [1987], at lower levels.

2.5.7 Scene interpretation by relaxation labeling

One of the first problems tackled by a relaxation-like method is the interpretation of line drawings [Waltz 1972, 1975]. Given an ideal line drawing of a scene with polyhedra, each line segment has three possible interpretations. It may be a line where two faces meet at a convex angle, a line where two faces meet at a concave angle or an edge of a face which occludes the objects lying behind it (an occluding edge). The line drawing, however, only allows a very limited number of interpretations for each line, because only a few combinations of line interpretations are consistent. For instance, three lines meet at a vertex and two lines are known to be convex. Then, the only possible interpretation of the third line is convex too. Rosenfeld *et al.* [1976] solved this labeling problem by formulating these local constraints and propagating them by an iterative application of the label discarding rule.

Continuous relaxation labeling has been applied to the interpretation of small scale aerial images by Nevatia and Price [1982]. They described their images with lines (representing bridges) and regions (representing cities, airports, parks and water surfaces) and used relations like neighbours, above and part-of to describe the spatial relationships. The lines and regions are represented by attributes like size, intensity, location, orientation, length to width ratio and other shape descriptors. The features are to be labeled by matching the image description to a symbolic description of the recorded area (in this case San Francisco and Oakland with bays and bridges) which has been made by hand.

The matching is performed with the relaxation method as proposed by Faugeras and Price [1981]. Their support function not only contains the compatibility of an assignment with the labels of the neighbouring units but also reflects the similarity between the attributes of the image (unit) primitive and the model (label) primitive. The weight vectors and the support function values are used to define local measures of inconsistency and ambiguity. The global match evaluation function, which is the sum of the local measures, is minimized by making small adjustments to the weight vectors in the direction which gives the largest improvement of the global measure. This steepest descent is obtained by a differentiation of the global measure.

Although both examples above use the relaxation method to classify image features, it is clear that relaxation techniques can also be used for image to image

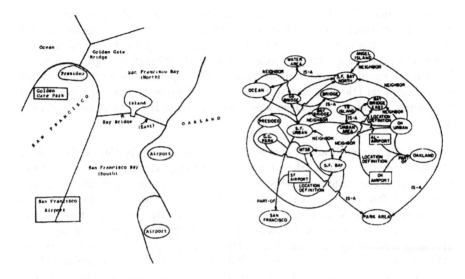

Figure 2.6: Map and symbolic description of San Francisco area (adopted from [Nevatia and Price 1982]).

matching. In fact, the model description used by Nevatia and Price is structured in the same way as the image description.

Davis [1979] presents another application of relaxation methods. He matches vectorized curved lines represented by the nodes and the angles between the adjacent lines elements. The support function is a function of the angle similarity, the node to node distance similarity and the number of unmatched nodes and thus measures the local tension in the node to node mapping. The space of the initially possible mappings is reduced by discrete relaxation.

This discrete relaxation is also useful as a preprocessing step for the tree search. Some of the branches of the tree that have an exponential complexity can be eliminated by the label discarding rule that only has a polynomial complexity.

2.5.8 Computational models of human stereo vision

Psychologists and psychophysicist are interested in getting an insight into the information processing humans perform to see stereo. Major research has been carried out at the Artificial Intelligence Laboratory of the M.I.T. [Marr and Poggio 1979, Marr and Hildreth 1980, Grimson 1981, 1985] and at the Department of Psychology of the University of Sheffield [Mayhew and Frisby 1981, Pollard et al. 1985].

In their computational studies they use the zero-crossings of the second derivative of a grey value image to describe the image. The zero-crossings are derived after filtering the image with the Laplacian of the Gaussian [Marr and Hildreth 1980, Hildreth 1983]. Using Gaussian filters of different strength, a pyramidal feature based description is obtained with only a few zero-crossings at the smoothest level (the top level). Psychophysical evidence has been found that the human visual system indeed uses 5 to 6 different smoothness levels [Wilson 1983].

Because the human brain of course knows the relative orientation of the eyes, the matching process can take advantage of the epipolar constraint. Starting at the smoothest description level, each pixel on a zero crossing in the left image only has a few matching candidates in the right image. The corresponding zero-crossings should have the same sign and roughly the same strength and orientation. The search is further constrained by the continuity of the zero-crossings across epipolar lines. This is the so-called figural continuity constraint [Mayhew and Frisby 1981, Grimson 1985]. The match of the zero-crossing pixels in a small area is judged by the percentage of correspondences in that area. Smoothness of the parallax field further constrains this exhaustive search.

Having found some match at the smoothest level, it is propagated down to the less smoothed levels. An interesting property of the zero-crossings is that zero-crossings existing at some smoothness level are preserved at all less filtered levels [Witkin 1983, Yuille and Poggio 1986]. Because the position of a zero-crossing, when using different smoothness levels, can only shift within a known fixed bound [Berzins 1984], the search at the less smoothed levels is tightly constrained by the correspondences of the higher levels. The complexity of this search strategy is shown to be of the order n^2 for images of nxn pixels [Grimson 1985]. The algorithm is capable of matching images of different types like random dot patterns and aerial images of natural and urban terrain.

2.6   Discussion

In paragraph 2.1 we have seen different levels of data descriptions. Data can be described by pixels, selected points, lines, regions, other, more complicated, features or even by relational structures. The question is: which type of description should one use for matching purposes. As Medioni and Nevatia [1984] argue, "the higher the level of descriptions at which matching is attempted, the more likely the descriptions are to be invariant to imaging changes, but this gain may be offset by the errors and deficiencies of the current programs that compute these descriptions". Indeed, the invariance of high level descriptions facilitates the matching process, but a good high level description often only can be extracted from an image after the image has been interpreted, that is, after another matching process. Medioni and Nevatia therefore use straight lines as primitives, considering this as the optimum between correctness and invariance of the description. For their application (stereo matching along epipolar lines) this may well be right, but this can not be generalized to other matching tasks.

For recognizing 3-dimensional objects, for example, one needs the contextual information of the relational descriptions to constrain the search space. Simple descriptions with points and lines are not invariant enough against imaging differences to be sufficient for object recognition. Because the extraction of high level descriptions from grey value images is so complicated, one nowadays sees that many researchers start to use range images (whose segmentation in physically meaningful parts is much easier) to recognize 3-dimensional objects [Oshima and Shirai 1983, Grimson and Lozano-Perez 1984, Horaud and Bolles 1984, Faugeras and Hebert 1986, Fan 1988].

In the case of image sequence analysis, one could do with less complicated primitives instead of the straight lines. Because the objects only move a few pixels from image to image, a simple area based description of points primitives will suffice for the matching process.

Such low level descriptions usually are very large. They can only be handled by a matching algorithm when good approximate values are available. If the type of transformation between the data descriptions is known (e.g. affine), least squares matching methods are very fast in determining the transformation parameters.

If no transformation type is known in advance, an additional smoothness constraint and the use of hierarchy are necessary to limit the search space. Only under these conditions one can match dense data, for instance with relaxation labeling or simulated annealing. When no approximate values are given, the parameters of simple transformations may be found by a generalized Hough transformation. To determine a more complex transformation, higher level descriptions and tree search methods are needed.

Concluding one may say that the relational matching should be applied to those problems where the approximate values are too bad to solve it with feature based methods. These are problems like 3-dimensional object recognition, stereo matching with unknown rotation between the images and bootstrapping of (stereo) image sequence tracking. Because the high level descriptions (derived from grey value images) on which the relational matching is operating is likely to have errors, this matching method has to be fault tolerant.

3   Formal description of relational matching

In this chapter we will give a more formal description of some idea's presented in
the previous chapter and review the early developments in relational matching.
First we will formally describe the data (the relational description). The matching algorithm has to find the mapping between two such descriptions. The mapping function maps one description onto the other description. This "mapped"
description is called the composition of the description with the mapping function. Having defined this composition, we can describe the requirements for an
exact match, a match where all relations tuples of one description correspond to
some relation tuple of the other description. In many cases, due to noise, image
segmentation errors or occlusion, an exact match will not be possible. Some
primitives and relations of the first description will not have corresponding oc-
currences in the other descriptions. The exact match definition therefore has to
be relaxed to an inexact match definition which allows for a certain number of
unmatched primitives and relations [Shapiro and Haralick 1981]. Finally a tree
search method is employed to find the mapping function that fulfils the requirements of the exact or inexact match definitions. Together, the use of relational
descriptions, the definition of a the match between relational descriptions and
the tree search method make up the relational matching method.

3.1   Definition of relational description

In this thesis we will use the formalism as introduced by Shapiro and Haralick
[1981] as they were the first to extensively use the relational descriptions for
tasks in image processing.

A relational description D is defined by primitives P and the interrelationships
R among the primitives.

$$D = (P, R) \tag{3-1}$$

The primitives p_i are represented in a set P

$$P = \{p_1, p_2, p_3, \ldots, p_i, \ldots, p_{N-1}, p_N\} \tag{3-2}$$

and each primitive p_i is described by a set of L attribute value pairs. Thus the
set P is a subset of all combinations of L attribute value pairs.

$$P \subseteq (A \times V)^L \tag{3-3}$$

where A is the set of attributes names and V is the set of possible values for
those attributes. E.g. a point primitive having three attributes ($L=3$), a row and
a column coordinate and a gradient strength attribute, could be represented as:

$$p_i = \{(row\ 119)(column\ 34)(strength\ 1.7)\}$$

Relational matching needs the contextual information of a description to solve the correspondence problem. This contextual information is stored in the relational part of a structural description, denoted by the symbol R. Usually there will be several different relations, e.g. a relation "contour" between a line and a region, a relation "angle" between two lines or a relation "collinear" between three points. Of each relation there will be multiple events, e.g. there will be several pairs of lines and regions that make an event of the "contour" relation. Each event of a relation is described by a tuple of the primitives that build the event and the attribute value pairs of the event of this relation. All events are collected in one set, denoted R_k for the kth relation. Paired with the name of the relation (NR_k), it is called a named relation and is denoted by the symbol PR_k. All named relations together are called the contextual information of the description.

More formally, R is a set of K named relations PR.

$$R = \{PR_1, PR_2, PR_3, \ldots, PR_k \ldots, PR_{K-1}, PR_K\} \qquad (3\text{-}4)$$

Each named relation PR_k is a pair of the name of the relation and the set of relation tuples.

$$PR_k = (NR_k, R_k) \qquad (3\text{-}5)$$

The set of relation tuples of relation k over M_k primitives and L_k attribute value pairs is a subset of all possible combinations.

$$R_k \subseteq P^{M_k} \times (A \times V)^{L_k} \qquad (3\text{-}6)$$

Taking the example of paragraph 2.1.2, we have a named relation, say PR_1, expressing all contour relationships between the polygons and the regions

$$PR_1 = (\text{ contour}, \quad (\quad \{ p_2\ p_5 \ (\text{ coverage } 100\ ) \ (\text{ distance } 10.3\ ) \}$$
$$\{ p_2\ p_4 \ (\text{ coverage } 34\ ) \ (\text{ distance } 5.7\ ) \}$$
$$\ldots$$
$$\{ p_1\ p_7 \ (\text{ coverage } 100\ ) \ (\text{ distance } 25.4\ ) \}))$$

which has the name "contour" and a set of relation tuples describing the events of the contour relationships. Each relation tuple of this set, e.g.

$$\{ p_2\ p_4 \ (\text{ coverage } 34\ ) \ (\text{ distance } 5.7\ ) \}$$

is a binary relation over the primitives, i.e. $M_1{=}2$, and has two attributes, i.e. $L_1{=}2$. Since the primitives in the relation tuples are tuples themselves, these relational descriptions are closely related to the relational models in the so-called *non first normal form* [Schek and Scholl 1986, 1987].

3.2 Compositions

Compositions are used to find out which relation tuples have to be compared with each other. If we would have the following mapping function from primitive set P to primitive set Q

$$h: \quad \begin{aligned} p_1 &\to q_1 \\ p_2 &\to q_3 \\ p_3 &\to q_7 \end{aligned}$$

and the primitives p_1, p_2 and p_3 would make up a tuple of a ternary relation, i.e. $\{ p_1 \; p_2 \; p_3 \}$, then, clearly, it has to be checked whether the relational part of the other description contains the tuple $\{ q_1 \; q_3 \; q_7 \}$. The latter tuple is called the composition of the first tuple with the mapping function. The composition operator is denoted by a small circle o

$$\{ p_1 \; p_2 \; p_3 \} \circ h = \{ q_1 \; q_3 \; q_7 \} \tag{3-7}$$

Similarly a composition of a set of tuples R_k is built by composing all tuples of the set. Formally this is described as follows. Let $D1 = (P, R)$ and $D2 = (Q, S)$ be two relational descriptions with primitive sets P and Q and relationships described in R and S. Let $h : P \to Q$ be a function that maps primitives of P to primitives of Q. Then the composition of the kth relation set R_k with h, denoted $R_k \circ h$, is defined by all tuples of primitives of Q of which the corresponding primitives in P form a tuple which is in R_k:

$$\begin{aligned} R_k \circ h \;=\; & \{(q_1, q_2, ..., q_N) \in Q^N \mid (p_1, p_2, ..., p_N) \in R_k \\ & \text{with } h(p_i) = q_i \text{ for } i = 1, 2, ..., N\} \end{aligned} \tag{3-8}$$

In the next four figures we will use two simple relational descriptions, $D1 = (P, R)$ and $D2 = (Q, S)$, to illustrate the principle of the composition and some exact match definitions. In these figures, the primitives of the descriptions, $p_i \in P$ resp. $q_j \in Q$, are represented by circles with their name written in them. The relational part of the descriptions, R resp. S, exist of only one binary relation without attributes. Thus,

$$R = \{PR_1\} \tag{3-9}$$
$$PR_1 = (N_1, R_1) \tag{3-10}$$
$$R_1 \subseteq P \times P \tag{3-11}$$

and

$$S = \{PS_1\} \tag{3-12}$$
$$PS_1 = (N_1, S_1) \tag{3-13}$$
$$S_1 \subseteq Q \times Q \tag{3-14}$$

If two primitives have a relation, this is visualized in the figures by a line between the primitives. Figure 3.1 gives an example of a composition of a relation set with a mapping function.

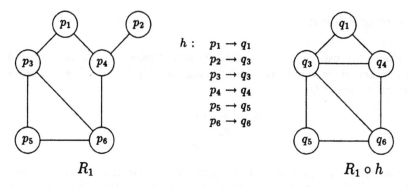

$$h : \quad p_1 \rightarrow q_1$$
$$p_2 \rightarrow q_3$$
$$p_3 \rightarrow q_3$$
$$p_4 \rightarrow q_4$$
$$p_5 \rightarrow q_5$$
$$p_6 \rightarrow q_6$$

Figure 3.1: The composition of R_1 with a mapping h

3.3 Exact matching

An exact match from description $D1$ to description $D2$ is a mapping that has a corresponding relation tuple in $D2$ for each relation tuple in $D1$. For the moment we will ignore any attribute of the primitives and the relations. An exact match of the two descriptions in figure 3.2 therefore is a mapping $h : P \rightarrow Q$ that maps each tuple in R_1 to a tuple in S_1. This is equivalent to saying that the composition of relation set R_1 with the mapping function h is a subset of the relation set S_1, i.e.,

$$R_1 \circ h \subseteq S_1 \tag{3-15}$$

A mapping fulfilling this requirement is called a relational homomorphism from R_1 to S_1 (figure 3.2). Having more relation types than just the one binary

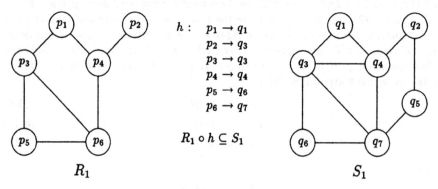

Figure 3.2: A relational homomorphism

relation in the example, one will require a mapping which is a relational homomorphism for each pair of relation sets R_i and S_j having the same name, i.e. $NR_i = NS_j$. Thus one looks for the mapping $h : P \rightarrow Q$ such that

$$R_i \circ h \subseteq S_j \qquad \forall i,j \text{ where } NR_i = NS_j \tag{3-16}$$

One might also consider the descriptions of the example to be two undirected graphs. The primitives are the vertices of the graph and the relations are the edges of the graph. In that case one also speaks of a graph homomorphism [Harary 1969]. In fact, the relational homomorphism is the natural extension of the graph homomorphism for graphs with multinary relations [Haralick and Kartus 1978].

The time needed for finding a homomorphism exponentially increases with the number of primitives involved. The homomorphism problem is *non polynomial complete* (usually abbreviated to NPC or NP complete) which means that there are no algorithms with polynomial time complexity that can solve all homomorphism problems. A tree search method is needed to find the solution to a homomorphism problem.

Whereas the relational homomorphism is the general case, the relational monomorphism and the relational isomorphism are two special cases of the relational homomorphism which pose extra requirements to a mapping function. A relational monomorphism is a relational homomorphism that is one to one. I.e. each primitive of set P is mapped to a unique primitive of set Q. Figure 3.3 gives an example. Note that the mapping in figure 3.2 is not a relational monomorphism. Although the relational monomorphism is a stronger match than the relational homomorphism, its worst case search complexity is still exponential. The relational isomorphism is an even stronger kind of match. A mapping h is a

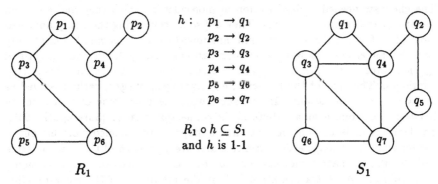

$$h : \quad p_1 \rightarrow q_1$$
$$p_2 \rightarrow q_2$$
$$p_3 \rightarrow q_3$$
$$p_4 \rightarrow q_4$$
$$p_5 \rightarrow q_6$$
$$p_6 \rightarrow q_7$$

$$R_1 \circ h \subseteq S_1$$
and h is 1-1

Figure 3.3: A relational monomorphism

relational isomorphism if h is a one-to-one homomorphism from relation set R_1 to relation set S_1 and h^{-1} is a one-to-one relational homomorphism from S_1 to R_1 (figure 3.4). Thus a relational isomorphism h is a one-to-one mapping from P to Q such that

$$R_1 \circ h \subseteq S_1 \quad \text{and} \quad S_1 \circ h^{-1} \subseteq R_1 \tag{3-17}$$

or equivalently

$$R_1 \circ h = S_1 \tag{3-18}$$

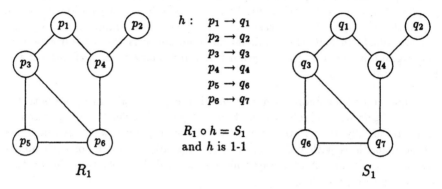

Figure 3.4: A relational isomorphism

The worst case search complexity of the relational isomorphism problem is polynomial in the number of primitives. If one excludes a class of very regular graphs, an efficient polynomial algorithm can be used (clearly not a tree search) of which the power is at worst five [Corneil and Gottlieb 1970].

The first applications of exact relational matching were not in image processing but in chemistry and mathematics [Unger 1964, Sussenguth 1965, Lynch 1968]. The chemists needed a classification of molecules of which they had analyzed the atoms and their connections. They did so by comparing the newly analyzed molecule (of which the name was still unknown) with a large number of already classified molecules that were stored in a database. All molecules were described by their atoms (the primitives) and the connections between the atoms (the relations). The type of the molecule, e.g. hydrogen, oxygen, carbon, served as an attribute to the atoms. In the same way, the bond type of a connection between two atoms is an attribute to the connection relation [Sussenguth 1965]. To classify a molecule, one needs to find a mapping to a named molecule out of the database that maps every primitive and every relation of the new molecule and the already named molecule one-to-one, i.e. one needs to find a relational isomorphism. An extra condition is that the attributes of the corresponding atoms and the corresponding connections should also agree of course. Since, for each atom type, this match requires that the number of atoms are the same, e.g. a molecule with six hydrogen atoms will not match with a molecule with seven hydrogen atoms, it is easy to rule out most of the molecules of the database by checking the sum-formula. However, several different molecules exist having the same sum-formula, like e.g. the amino-acids in figure 3.5. These two molecules can only be discerned by checking their structure, i.e. their relational description. So, if a chemist would analyze a molecule and find a structure as in figure 3.6, he needs a relational matching to classify it. Another task chemists are interested in is to find all molecules which contain a certain subcompound, e.g. the **COOH**-group in the figures of the amino-acids. This is a typical example of a relational

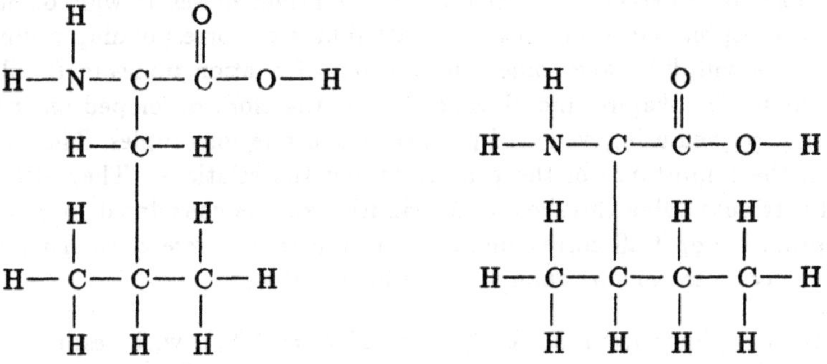

Figure 3.5: Two amino-acids with the same atoms

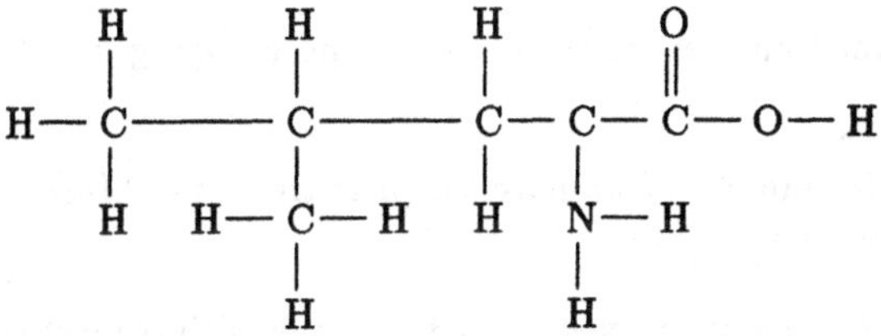

Figure 3.6: Leucine or Isoleucine ?

monomorphism. It is a one-to-one homomorphism from the subcompound to a compound in the database, but not vice-versa, because not all primitives of the compound will be mapped to by a primitive of the subcompound. Thus it is not a relational isomorphism. If the relational descriptions are graphs (like in the examples above), the mapping that maps a small graph to a part of a larger graph is also called a subgraph-isomorphism. The reason for this is obvious. Letting away the primitives of the larger graph which are not mapped to and the relations these primitives are involved in, there is a graph-isomorphism between the small graph and the remaining part of the larger graph.

3.4 Inexact matching

Although the above concepts of homomorphisms might well work for finding chemical compounds or the interpretation of line drawings [Waltz 1972], they will fail when being applied to matching images with other images, models or maps. Due to noise or differences in orientation, primitives of set P will sometimes have no corresponding primitives in Q, attributes of corresponding primitives and relations will differ and some compositions of relation tuples in R will not be present in S. Shapiro and Haralick [1981] therefore developed an inexact matching approach using weighted primitives and relations tuples. The weights represent the importance of the primitives and the relations. They also used a set of attribute value thresholds. A primitive p_i was considered to inexactly match primitive q_j if all corresponding attribute values were close enough, i.e. the differences were smaller than the thresholds values.

An ε-homomorphism from R_i to S_j (with $NR_i = NS_j$), with respect to the relation tuple weights $w(r)$, was defined as a mapping $h : P \rightarrow Q$ such that the weighted number of tuples in R_i that do not have corresponding tuples in S_j is below the threshold ε_i:

$$\sum_{\substack{r \in R_i \\ r \circ h \notin S_j}} w(r) \leq \varepsilon_i \qquad (3\text{-}19)$$

Finally they defined an inexact match to be the mapping $h : P \rightarrow Q \cup \emptyset$ such that

1. the weighted number of unmatched primitives (i.e. $h(p_i) = \emptyset$) is below a certain threshold,

2. the corresponding primitives inexactly match with respect to the attribute value thresholds and

3. h is an ε_i-homomorphism from R_i to S_j for all sets of relation tuples having the same name ($NR_i = NS_j$).

3.5 Tree search

The final component of the relational matching method is the tree search. Using the inexact matching definition of Shapiro and Haralick, one has to test for the attribute value differences and the percentages of unmatched primitives and relations at every node in the tree. These tests then give the answer to the question whether or not to continue the search at the sons of the current node. The backtracking tree search, which is a standard method to process a search tree and was briefly described in paragraph 2.3.1, is quite inefficient in finding an acceptable mapping. Ullman [1976], Rosenfeld et al. [1976], Haralick and Elliot [1980] and others made several improvements to this method by using heuristics in order to find a more efficient way of scanning the search space. Haralick and Elliot also made a comparative study on the efficiency of several heuristics by testing them on the so-called N-Queens problem.

3.6   Some problems using relational matching

Despite the popularity of the relational matching method, there still are quite some problems that have to be solved before this method can be of practical use. The major problems are shortly outlined below.

- Relational matching requires high level descriptions of the data to be matched. The extraction of high level description, however, often needs a lot a priori knowledge. The grey values of an image as analyzed by a line detector that operates locally do not contain enough information to find all edges. The extracted edges have to be combined with knowledge about the global structures of the objects in the image in order to obtain high level descriptions. The representation and integration of such knowledge in feature extraction processes still is a problem. First experiment, however, show encouraging results [Fua and Hanson 1987, 1988, Mohan and Nevatia 1989, Straforini *et al.* 1990].

- The inexact matching as described above uses many weights to define the ϵ-homomorphisms and the allowed number of unmatched primitives. There is no sound theory describing the way all these weights and thresholds have to be determined.

- The inexact matching uses a lot of tests to decide whether a mapping is acceptable or not. Given two mappings it is hard to decide which mapping is the best one, since this would require a comparison of the test values of all tests.

- All tests only decide whether a (partial) mapping is acceptable or not. This doesn't inform the search method about the locations in the search tree where it will be likely to find a good mapping.

- As a consequence, the inexact matching only uses so-called blind search methods. Although heuristics can improve their performance to a certain extent, more intelligent search methods certainly could bring a larger decrease in search time.

In the next chapter we will elaborate on these problems and describe the contribution of this thesis in solving them.

4 Problem definition and contributions of the thesis

Although relational matching nowadays is a widely applied technique, especially for object recognition tasks, only few attempts have been made to further develop the theory. In this thesis we will improve several aspects of the relational matching method using the results of the well established probability and information theory.

The first aspect, the extraction of high level descriptions from digital grey value images, still is a problem. A high level description usually requires a (partial) interpretation of the image, which is a matching process itself. Although good high level relational descriptions are important to the relational matching method - the higher the level of description, the smaller the search space -, extracting such descriptions is not a specific task to the relational matching. Virtually all matching methods benefit from high level descriptions. This thesis will not further investigate this theme, but focus on the other two components which both are specific to the relational matching method: comparing relational descriptions and searching for the best match between them.

4.1 Evaluation of mappings

In the first applications of relational matching the quality of a mapping was only judged by the percentage of relation tuples that could be matched (like in the examples of the homomorphism, monomorphism and isomorphism). Later symbolic attributes were added to the primitives as well as to the relations, giving extra constraints in the search process (like in the example of the chemical compounds). Finally numeric attributes were introduced and, because of the stochastic nature of the measurements producing the attribute values, the inexact matching was defined.

In the definition of inexact matching a good mapping is a mapping that is acceptable with respect to the imposed threshold on the percentage of unmatched primitives, the thresholds on the differences of the attribute values and the thresholds on the percentages of not corresponding relation tuples. There are several disadvantages in proceeding this way:

- The definition of the inexact match is for a mapping that is good enough, not for the best possible match. However, often it will be impossible to specify what is good enough. For instance, in image to image matching one tries to find the corresponding primitives of two overlapping images. But, if it is not known to what extent the images overlap each other, one can not specify an appropriate threshold for the allowed percentage of unmatched primitives. This forces one to look for the best mapping.

- The definition uses many thresholds (one for each attribute type, one for each relation type and one for the unmatched primitives). All test values have to pass the threshold before a mapping is accepted. This means that if only one test fails, whereas all other test values are good, a mapping will be rejected. This even happens if the good test values give such a strong support for the correctness of the mapping that one failing test would not matter. To prevent this, one has to set all thresholds to a very generous value, but this clearly diminishes the discriminating power of the search.

- The tests always give a binary answer: a value is good or not good. This implies that the test values themselves are not used to tell the search algorithm where it will be more likely or less likely to find a good mapping. It also disables the search algorithm to use attributes which can not give a good/not good answer. For example, a 3D object model consists of a few short straight lines and a few long straight lines. The object has been recorded in a digital image and the task is to determine the location and orientation of the object in the image. Suppose the attribute linelength is used to guide the search. If the length of an image line would be relatively small compared to the other lines, it is likely that this line corresponds to a short object line. However, it may well be that, due to the projection, the short image line corresponds to a long object line. Thus, the attribute linelength can not be used to decide whether a mapping is good or wrong, but certainly indicates which mapping is likely and which one is not.

The solution to these problems is the use of an evaluation function which combines all test values. The definition of an evaluation function for mappings of relational descriptions is one of the main topics of this thesis.

Several functions already have been suggested [Sanfeliu and Fu 1983, Shapiro and Haralick 1985, Boyer and Kak 1986], but they all have some drawbacks. These functions either are mixtures of many weights, thresholds and normalization factors or do not comprise all aspects of a mapping that should be reflected by such a function. Boyer and Kak [1986], for instance, do not consider the effect of unmapped primitives in their evaluation function. Their measure is, however, the only one of those cited above that models the similarity between attributes by probabilities. As shown in chapter 2 this is the only way one can combine the evaluation of numerical and symbolical attribute correspondences. Using some of the ideas on which this function is based, we will propose a new measure. This new function contains all components the evaluation function should have, is also based on the probability/information theory and needs no weights or other hard to tune control parameters. Furthermore it will be shown that optimizing this function leads to the maximum likelihood estimation of the mapping.

4.2 Tree search methods

The last component of relational matching is the tree search. Beside the improvements of the backtracking search which could be made by the use of heuristics, the use of a single evaluation function also can be used to speed up the search and opens up the possibility to use a variety of search methods developed in the area of artificial intelligence [Nilsson 1971, 1982, Winston 1977, Barr and Feigenbaum 1981]. These so-called informed search methods use the evaluation function to guide the search.

Evaluation functions can be either cost functions or merit functions. The value of a cost function is to be minimized, that of a merit function to be maximized. All evaluation functions that have been suggested before are cost functions. Our new evaluation function, however, will be a merit function. The informed search methods are all designed for evaluation functions that are cost functions. We will show that using these search methods with a merit function is possible but that the definition of some of these methods needs to be slightly changed. We will analyze the behaviour of the search methods when being applied to relational matching problems.

The heuristics in [Haralick and Elliott 1980] and others were developed for blind search methods, but they can also be used for informed search methods. We will describe how these heuristics efficiently can be combined with the calculation of the evaluation function.

This chapter concludes the introductory part of this thesis. In the next part we will develop the new evaluation function and combine this function with the well-known search methods. In the third and last part we will then apply the new theories to the object location problem.

Part II

Theory of relational matching

The evaluation of mappings, or more general, the evaluation of results of computer vision algorithms, has been grossly undervalued. Only in recent years the qualitative analysis of algorithms and their results has gained in interest. The probability theory is pre-eminently suitable for this analysis and is increasingly applied to computer vision problems. Maximum likelihood estimators can be used to select the best solution (e.g. the best mapping), whereas statistical tests can be invoked for the decision whether the solution can be accepted or has to be rejected.

Closely related to the probability theory is the information theory. Originally developed for optimizing communication systems, the information theory nowadays is a widely applied tool. Like the probability theory, it can also be used for decision making. The information theory gives an alternative view on probabilities. Because the information theory will be important for the definition of the new measure for comparing relational descriptions, the first chapter of this more theoretical part will be devoted to this theory.

In chapter 6 we will discuss the information-theoretic measure of Boyer and Kak and present a new measure for the evaluation of mappings between relational descriptions. This measure will be integrated into the tree search methods in chapter 7.

5 Information theory: selected topics

Information theory has been developed in order to optimize the transmission of information over communication channels. Communication systems, like telegraph, telephone and television, usually can be characterized by the following scheme (figure 5.1). A message is to be sent from the information source to some destination. First the message (e.g. a written text) is sent to the transmitter which encodes the message in a signal that is suitable for sending over the system channel between the transmitter and the receiver (e.g. a sequence of electric pulses over a wire). During the transmission over the system channel, the signal may be exposed to disturbing influences. So, the input to the receiver is a mixture of the signal sent by the transmitter and the noise on the system channel. The task of the receiver is to decode this noisy signal, thereby filtering out as much of the noise as possible and so making an estimate of the original message which was the input to the transmitter.

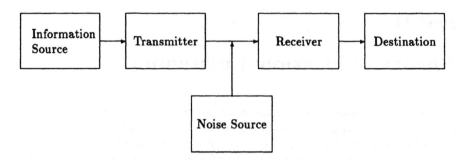

Figure 5.1: A sketch of a communication channel

The main objective of the information theory is to develop efficient codes for the transmission of signals over a communication channel. On the one hand, the transmission speed is to be maximized. This requires a code which encodes the message into the shortest possible signal. On the other hand, however, the receiver should be able to filter out the noise. This pleads for a certain amount of redundancy in the transmitted signal, depending on the amount of noise to be expected and the necessity of error-free transmission.

The first prerequisite for making a quantitative analysis of communication systems and encoding schemes is to have a quantitative measure for the information of a signal. In 1948, Claude E. Shannon first published such a measure and described several other quantities of interest, like for instance the capacity of a communication channel, in his paper "Mathematical theory of communication".

In this chapter we will first describe this measure of information and some related measures for both discrete and continuous signals. Based on these definitions, we then show how the length of an optimal coded message is related to the probability. This principle of the *minimal description length* will be used to improve the relational image descriptions that will be matched to 3-D models in part III of this thesis, where the relational matching method is applied to the object location problem.

The last paragraph of this chapter deals with the problem of discretization. Many attributes of primitives and relations have continuous attribute value ranges (e.g. length or angle). Often it will not be possible to specify a continuous function of two attribute values that outputs a value for the similarity between these attribute values. In that case one has to discretize the value range and to somehow determine the similarity for a (large) number of discrete values. A discretization, however, always implies a loss of information, and therefore a loss in the accuracy of the similarity value. We will show that, for a certain type of information, this loss can be limited to an arbitrarily low percentage.

5.1 Information measures for discrete signals

A channel is called discrete if it can only transmit a countable number of symbols. These symbols can be selected from a predefined alphabet. A signal which is made up by a sequence of symbols from this alphabet is therefore called a discrete signal. The measure of information content of a symbol follows from the following considerations (also see [Koch 1990], p.16):

- The information of a symbol or a sequence of symbols will be high if the probability this symbol or sequence will be selected is small. The information is a measure of surprise. The information of the message "it is snowing outside" will be higher in the summer than in the winter, because it is less likely to snow in the summer.

- If there is only one symbol that can be selected, there is no uncertainty in the outcome of this selection. So, if the probability of a message is one, the message contains no information.

- The information a message reveals to us is an additive quantity. If we had received a certain message and after that receive another, equally informative, message which is statistically independent of the first message, we say that we now have received twice as much information as we had after receiving only the first message. Thus the information of independent messages can be added. To calculate the probability of receiving two independent messages, however, one has to multiply the probabilities of the individual messages.

Combining the above considerations, the logarithm is the only possible functional relation between information and probability. The information of a selecting a certain symbol a_i, which is selected with a probability $P(a_i)$, is defined by

$$I(a_i) = \log_b \frac{1}{P(a_i)} = -\log_b P(a_i) \tag{5-1}$$

where b is the constant base of the logarithm which determines the unit of information [Shannon and Weaver 1949]. If it is two, the unit is a bit, if we use the natural logarithm, the unit is called a nat and if the base is ten, the information is expressed in Hartley's. We will use the bit as the unit of information and omit the base indication of the logarithm.

Suppose the alphabet of a transmitter (source) A would contain the symbols $\{a_1, a_2, \ldots, a_N\}$ and for each symbol a_i the probability that the symbol will be sent, $P(a_i)$, would be known. Then one can calculate the average information per symbol that the source A sends by the weighted sum of the information of the individual symbols.

$$H(A) = \sum_{i=1}^{N} P(a_i) \cdot I(a_i) = \sum_{i=1}^{N} -P(a_i) \log P(a_i) \tag{5-2}$$

$H(A)$ is also called the entropy [3] of the source and expresses the uncertainty in the selection of the symbol which is to be transmitted [Shannon and Weaver 1949]. It also is the expected amount of information. If only one symbol a_k were possible, i.e. $P(a_k) = 1$ and all other probabilities were zero, the entropy would be zero too. In this case there is no uncertainty. It can be proven that the maximum uncertainty occurs in case all symbols are equally likely [Ingels 1971].

The symbols received by the receiver also constitute an alphabet, say $\{b_1, b_2, \ldots, b_M\}$ and the probability that symbol b_j is received is denoted $P(b_j)$. The noise characteristics of the channel can be modeled by the conditional probabilities of the transmitted symbols, given the received symbols. In an ideal channel there is a one to one correspondence between the symbols of the source alphabet and the symbols of the receiver alphabet. I.e. knowing the symbol that has been sent, one also knows the symbol that will be received and, vice versa, knowing the symbol that has been received, one also knows which symbol has been sent. If a source sends symbol a_k over an ideal channel and the symbol b_l is received, the conditional probabilities of the symbols of source alphabet A given that b_l has been received is one for symbol a_k and zero for all other symbols. In case of a noisy channel these probabilities may take all values between one and zero. The surprise when being told that symbol a_i has been transmitted, whereas it is known that symbol b_j has been received is measured by the conditional information [Ingels 1971, Blahut 1987]

$$I(a_i|b_j) = -\log P(a_i|b_j) \tag{5-3}$$

The surprise will be low for high probabilities. The conditional information will even be zero if the probability is one, since, after receiving b_j over an ideal channel, we can conclude that a_i must have been transmitted. Hence, the message that a_i has been transmitted is no surprise to us and contains no information that we didn't already have.

The uncertainty about the symbol which has been sent when having received b_j is found by averaging over the symbols of the source alphabet, thereby weighting the conditional information with the probability that a source symbols is sent:

$$H(A|b_j) = \sum_{i=1}^{N} P(a_i) \cdot I(a_i|b_j) = \sum_{i=1}^{N} -P(a_i)\log P(a_i|b_j) \tag{5-4}$$

For the ideal channel, with all conditional probabilities being either 0 or 1, it is clear that the uncertainty is zero[4].

The conditional entropy is defined by the weighted sum of the conditional information over all combinations of input and output symbols [Ingels 1971, Blahut

---

[3] Since the average information per symbol has the same mathematical expression as the physical entropy as defined by Boltzmann in the theory on thermodynamics, Shannon also called it entropy.

[4] Defining $0\log 0 = \lim_{x \downarrow 0} x \log x = 0$.

1987].

$$H(A|B) = \sum_{i=1}^{N}\sum_{j=1}^{M} -P(a_i, b_j)\log P(a_i|b_j)$$

$$= \sum_{j=1}^{M} P(b_j)\sum_{i=1}^{N} -P(a_i|b_j)\log P(a_i|b_j) \qquad (5\text{-}5)$$

The conditional entropy is also called the noise entropy (or equivocation) since it expresses the average uncertainty about the transmitted symbol, average over all received symbols. It measures the average loss of information in the channel.

The most important quantity is the mutual information between two symbols, defined as the difference of the self information and the conditional information [Ingels 1971, Blahut 1987].

$$I(a_i; b_j) = I(a_i) - I(a_i|b_j) \qquad (5\text{-}6)$$

This is the amount of information one symbol gives about the other. An interesting property of the mutual information is that it is a symmetric function of the input and the output symbol.

$$\begin{aligned} I(a_i; b_j) &= I(a_i) - I(a_i|b_j) \\ &= -\log P(a_i) + \log P(a_i|b_j) \\ &= \log \frac{P(a_i, b_j)}{P(a_i)\ P(b_j)} \end{aligned} \qquad (5\text{-}7)$$

Clearly, the last expression is symmetric.

Averaging over all input and output symbols we obtain the average mutual information. This is the difference between the entropy and the noise entropy.

$$H(A; B) = H(A) - H(A|B) \qquad (5\text{-}8)$$

Since $H(A)$ is the average information per transmitted symbol and $H(A|B)$ is the average loss of information, the average mutual information is the average amount of information received per symbol transmitted. Hence, it is an important measure for analyzing the performance of communication systems and for designing communication systems. The average mutual information is also called the transinformation, since it is a measure for the information transmitted through the channel. Like the mutual information the transinformation is symmetric in its arguments.

$$\begin{aligned} H(A; B) &= H(A) - H(A|B) \\ &= \sum_{i=1}^{N} -P(a_i)\log P(a_i) + \sum_{i=1}^{N}\sum_{j=1}^{M} P(a_i, b_j)\log P(a_i|b_j) \end{aligned}$$

$$= \sum_{i=1}^{N} \sum_{j=1}^{M} -P(a_i, b_j) \log P(a_i) + \sum_{i=1}^{N} \sum_{j=1}^{M} P(a_i, b_j) \log P(a_i|b_j)$$

$$= \sum_{i=1}^{N} \sum_{j=1}^{M} P(a_i, b_j) \log \frac{P(a_i, b_j)}{P(a_i) \ P(b_j)} \qquad (5\text{-}9)$$

5.2 Information measures for continuous signals

Up to now it has been assumed that the alphabet from which the source can choose a symbol has a countable number of symbols. It may, however, be that one wants to transmit an event of a random real variable. In practice one will always send a rounded-off value of course, but, in order to analyze the information contents of real variables, let us for the moment consider that there is an infinite number of signals that may be transmitted. Let these events be modeled by a random variable A with probability density function $p(a)$[5].

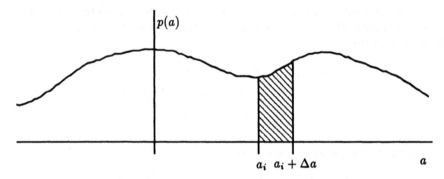

Figure 5.2: A probability density function

The probability of A taking a value between a_i and $a_i + \Delta a$ can be approximated by $p(a_i)\ \Delta a$ (figure 5.2). The information of a value lying in this interval would therefore be $-\log p(a_i)\ \Delta a$. For indefinitely small intervals (i.e. no discretization), it is clear that the above probability becomes zero and the corresponding information becomes infinite. To be able to compare the information of different continuous signals, one therefore defines the differential information, which is the negative logarithm of the probability density [Ingels 1971].

$$I_{dif}(a_i) = -\log p(a_i) \qquad (5\text{-}10)$$

Note that an amount of differential information can not be compared with an amount of information from a discrete source. Also, unlike the information of a

---

[5]Note that throughout this thesis we will use the uppercase P for probability and the lowercase p for probability density.

discrete source, the differential information may take a negative value, since a probability density may be larger than one. Thus the differential information can only be used for sorting the information of continuous signals or for calculating a difference in information content.

The entropy of a continuous random variable according to formula 5-2 becomes

$$
\begin{aligned}
H(A) &= \lim_{\Delta a \to 0} - \sum_{i=-\infty}^{\infty} p(a_i) \Delta a \log p(a_i) \Delta a \\
&= \lim_{\Delta a \to 0} \left[- \sum_{i=-\infty}^{\infty} p(a_i) \Delta a \log p(a_i) - \sum_{i=-\infty}^{\infty} p(a_i) \Delta a \log \Delta a \right] \\
&= - \int_{-\infty}^{\infty} p(a) \log p(a) da - \lim_{\Delta a \to 0} \log \Delta a
\end{aligned}
\tag{5-11}
$$

From the last term it becomes evident that the entropy of any continuous random variable approaches infinity. Like for the differential information, a differential entropy has been defined by only considering the probability density [Ingels 1971].

$$
\begin{aligned}
H_{dif}(A) &= \int_{-\infty}^{\infty} p(a) I_{dif}(a) da \\
&= - \int_{-\infty}^{\infty} p(a) \log p(a) da
\end{aligned}
\tag{5-12}
$$

This makes it possible to compare the entropies of different continuous sources.

Similar definitions can be made for the conditional probability density function. The differential conditional information is defined by

$$
I_{dif}(a_i|b_j) = - \log p(a_i|b_j)
\tag{5-13}
$$

and the differential conditional entropy by

$$
\begin{aligned}
H_{dif}(A|B) &= \int_{-\infty}^{\infty} \int_{-\infty}^{\infty} p(a,b) I_{dif}(a|b) \ da \ db \\
&= \int_{-\infty}^{\infty} \int_{-\infty}^{\infty} -p(a,b) \log p(a|b) \ da \ db \\
&= \int_{-\infty}^{\infty} -p(b) \int_{-\infty}^{\infty} p(a|b) \log p(a|b) \ da \ db
\end{aligned}
\tag{5-14}
$$

Finally the differential mutual information is defined as the difference between the differential information and the differential conditional information. Since $P(a_i) = p(a_i)\ \Delta a$ and $P(a_i|b_j) = p(a_i|b_j)\ \Delta a$, it follows that (cf. [Ingels 1971])

$$
\begin{aligned}
I(a_i; b_j) & = I(a_i) - I(a_i|b_j) = \log \frac{P(a_i|b_j)}{P(a_i)} \\
& = \log \frac{p(a_i|b_j)\Delta a}{p(a_i)\Delta a} = \log \frac{p(a_i|b_j)}{p(a_i)} \\
& = I_{dif}(a_i) - I_{dif}(a_i|b_j) = I_{dif}(a_i; b_j)
\end{aligned}
\tag{5-15}
$$

Hence the mutual information takes the same form for both discrete and continuous signals.

Clearly, the same holds for the average mutual information

$$
\begin{aligned}
H(A; B) & = \lim_{\Delta a \to 0} \lim_{\Delta b \to 0} \sum_{i=-\infty}^{\infty} \sum_{j=-\infty}^{\infty} P(a_i, b_j) \log \frac{P(a_i|b_j)}{P(a_i)} \\
& = \lim_{\Delta a \to 0} \lim_{\Delta b \to 0} \sum_{i=-\infty}^{\infty} \sum_{j=-\infty}^{\infty} p(a_i, b_j) \Delta a \Delta b \log \frac{p(a_i|b_j)\Delta a}{p(a_i)\Delta a} \\
& = \int_{-\infty}^{\infty} \int_{-\infty}^{\infty} p(a, b) \log \frac{p(a|b)}{p(a)}\ da\ db \\
& = -\int_{-\infty}^{\infty} \int_{-\infty}^{\infty} p(a, b) \log p(a)\ da\ db + \\
& \quad\ \int_{-\infty}^{\infty} \int_{-\infty}^{\infty} p(a, b) \log p(a|b)\ da\ db \\
& = -\int_{-\infty}^{\infty} p(b|a) \int_{-\infty}^{\infty} p(a) \log p(a)\ da\ db + \\
& \quad\ \int_{-\infty}^{\infty} \int_{-\infty}^{\infty} p(a, b) \log p(a_i|b_j)\ da\ db \\
& = H_{dif}(A) - H_{dif}(A|B) \\
& = H_{dif}(A; B)
\end{aligned}
\tag{5-16}
$$

This implies that, except for a noise-free channel, the information of a continuous signal received per signal transmitted is always finite, although the information at the source side may be infinite.

From these equations one can also conclude that for probability density functions that are discretized, such that the probability density function is constant on each interval, the mutual information between the continuous signals is the same as the mutual information between the discretized signals. We will come back on the mutual information of discretized signals later.

5.3   The minimum description length principle

The minimum description length principle states that the shortest description of a data set is not only optimal because it can be transmitted in a short time, but also because it gives the best possible explanation of the data set. For example, if

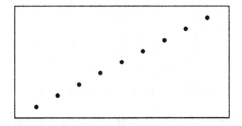

Figure 5.3: Points on a straight line

one looks at the set of points of fig. 5.3, one immediately notices that the points are equi-distantly distributed along a straight line. Hence, a complete description of the points is given by the coordinates of the first point, the direction of the line, the number of points and the distance between the points. This description clearly is much shorter than the tabulation of the coordinates of all points (a strategy that even can be used for randomly distributed points), and thus it is also the more plausible interpretation of the figure. In this paragraph we first further specify this relation between likelihood and description length. Then we extend the above example to noisy point distributions and finally show the relation between the minimum description length principle, the maximum a posteriori and maximum likelihood estimation.

5.3.1   The optimal code

Suppose a source has a set of messages $\{a_1, a_2, \ldots, a_N\}$ which are sent with probabilities $P(a_1), P(a_2), \ldots, P(a_N)$ and that the communication channel can only transmit a 0 or a 1. Any message then has to be coded as a string of 0's and 1's. A code is said to be optimal if there is a one-to-one relation between the messages and the strings and if the average length of the strings is minimal [Ingels 1971]. It is easy to prove that optimal codes use a shorter string for the message that have a high probability. A well known example for this is the Morse code, which uses a single dot for the most frequent letter "e" and the code "-.." for the less frequent letter "z". A necessary and sufficient condition for strings to be decoded is the so-called *Kraft inequality* [Ingels 1971, Rissanen 1985].

$$\sum_{a_i \in A} 2^{-L(a_i)} \leq 1 \tag{5-17}$$

A code fulfilling the prefix property, the property that no bit sequence is a prefix to another sequence, also fulfils the Kraft inequality. Consider, for instance, the following source that can send four different messages. In this example, there

a_i	$P(a_i)$	Code	$L(a_i)$
a_1	$\frac{1}{2}$	1	1
a_2	$\frac{1}{4}$	01	2
a_3	$\frac{1}{8}$	001	3
a_4	$\frac{1}{8}$	000	3

Table 5.1: An ideal coded source

is no code that is a prefix of another code. This implies that one always knows how to separate a long sequence into the codes of the individual messages.

Another important inequality states that if $\{x_i\}, \{y_i\}, i = 1, 2, \ldots, n$ are two sets of non-negative numbers such that $\sum_{i=1}^{n} x_i = \sum_{i=1}^{n} y_i = 1$

$$-\sum_{i=1}^{n} x_i \log y_i \geq -\sum_{i=1}^{n} x_i \log x_i \tag{5-18}$$

and are only equal if $x_i = y_i$, $i = 1, 2, \ldots, n$ [Ingels 1971].

Searching for the shortest average code length $\bar{L} = \sum_{i=1}^{n} P(a_i) \, L(a_i)$, it follows that

$$\bar{L} = -\sum_{i=1}^{n} P(a_i) \log_2 2^{-L(a_i)} \geq -\sum_{i=1}^{n} P(a_i) \log_2 P(a_i) = H(A) \tag{5-19}$$

This implies that the ideal way to encode the messages a_i relative to a given distribution is to use a code string with length $-\log P(a_i)$. It also gives a different view on the definition of information. Information is not just a measure of surprise, but also the length of the message when optimally encoded [Rissanen 1985].

Since the information is proportional to the length of a code string, each bit that is sent, contains a fixed quantity of information. This quantity is independent of the message that is sent. This implies that all code symbols (0 and 1 for a binary code) are equally likely to be sent, and, furthermore, that the entropy

59

of the transmitter is therefore maximized. Hence, the optimal code allows the transmitter to send as much information per symbol as possible. Table 5.1 gives an example of such an optimal code: the length of the code strings equals their information content.

5.3.2 Interpretation of noisy point distributions

The principle of minimum description length uses this relation between the probability of a message (event) and the length of its description in the optimal code, when trying to find the best explanation for a set of data. It says that the best, i.e. the most likely, explanation, using an optimal encoding scheme, is given by the explanation, i.e. description, of the smallest length [Rissanen 1985, 1987, Leclerc 1988].

The interpretation of sets of points was first introduced by Georgeff and Wallace [1984]. After hypothesizing several models (e.g. one line, two lines or just noise), the best interpretation is said to be the one with the shortest description. This selection not only reflects the deviations of the data from the model, but also comprises a measure for the complexity of the model in order to avoid unnecessarily complex explanations. For example, describing the points in figure 5.4 it

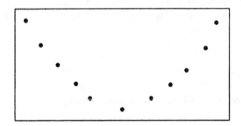

Figure 5.4: Shortest description by a parabola

is clear that a parabola will do to describe the points. A fourth order polynomial certainly will fit better, but the smaller deviations from the model will not pay off against the increased effort in describing the extra model parameters.

Another example is given in figure 5.5, taken from Förstner [1989] who shows that the left picture is best explained by a straight line, some noise and a few outliers, whereas the right picture is shorter described by the list of coordinates of all points. Using this randomness assumption, i.e. the assumption that there is no model behind the data, it takes $2n \log \frac{R}{\epsilon}$ bits to describe the set of n points with coordinate range R and resolution ϵ. Because the tabulation of the coordinates is the best way to describe the points in case they are randomly distributed, the above description length is equivalent to the information of the

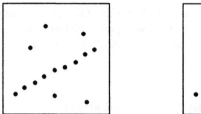 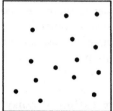

Figure 5.5: Left: Straight line with outliers. Right: Random point distribution.

point coordinates under the randomness assumption.

$$I(\text{data}|\text{randomness}) = 2n \log \frac{R}{\varepsilon} \tag{5-20}$$

For the one line assumption, the optimal description contains the following components [Förstner 1989]:

• The points either are noisy events of points on a line or outliers. It takes one bit for each point to classify the points into one of these categories.

n

• Suppose there are n_0 outliers and n_1 points along the line, so that $n = n_0 + n_1$. The outliers are described by their coordinates.

$2n_0 \log \frac{R}{\varepsilon}$

• The other points can efficiently be described by a component along the line and a component perpendicular to the line. The first component again is equally distributed (i.e. all positions are equally likely).

$n_1 \log \frac{R}{\varepsilon}$

• The perpendicular part is normal distributed in case of white noise. The term on the right gives the expected number of bits needed to code this component in case of a standard deviation of σ.

$\frac{1}{2} n_1 \log 2\pi e \left(\frac{\sigma}{\varepsilon}\right)^2$

The information of the data under the one line assumption therefore is

$$I(\text{data}|\text{one line}) = n + 2n_0 \log \frac{R}{\varepsilon} + n_1 \log \frac{R}{\varepsilon} + \frac{1}{2} n_1 \log 2\pi e \left(\frac{\sigma}{\varepsilon}\right)^2 \tag{5-21}$$

The one line assumption, however, also requires that we describe the parameters of the line. Rissanen [1978] showed that $\frac{k}{2} \log n$ bits are needed to code k parameters of a function describing n observed values. So, to code the two line parameters it takes

$$I(\text{one line}) = \log n_1 \tag{5-22}$$

bits.

The one line hypothesis is considered the best of the two hypotheses if

$$I(\text{data}|\text{one line}) + I(\text{one line}) < I(\text{data}|\text{randomness}) \qquad (5\text{-}23)$$

or

$$n + 2n_0 \log \frac{R}{\varepsilon} + n_1 \log \frac{R}{\varepsilon} + \frac{1}{2} n_1 \log 2\pi e \left(\frac{\sigma}{\varepsilon}\right)^2 + \log n_1 < 2n \log \frac{R}{\varepsilon} \qquad (5\text{-}24)$$

which evaluates to the admissibility criterion:

$$n + \log n_1 + \frac{1}{2} n_1 \log 2\pi e \left(\frac{\sigma}{R}\right)^2 < 0 \qquad (5\text{-}25)$$

It is interesting to note that this criterion is independent of the discretization resolution ε. Omitting the ε in all above expressions would mean that we are using the differential information. In this case this is allowed because there will be the same number of differential expressions on both sides of the inequality.

In contrast to formula 5-22, Förstner [1989] used $2 \log \frac{R}{\varepsilon}$ to describe the line parameters. His admissibility criterion therefore still depended on the discretization interval ε, although this interval intuitively should be of no importance for the interpretation of the points.

5.3.3 Relation to maximum a posteriori and maximum likelihood estimation

The maximum a posteriori strategy selects the ith model M_i that maximizes the conditional probability of the model given the data D: $P(M_i|D)$ [Leclerc 1988]. Since Bayes' rule states

$$P(M_i|D) = \frac{P(D|M_i) \ P(M_i)}{P(D)} \qquad (5\text{-}26)$$

and $P(D)$ is constant, the numerator $P(D|M_i) \ P(M_i)$ is to be maximized.

The minimum description length principle selects the model M_i giving the shortest complete description of the data. This description contains the description of the model and the description of the deviations of the data from that model. When the code used for these description is optimal, the length of the description is equivalent to their information content. Thus the minimum description length principle minimizes (cf. left side of equation 5-23):

$$I(D|M_i) + I(M_i) \qquad (5\text{-}27)$$

which can also be written as

$$-\log P(D|M_i) - \log P(M_i) \qquad (5\text{-}28)$$

Hence, like the maximum a posteriori strategy, the minimum length description strategy also maximizes

$$P(D|M_i) \; P(M_i) \tag{5-29}$$

In case all models are equally likely, i.e. $P(M_i)$ is constant, no attention is payed to the length of the model description. This leads to the maximum likelihood estimation, selecting the model which fits best to the data.

5.4 Discretization of continuous signals

The influence of discretizations onto the evaluation is of importance for the function that measures the similarity between relational descriptions. As argued above, it may not be possible to define similarity functions for *all* continuous attributes. A discretization of the attribute value ranges, however, causes a loss of information and decreases the accuracy of the evaluation.

Below we will show that the mutual information between a continuous signal and a discretized noisy observation of this signal *does* depend on the discretization interval, but that the involved loss of information can be limited to an arbitrarily low amount by choosing an appropriate interval range. We will use this result for the definition of the new evaluation function.

Continuous values often arise as the outcome of a measurement process. E.g. the measurement of a distance between two points. The observed value contains information about the 'true' value, but it usually isn't identical with it because of noise. The mutual information expresses the information that one value contains about another value and, as stated above, is always finite in case of noise. Hence, the information the observed value gives us about the 'true' value is already limited.

In order to transmit the observed value, it needs to be discretized. In all cases, rounding off will cause a loss of information about the 'true' value. But if one chooses a small discretization interval compared to the noise, the percentage of information that is lost with respect to the information that the observed value contains about the 'true' value can be limited. This also agrees with the way observations are registered. If, for example, the noise of a distance measurement is known to be about 1 cm, one usually will write down the observed number of millimeters, but neglect all further decimals. The neglected decimals contain a too small amount of information to be worth to be noted.

To justify this approach with the information theory, we introduce a 'true' signal A which is to be observed. All values of A are assumed to occur equally frequent and within a range from x_1 to x_2. E.g. the measurements with a theodolite of the directions to a large number of randomly distributed points are equally distributed between 0 and 360 degrees. All directions are equally likely. Thus,

$$p(a) = \frac{1}{x_2 - x_1} \qquad \text{on } [x_1, x_2] \qquad (5\text{-}30)$$

The noise source N is also modeled by a simple equal distribution on an interval of width Δn.

$$p(n) = \begin{cases} \frac{1}{\Delta n} & \text{on } [-\tfrac{1}{2}\Delta n, \tfrac{1}{2}\Delta n] \\ 0 & \text{elsewhere} \end{cases} \qquad (5\text{-}31)$$

The probability density function of the noisy observation B is found by the convolution of the two above functions and results in another equal distribution on the interval $[x_1, x_2]$ when the effects at the boundaries of the range are ignored.

$$p(b) = \frac{1}{x_2 - x_1} \qquad \text{on } [x_1, x_2] \qquad (5\text{-}32)$$

The conditional probability density function of the 'true' value given an observation is given by

$$p(a|b) = \begin{cases} \frac{1}{\Delta n} & b - \tfrac{1}{2}\Delta n \le a < b + \tfrac{1}{2}\Delta n \\ 0 & \text{elsewhere} \end{cases} \qquad (5\text{-}33)$$

The average information that an observed value contains about a 'true' value is given by the transinformation $H(A; B)$

$$
\begin{aligned}
H(A; B) &= \int_{x_1}^{x_2} p(b) \int_{x_1}^{x_2} p(a|b) \log \frac{p(a|b)}{p(a)} \; da \; db \\
&= \int_{x_1}^{x_2} \frac{1}{x_2 - x_1} \int_{b-\frac{1}{2}\Delta n}^{b+\frac{1}{2}\Delta n} \frac{1}{\Delta n} \log \frac{\frac{1}{\Delta n}}{\frac{1}{x_2-x_1}} \; da \; db \\
&= \int_{x_1}^{x_2} \frac{1}{x_2 - x_1} \log \frac{x_2 - x_1}{\Delta n} \; db \\
&= \log \frac{x_2 - x_1}{\Delta n} \qquad (5\text{-}34)
\end{aligned}
$$

The average mutual information between the observed value and the 'true' value is the logarithm of the quotient of the value range and the noise range. Given a certain noise level, the observed value on the average can contain no more information about the 'true' value than given by the mutual information.

The discretization of the observation will even reduce this information, i.e. the mutual information between the discretized observation and the 'true' value will be smaller than the above expression. However, the information loss can be limited to an arbitrarily small percentage by choosing the appropriate discretization interval. Let C be the discretized observation B, where the interval $[x_1, x_2]$ is divided into n intervals of width Δx. Since B has an equal distribution, we have

$$P(c_i) = \frac{\Delta x}{x_2 - x_1} \qquad \text{for } i = 1, 2, \ldots, n \tag{5-35}$$

The conditional probability density function of the observation, given its rounded value is

$$p(b|c_i) = \begin{cases} \frac{1}{\Delta x} & c_i - \frac{1}{2}\Delta x \le b < c_i + \frac{1}{2}\Delta x \\ 0 & \text{elsewhere} \end{cases} \tag{5-36}$$

In order to calculate the mutual information between the rounded observed value and the 'true' value, one needs the conditional probability density function of these two.

$$p(a|c_i) = \int_{x_1}^{x_2} p(a|b, c_i) \; p(b|c_i) \; db \tag{5-37}$$

Since the knowledge of the real observation implies the knowledge of the rounded observation, it follows that

$$p(a|b, c_i) = p(a|b) \tag{5-38}$$

and

$$p(a|c_i) = \int_{x_1}^{x_2} p(a|b) \; p(b|c_i) \; db \tag{5-39}$$

So, this conditional probability density function is obtained by the convolution of the two box functions $p(a|b)$ and $p(b|c_i)$. To simplify the formulas below, the larger of both intervals Δn and Δx is denoted Δmax and the smaller with Δmin.

Mathematically, this function is described by

$$p(a|c_i) = \begin{cases} 0 & : a < c_i - \frac{1}{2}\Delta max - \frac{1}{2}\Delta min \\[2mm] \dfrac{a - c_i + \frac{1}{2}\Delta max + \frac{1}{2}\Delta min}{\Delta max \cdot \Delta min} & : \begin{array}{l} c_i - \frac{1}{2}\Delta max - \frac{1}{2}\Delta min \le a \\ a < c_i - \frac{1}{2}\Delta max + \frac{1}{2}\Delta min \end{array} \\[2mm] \dfrac{1}{\Delta max} & : \begin{array}{l} c_i - \frac{1}{2}\Delta max + \frac{1}{2}\Delta min \le a \\ a < c_i + \frac{1}{2}\Delta max - \frac{1}{2}\Delta min \end{array} \\[2mm] \dfrac{-a + c_i + \frac{1}{2}\Delta max + \frac{1}{2}\Delta min}{\Delta max \cdot \Delta min} & : \begin{array}{l} c_i + \frac{1}{2}\Delta max - \frac{1}{2}\Delta min \le a \\ a < c_i + \frac{1}{2}\Delta max + \frac{1}{2}\Delta min \end{array} \\[2mm] 0 & : c_i + \frac{1}{2}\Delta max + \frac{1}{2}\Delta min \le a \end{cases} \tag{5-40}$$

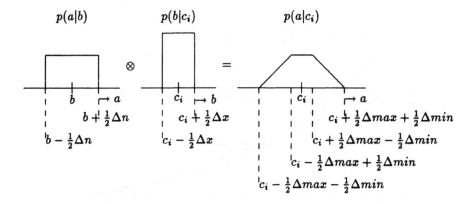

Figure 5.6: Convolution of conditional probability density functions

Finally, the average amount of information that the rounded observation contains about the 'true' value can be calculated (the complete derivation is given in appendix A).

$$
\begin{aligned}
H(A;C) &= \sum_{i=1}^{n} P(c_i) \int_{x_1}^{x_2} p(a|c_i) \log \frac{p(a|c_i)}{p(a)} \, da \\[2mm]
&= \log \frac{x_2 - x_1}{\Delta max} - \frac{1}{2} \frac{\Delta min}{\Delta max} \\[2mm]
&= \begin{cases} \log \frac{x_2 - x_1}{\Delta n} - \frac{1}{2} \frac{\Delta x}{\Delta n} & \Delta x \le \Delta n \\[2mm] \log \frac{x_2 - x_1}{\Delta x} - \frac{1}{2} \frac{\Delta n}{\Delta x} & \Delta x > \Delta n \end{cases} \\[2mm]
&= \begin{cases} H(A;B) - \frac{1}{2} \frac{\Delta x}{\Delta n} & \Delta x \le \Delta n \\[2mm] H(A;B) - \log \frac{\Delta x}{\Delta n} - \frac{1}{2} \frac{\Delta n}{\Delta x} & \Delta x > \Delta n \end{cases}
\end{aligned}
\tag{5-41}
$$

From the above equation it is clear that the discretization of the observation on the average always causes some loss of information. Figure 5.7 gives two examples of this mutual information as a function of the discretization interval Δx. The value range $x_2 - x_1$ in this figure is 100 and the two curves are drawn for noise levels $\Delta n = 10$ and $\Delta n = 20$ respectively. The maximum mutual information between the 'true' value and the discretized observation is a monotone decreasing function of the discretization interval and has its maximum for an infinitesimal discretization interval. This maximum equals the mutual information between the 'true' value and the real observation.

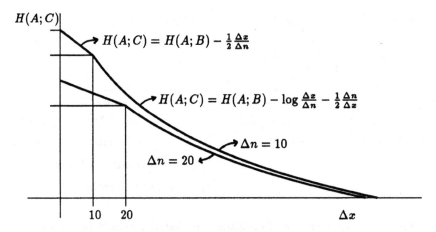

Figure 5.7: Mutual information between the 'true' value and the discretized observation as a function of the discretization interval

The percentage of information that is lost, denoted PL, is given by

$$
PL = \begin{cases} \dfrac{\frac{1}{2}\frac{\Delta x}{\Delta n}}{\log \frac{x_2 - x_1}{\Delta n}} & \Delta x \leq \Delta n \\[3ex] \dfrac{\log \frac{\Delta x}{\Delta n} + \frac{1}{2}\frac{\Delta n}{\Delta x}}{\log \frac{x_2 - x_1}{\Delta n}} & \Delta x > \Delta n \end{cases} \tag{5-42}
$$

In case a maximum percentage of loss PL is given, the appropriate discretization interval Δx is found by

$$
\Delta x = 2\ \Delta n\ PL\ \log \frac{x_2 - x_1}{\Delta n} \qquad \text{for } \Delta x \leq \Delta n \tag{5-43}
$$

If the discretization interval exceeds the noise interval Δn, the solution must be calculated with a numerical method.

In this paragraph it was shown that, in case of noise, continuous signals can be discretized with an arbitrarily low percentage of loss of information about the original signal. We will use this result for the development of the new evaluation function that will be described in the next chapter. The discretization of attribute values will only have a limited influence on the value of this function.

We will take advantage of this property of the new function in chapter 9 (part III). For the location of 3-D objects in grey value images, we will use the similarity of the angle between two lines of the 3-D model (the 'true' value) with the angle of the corresponding lines in the image (the 'observed' value). As it is difficult to derive the similarity as a function of these two angles, we will discretize the values of the angles in the image and calculate the similarity between a large number of these rounded off values and the angles in the model.

6 Evaluation of mappings between relational descriptions

In this chapter we will present the new evaluation measure for comparing relational descriptions. This measure is based on the measure suggested by Boyer and Kak [1986, 1988], which uses the logarithm of the conditional probabilities as a cost function. Although their measure already includes many features which are necessary for evaluating mappings of relational descriptions, it still has some drawbacks. These disadvantages are eliminated in the new evaluation function. This function is not a distance between two relational descriptions or a cost function of the corresponding features, but measures the support which the two descriptions give to the mapping. Before coming to this new function, we first sketch two traditional distance measures and then follow the lines of thought which led Boyer and Kak to their information-theoretic measure.

6.1 Two traditional distance measures on graphs and relations

A nowadays quite popular distance measure between attributed graphs was introduced by Sanfeliu and Fu [1983]. They defined a grammar by which the graphs could be described and defined the distance measure on graphs to be the weighted sum of several costs which incur when transforming one graph into the other graph using the rules of the grammar.

$$\text{Distance} = w_{nr} \cdot C_{nr} + w_{ni} \cdot C_{ni} + w_{nd} \cdot C_{nd} + w_{bi} \cdot C_{bi} + w_{bd} \cdot C_{bd} \qquad (6\text{-}1)$$

In case of relational descriptions, the nodes of the graphs are the primitives and the branches of the graph represent the (binary) relations between the primitives. Costs C_x arise for node recognition (nr), node insertion (ni), node deletion (nd), branch insertion (bi) and branch deletion (bd). The first component is a measure for the similarity of the attributes of the corresponding primitives and is calculated from differences between normalized attribute values. The last four costs factors represent the structural differences between the graphs and are determined by merely counting the number of required transformations of those kinds.

Another distance measure for comparing relational descriptions without attributes was presented by Shapiro and Haralick [1985]. They define the structural error of a mapping function h between two sets of relation tuples R_k and S_k with the same name ($NR_k = NS_k$) to be the number of tuples in R_k that is not mapped by h to tuples in S_k plus the number of tuples in S_k that is not mapped by the inverse mapping function h^{-1} to tuples in R_k.

$$E^k(h) = |R_k \circ h - S_k| + |S_k \circ h^{-1} - R_k| \qquad (6\text{-}2)$$

The total error of h is given by the sum over all relation sets.

$$E(h) = \sum_{k=1}^{K} E^k(h) \tag{6-3}$$

Later Shapiro and Haralick extended this measure to attributed relation tuples by adding a normalized distance (between 0 and 1) for each corresponding pair of relation tuples [Shapiro and Haralick 1987]. In this way, two tuples, one of R_k and one of S_k, which have very different attributes (distance 1) cause the same error as tuples that do not have corresponding tuples in the other relation set.

Both the measures of Sanfeliu and Fu and of Shapiro and Haralick have disadvantages:

- The similarity of attributes are calculated from normalized differences between the attribute values. Clearly, some attributes will be more important than others and thus should have a larger impact on the similarity value. To achieve this, both measures need to be extended with weight parameters for the attributes. The only way these weights can be determined is by extensive training samples.

- Relations between primitives either exist or not. E.g., a point may be connected with a line, in which case the relation set "connected" contains a tuple of the point and the line, or it is not connected with a line, in which case there is no such tuple. Matching two descriptions, one requires that if a relation tuple exists in one description, the composed tuple should exist in the other description. If this is not true, a penalty is added to the distance function. As for attributes, the different relations also are of different importance. For instance, when matching two images in order to determine the relative orientation, a relation describing the relative position of two primitives (primitive 1 left of primitive 2, or, primitive 1 above primitive 3) will be of minor importance since the rotation between the images, being one of the orientation parameters, is unknown. The relation "connected", however, is independent of the transformation and thus is more valuable to the matching process. The relative importance of the relations again may be expressed by weight factors. E.g. a high weight for the relation "connected" and a low weight for the relations "left of" and "above". This only affects the costs in case a relation tuple has no corresponding tuple in the other relation set. If there are corresponding tuples, however, both the important and the unimportant tuple correspondences contribute the same amount to the evaluation function (namely nothing). But shouldn't a corresponding "connected" tuple be a clearer indication for a correct mapping than a corresponding "above" tuple?

6.2 Mapping as an information channel

A communication system transfers information over the system channel. It sends messages which contain information from the transmitter to the receiver. Letters from the source alphabet are selected and sent over the channel. The letters that can be received constitute the receiver alphabet. One can also say that the input letters are mapped onto the output letters. An ideal channel permits us to fully reconstruct the input message from the output message. I.e. there is no difference between the input message and the reconstructed input message. In case of noise, the best channel would be the channel which gives the best possible reconstruction of the input message, i.e. the smallest difference between the input message and the reconstructed message.

The problem of finding the best channel can be considered equivalent to the problem of finding the best mapping between two descriptions as has been suggested by Boyer and Kak [1986, 1988]. Mapping description D_1 to description D_2, one looks for the transformation that converts description D_1 into a description that is most similar to description D_2. Vice versa, one can consider the correspondence as a communication system. The input to the communication system then is description D_1 and the output is description D_2. The fact that the composition of D_1 with the best possible mapping function, i.e. the message as transmitted by the best channel, is not identical with description D_2, i.e. the message that is actually received, is due to noise in the communication system.

Before analyzing the efficiency of the communication system, we first have to determine the information of relational descriptions.

6.2.1 The information content of a relational description

The primitives of a description are described by their attribute value pairs. Some attributes will be more stable under the mapping, and therefore are more important to the mapping process, than other attributes. For instance, remember the example in paragraph 2.2.1 where the hue attribute was a more important clue than the size attribute. In terms of a communication system, the hue attribute is less corrupted by noise on the communication channel than the size attribute. To model these differences in corruption properly, each attribute transmission needs to be described by its own communication channel. Hence the communication system modeling the correspondence of relational descriptions is a multi-channel communication system.

The information of an attribute value depends on the probability that the attribute of a primitive takes this value. Suppose a primitive p_i has L attributes a_l and that attribute a_l may assume values $v_l \in V_l$, i.e. V_l is the alphabet of a_l.

Then the information content of attribute a_l is

$$I(a_l) = -\log P(a_l = v_l) \tag{6-4}$$

where $P(a_l = v_l)$ is the probability that attribute a_l will take value v_l.

Assuming that all attributes are independent of each other, the information of a single primitive is found by the sum over the attributes.

$$I(p_i) = \sum_{l=1}^{L} I(a_l) \tag{6-5}$$

The total information of the primitives is given by the sum over the primitives.

$$I(P) = \sum_{i=1}^{N} I(p_i) \tag{6-6}$$

In order to describe the information of the relational part of a relational description, we need to slightly change the notion of a relation. In the previous paragraphs a tuple of the primitives involved was only registered if a relation existed. E.g. if line primitive p_3 was connected to point primitive p_5, the tuple $(p_3 \; p_5)$ was part of the relation set of relation "connected". In the following we will store all primitive combinations as a tuple and add an attribute value to the tuples indicating whether the relation holds or not. Thus, the above example relation is denoted as $(p_3 \; p_5 \; \text{true})$. If the relation holds, additional attributes may be added to the tuple. If it does not, there is only one attribute which value is false.

The information of an attribute value of a relation tuple again depends on the probability that the attribute takes that value. Let r_{k_i} be the ith tuple of relation set R_k and have L_k attributes a_{k_l} which can take values v_{k_l}. The information of attribute a_{k_l} is

$$I(a_{k_l}) = -\log P(a_{k_l} = v_{k_l}) \tag{6-7}$$

The information of the relation tuple r_{k_i} is found by summing up over the attributes (for sofar they exist)

$$I(r_{k_i}) = \sum_{l=1}^{L_k} I(a_{k_l}) \tag{6-8}$$

The information of all tuples of this relation is

$$I(R_k) = \sum_{i=1}^{N_k} I(r_{k_i}) \tag{6-9}$$

and the information of the relational part of the description is found by summing up over all relation sets

$$I(R) = \sum_{k=1}^{K} I(R_k) \qquad (6\text{-}10)$$

All summations are again under the assumption that all attributes of all relation tuples are independent. Finally the information of the description $D_1 = (P, R)$ is found by

$$I(D_1) = I(P) + I(R) \qquad (6\text{-}11)$$

6.2.2 Modeling the transfer of information over a communication channel

The matching process is driven by the similarity between the attributes of the primitives and the relations. Knowing that two primitives correspond, we expect that their attributes have similar values. That is, usually they will be very similar, but sometimes, due to noise, they may be a little different. In terms of a communication system, the attribute channels usually will transfer the messages correctly, but sometimes will cause small corruptions. This channel behaviour can be modeled by transition probabilities. These are the conditional probabilities that a value, say b_j, will be received knowing that some value, say a_i, has been sent. To illustrate this, we now sketch an example taken from Boyer and Kak [1986]. They want to match two epipolar images which are taken from slightly different viewpoints. One of the attributes they use is the orientation of the extracted edges. The attribute values were quantized in intervals of $\pi/8$ radians. Suppose that they could determine by experiment or analysis that, for their typical images, there is a 0.8 probability that the orientation values of two corresponding edges are the same and that they are differing by one interval with a probability of 0.1 for both adjacent intervals. The orientation channel then can be characterized by the matrix of transition probabilities, also called the channel matrix, as given in table 6.1. The fact that some probabilities in this matrix are zero means that it is considered impossible that corresponding primitives will have such combinations of attribute values.

If, for some reason, the relative orientation of the two images could not be determined very accurate, the orientation becomes a less valuable attribute for the matching. This could result, for example, in the transition matrix of table 6.2, showing an increased transition uncertainty and a corresponding larger "bandwidth".

The transition matrices not only model the uncertainty in the attribute transmission, but can also be used to model systematical deformations between the attributes. If, for instance, it would be known that the two cameras recording

$P(b_j|a_i)$	0	$\pi/8$	$2\pi/8$	$3\pi/8$	$4\pi/8$	$5\pi/8$	$6\pi/8$	$7\pi/8$
0	.8	.1	0	0	0	0	0	.1
$\pi/8$	.1	.8	.1	0	0	0	0	0
$2\pi/8$	0	.1	.8	.1	0	0	0	0
$3\pi/8$	0	0	.1	.8	.1	0	0	0
$4\pi/8$	0	0	0	.1	.8	.1	0	0
$5\pi/8$	0	0	0	0	.1	.8	.1	0
$6\pi/8$	0	0	0	0	0	.1	.8	.1
$7\pi/8$	.1	0	0	0	0	0	.1	.8

Table 6.1: A probability transition matrix for orientation values

$P(b_j|a_i)$	0	$\pi/8$	$2\pi/8$	$3\pi/8$	$4\pi/8$	$5\pi/8$	$6\pi/8$	$7\pi/8$
0	.4	.2	.1	0	0	0	.1	.2
$\pi/8$	.2	.4	.2	.1	0	0	0	.1
$2\pi/8$	.1	.2	.4	.2	.1	0	0	0
$3\pi/8$	0	.1	.2	.4	.2	.1	0	0
$4\pi/8$	0	0	.1	.2	.4	.2	.1	0
$5\pi/8$	0	0	0	.1	.2	.4	.2	.1
$6\pi/8$	.1	0	0	0	.1	.2	.4	.2
$7\pi/8$	.2	.1	0	0	0	.1	.2	.4

Table 6.2: A probability transition matrix for orientation with increased uncertainty

the images are rotated by 45 degrees in the image plane against each other, one expects an edge with an orientation of k degrees to correspond with an edge with an orientation of k+45 degrees. The channel matrix in table 6.3 reflects such a transformation.

$P(b_j|a_i)$	0	$\pi/8$	$2\pi/8$	$3\pi/8$	$4\pi/8$	$5\pi/8$	$6\pi/8$	$7\pi/8$
0	0	.1	.8	.1	0	0	0	0
$\pi/8$	0	0	.1	.8	.1	0	0	0
$2\pi/8$	0	0	0	.1	.8	.1	0	0
$3\pi/8$	0	0	0	0	.1	.8	.1	0
$4\pi/8$	0	0	0	0	0	.1	.8	.1
$5\pi/8$	.1	0	0	0	0	0	.1	.8
$6\pi/8$	.8	.1	0	0	0	0	0	.1
$7\pi/8$	.1	.8	.1	0	0	0	0	0

Table 6.3: A probability transition matrix for orientation with systematic differences

6.3 The conditional information as a distance function (after Boyer and Kak)

The probabilities in a channel matrix state how likely it is that the attribute of a primitive or a relation tuple takes a certain value given the value that the attribute of the corresponding primitive or relation tuple has. The information of this attribute correspondence, being the negative logarithm of the probability, is a measure for the surprise that an attribute assumes a certain value given the value of the corresponding attribute. It also is a measure for the difference between the attribute values. Boyer and Kak [1986, 1988] use this conditional information of the attributes to measure distances between relational descriptions. They define the best correspondence to be the mapping that minimizes the distance between the two descriptions. The distance $D_h(D_1, D_2)$, which of course is a function of the mapping h, is the sum of the conditional information between the primitives $I_h(Q|P)$ and the distance between the relational parts of the descriptions $I_h(S|R)$.

$$D_h(D_1, D_2) = I_h(D_2|D_1) = I_h(Q|P) + I_h(S|R) \qquad (6\text{-}12)$$

6.3.1 The distance between the primitives

Boyer and Kak start to note that the contribution of a single attribute a to the distance between the primitives p_i and q_j is the information we receive when being told that the attribute of q_j takes the value v_2 knowing that primitive p_i has attribute value v_1.

$$I(a(q_j)|a(p_i)) = -\log p(a(q_j) = v_2|a(p_i) = v_1) \qquad (6\text{-}13)$$

Assuming the attributes to be independent, the distance between two primitives p_i and q_j is found by summing up the conditional information over all the L attributes under the mapping h.

$$I_h(q_j|p_i) = \sum_{l=1}^{L} I(a(q_j)|a(p_i)) \qquad (6\text{-}14)$$

The distance between the two primitive sets P and Q is defined as the sum of the distances between all primitive pairs that are corresponding under the mapping

$$I_h(Q|P) = \sum_{(i,j)\in h} I_h(q_j|p_i) \qquad (6\text{-}15)$$

6.3.2 The distance between the relations

The conditional information of the mapping between the relational parts of the descriptions is calculated along the same lines as the information of the relational parts was calculated. Under the assumption that all attributes of the relation tuples are independent, the distance is found by summing up the attribute surprises over the attributes, the tuples in a relation set and the relation sets.

The contribution of a single attribute a of relation k to the overall distance measure again is the negative logarithm of the conditional probability of an attribute value v_2 of a relation tuple s_{k_j} given the value v_1 of the corresponding tuple r_{k_i}.

$$I(a(s_{k_j})|a(r_{k_i})) = -\log P(a(s_{k_i}) = v_2|a(r_{k_i}) = v_1) \tag{6-16}$$

The distance between two relation tuples is the sum of the contributions from the attributes.

$$I_h(s_{k_j}|r_{k_i}) = \sum_{l=1}^{L_k} I(a(s_{k_j})|a(r_{k_i})) \tag{6-17}$$

The distance between two relation sets (with the same name $NR_k = NS_k$) is the sum over all distances between the corresponding tuples

$$I_h(S_k|R_k) = \sum_{i=1}^{N_k} I_h(s_{k_j}|r_{k_i}) \tag{6-18}$$

and the distance between the relational parts of the descriptions is found by summing up over all relation sets

$$I_h(S|R) = \sum_{k=1}^{K} I_h(S_k|R_k) \tag{6-19}$$

6.3.3 Analysis of the conditional information as an evaluation function

The information-theoretic function for evaluating mappings of relational descriptions, as proposed by Boyer and Kak, certainly comprises many improvements compared to the traditional distance measures. However, it also has some disadvantages inherent. In this paragraph both will be discussed in order to substantiate the need for a new enhanced evaluation function.

+ The information-theoretic measure reflects the probabilistic nature of the attribute values and therefore should be superior to the traditional techniques which calculate distances between vectors of normalized attribute values. The probabilities give a direct insight into the stability of the attribute values and by that also into the usefulness of that attribute for the correspondence problem. Suppose a primitive attribute may assume two values: a and b. If all conditional probabilities are 0.5 $(P(a|a) = P(a|b) = P(b|a) = P(b|b) = 0.5)$, the attribute value of a primitive will tell nothing about the attribute value of its corresponding primitive. Hence it is useless to use such an attribute for the matching. The most valuable attributes are those attributes for which the values of the primitive are known, given the attribute value of the corresponding primitive. E.g. with conditional probabilities $P(a|a) = P(b|b) = 1.0$ and $P(a|b) = P(b|a) = 0.0$. The appropriate measure to determine the uncertainty of the attribute value transfer over the attribute channels is the average conditional information, i.e. the conditional entropy. A low conditional entropy indicates a low loss of information during transfer over the channel and therefore indicates a high value for the matching.

+ Unlike Eucledian distances and Mahanolobis distances, the information-theoretic distance measure can combine numerical and symbolical attributes in one and the same scheme.

+ The measures of Sanfeliu and Fu and the original one of Shapiro and Haralick only allow relation tuple correspondences to be good or not good and, unlike the measure of Boyer and Kak, do not differentiate between good correspondences of stable relation tuples and good correspondences of unstable relation tuples.

+ The attribute channels offer an elegant way to model the structural changes of the attributes between two data sets. E.g. a known rotation between two images.

- The information-theoretic distance measure is not symmetric in the two relational descriptions. I.e., the distance between description D_1 and description D_2 may differ from the distance between description D_2 and description D_1. As a consequence, the search for the best mapping from D_1 to D_2 may result in another solution to the correspondence problem than the search for the best mapping from D_2 to D_1. Both the measures of Sanfeliu and Fu and of Shapiro and Haralick are symmetric.

- Whereas these two traditional measures use many weights, the information-theoretic measure requires extensive modeling of all transition probabilities. Like for the weights these may be determined by examining training matches. Unlike other measures, however, some channel matrices may be derived analytically.

- The measure of Boyer and Kak can not handle real-valued attributes. The conditional probability of a real attribute value, given the real attribute value of the corresponding primitive, is zero and hence results in an infinite information for all real-valued attributes. The transition behaviour of such attributes can only be modeled by conditional probability density functions. Using the logarithm of these densities, however, would imply that the distance measure becomes an uninterpretable mixture of information and differential information. Boyer and Kak try to avoid this by discretizing the real values, i.e. by turning the probability density functions into probability functions. An example of this, already given in table 6.1 and repeated here, is the channel matrix of the edge attribute orientation. The range of possible values between 0 and π is divided into 8 intervals of $\pi/8$ radians.

$P(b_j|a_i)$	0	$\pi/8$	$2\pi/8$	$3\pi/8$	$4\pi/8$	$5\pi/8$	$6\pi/8$	$7\pi/8$
0	.8	.1	0	0	0	0	0	.1
$\pi/8$	.1	.8	.1	0	0	0	0	0
$2\pi/8$	0	.1	.8	.1	0	0	0	0
$3\pi/8$	0	0	.1	.8	.1	0	0	0
$4\pi/8$	0	0	0	.1	.8	.1	0	0
$5\pi/8$	0	0	0	0	.1	.8	.1	0
$6\pi/8$	0	0	0	0	0	.1	.8	.1
$7\pi/8$	.1	0	0	0	0	0	.1	.8

Table 6.4: A probability transition matrix for orientation values

So, if, for example, the orientation of an edge would lie in the second interval and the orientation of the corresponding edge would also lie in the second interval, the orientation of this edge would contribute

$$- \log P(\pi/8|\pi/8) = - \log(0.8) = 0.32 \text{ bits} \qquad (6\text{-}20)$$

to the overall distance measure. If, however, we would have chosen to segment the orientation range in pieces of $\pi/4$ radians, the channel matrix would look like

$P(b_j|a_i)$	0	$\pi/4$	$2\pi/4$	$3\pi/4$
0	.9	.05	0	.05
$\pi/4$	.05	.9	.05	0
$2\pi/4$	0	.05	.9	.05
$3\pi/4$	.05	0	.05	.9

Table 6.5: Another probability transition matrix for orientation values

and the contribution of the same orientation attribute values (which would now lie in the first interval) would be

$$- \log P(0|0) = - \log(0.9) = 0.15 \text{ bits} \qquad (6\text{-}21)$$

So, the amount of information a real-valued attribute contributes to the overall measure strongly depends on the discretization interval chosen. This clearly is unacceptable and may lead to curious mismatches as exemplified below.

Suppose a relation "contour" is used to guide the matching of two images which are described by lines and regions. The contour relation states if a line is part of the contour of a region and has one attribute which is the percentage of the region contour covered by the line. Let the following channel matrices be obtained by the analysis of many training samples.

contour	true	false
true	.65	.35
false	.35	.65

perc.	0-50	50-100
0-50	.8	.2
50-100	.2	.8

Table 6.6: Probability transition matrices for the relation contour

The left table gives the probability that a relation tuple will be present in an image given its presence in the other image. The right table gives the conditional probabilities of the coverage percentage. The percentage range is split into two intervals of 50%. Now suppose that one image has an occurrence of the contour relation with an attribute value of 40%. Using the channel matrices, the measure of Boyer and Kak determines the most likely appearance of this relation in the other image by minimizing the conditional information over all possible combinations of the attributes. There are three such combinations: the corresponding relation tuple may not exist in the other image (a), it may exist with an attribute value between 0 and 50% (b) and it may exist with an attribute value between 50 and 100% (c). The information of these possibilities is calculated straightforward.

(a)	$-\log P(\text{false}\vert\text{true})$	= 1.54	bits
(b)	$-\log P(\text{true}\vert\text{true}) - \log P(0\text{-}50\vert 0\text{-}50)$	= 0.94	bits
(c)	$-\log P(\text{true}\vert\text{true}) - \log P(50\text{-}100\vert 0\text{-}50)$	= 2.94	bits

Clearly, it will be most likely that the relation tuple does have a corresponding tuple in the other image and that the attribute value of this tuple will be between 0 and 50%.

If, however, one would have chosen to divide the percentage range into four intervals, the channel matrix could be the one in table 6.7.

perc.	0-25	25-50	50-75	75-100
0-25	.6	.3	.1	.0
25-50	.3	.4	.2	.1
50-75	.1	.2	.4	.3
75-100	.0	.1	.3	.6

Table 6.7: Another probability transition matrix for the percentage channel

Here, there would be five possible appearances of this tuple in the other image, namely with membership value false (a), or with membership value true and four different attributes (b-e).

(a) $-\log P(\text{false}|\text{true})$ $= 1.54$ bits
(b) $-\log P(\text{true}|\text{true}) - \log P(0\text{-}25|25\text{-}50)$ $= 2.36$ bits
(c) $-\log P(\text{true}|\text{true}) - \log P(25\text{-}50|25\text{-}50)$ $= 1.94$ bits
(d) $-\log P(\text{true}|\text{true}) - \log P(50\text{-}75|25\text{-}50)$ $= 2.94$ bits
(e) $-\log P(\text{true}|\text{true}) - \log P(75\text{-}100|25\text{-}50)$ $= 3.94$ bits

It now results that it will be most likely that the contour relation will not exist in the other image. For this attribute discretization the minimization of the conditional information will prefer mappings that have no correspondence for the tuple, no matter how similar the attributes are. The selection of the discretization interval strongly interferes with the selection of the best mapping.

The problems sketched above are closely related to the fact that, unlike the measures of Sanfeliu and Fu and of Shapiro and Haralick, the measure of Boyer and Kak does not contain a component for the primitives and relations that do not have a corresponding element in the other description. If a primitive of description D_1, mapping from D_1 to D_2, has no corresponding primitive in D_2, it is assigned a wildcard. This is a dummy primitive that may be considered an extension to the set of primitives in D_2. It ensures that every primitive in D_1 has some primitive to be mapped to. Clearly, no attribute comparison can be made between a primitive and a wildcard, and, hence, such a correspondence does not contribute to the distance between the descriptions. Assigning no costs (distance contribution) to the instantiation of a primitive with a wildcard in the limit leads to the conclusion that the best mapping from D_1 to D_2 is a mapping that maps all primitives of D_1 to a wildcard.

This, of course, is not desirable. Sanfeliu and Fu and Shapiro and Haralick therefore impose costs for wildcard assignments. The appropriate height of such costs, however, is difficult to determine, depends on the number of primitives and relations, and it again requires many test matches to get some insight into the influence of wildcard costs on the selection of the best mapping.

Boyer and Kak employ a complicated search scheme in order to find a mapping that uses as few wildcards as possible. For all primitives of description D_1 they first determine the group of candidate primitives of D_2 that could possibly match the primitive of D_1 by thresholding the distances between the primitives of D_1 and the primitives of D_2. They only allow a wildcard to be assigned to those primitives of D_1 which have relatively large distances to all candidate primitives. Furthermore they use the wildcard assignment as the last opportunity in a depth-first backtracking tree search and after having found a solution with, say, N wildcards, they require that all future solutions which have a lower conditional information do not have more than those N wildcards. Certainly, it would be more elegant to have a cost function for such wildcard assignments, but such a function hasn't been found yet.

6.4   The mutual information as a merit function

We now describe the mutual information as a new function for the evaluation of mappings of relational descriptions. Opposed to the function of Boyer and Kak, which is a cost function, the mutual information is a merit function. It measures the support that the attributes of the corresponding primitives and relation tuples give to the mapping. This support should be high for a good mapping, is expected to be zero if the two descriptions are independent, and also can be negative if the primitives and the relation tuples are highly unlikely to correspond in the way it is indicated by the mapping. We therefore define the best mapping to be the mapping with the highest mutual information between the corresponding description elements.

The mutual information between two descriptions can be calculated in the same way Boyer and Kak calculate the conditional information between two descriptions. Boyer and Kak sum up the conditional information between the attributes of corresponding primitives and relation tuples over all attributes of all primitive and relation tuple correspondences.

$$I_h(D_2|D_1) = \sum_{(i,j)\in h} \sum_{l=1}^{L} I(a(q_j)|a(p_i)) + \sum_{k=1}^{K}\sum_{i=1}^{N_k}\sum_{l=1}^{L_k} I(a(s_{k_j})|a(r_{k_i})) \qquad (6\text{-}22)$$

We now sum up the mutual information between the attributes instead. Again the assumption is made that all attributes are independent.

$$I_h(D_1;D_2) = \sum_{(i,j)\in h} \sum_{l=1}^{L} I(a(p_i);a(q_j)) + \sum_{k=1}^{K}\sum_{i=1}^{N_k}\sum_{l=1}^{L_k} I(a(r_{k_i});a(s_{k_j})) \qquad (6\text{-}23)$$

The measure of Boyer and Kak was based on minimizing the surprise of the mapping. In terms of a communication system, they looked for the channels with as less noise as possible. Maximizing the mutual information means maximizing the amount of received information per unit of information transmitted. Since the (self-)information of the transmitted message is constant (the description D_1 that is sent is constant) and the mutual information is the difference between the self-information and the conditional information, maximizing the mutual information in fact is identical to minimizing the conditional information. The information of the descriptions is, however, a very useful constant to get around many of the problems sketched in the previous paragraph.

6.4.1 A probabilistic view

Using the maximum likelihood approach we want to find the best mapping by maximizing over all possible mappings the conditional probability of the mapping given the two descriptions that are to be matched. More formally, given two descriptions D_1 and D_2, we look for the mapping h_{opt} such that

$$h_{opt} : \max_h P(h|D_1, D_2) \qquad (6\text{-}24)$$

Applying Bayes' rule, it follows that

$$P(h|D_1, D_2) = \frac{P(D_1, D_2|h) \cdot P(h)}{P(D_1, D_2)} \qquad (6\text{-}25)$$

[Koch 1990], with $P(h)$ being the a priori probability of the mapping. Without knowing the descriptions all mappings are equally likely and, hence, $P(h)$ is constant. $P(D_1, D_2)$ is the joint probability of both descriptions without knowing the mapping function. Under the assumption that the primitives of the descriptions show a large variety in attribute values, there will be no correlation between these values when not knowing the mapping function. I.e. the attributes of the description elements and by them the descriptions themselves are considered to be independent. This leads to the following expression which is to be maximized

$$\frac{P(D_1, D_2|h)}{P(D_1) \cdot P(D_2)} \qquad (6\text{-}26)$$

The logarithm of the above expression exactly is the mutual information between the two descriptions as it can be derived from the channel matrices and the probabilities of the attribute values of a description. The channel matrices express the transition probabilities while knowing the correct mapping. Knowing the probabilities of the attribute values of a description, the joint probability in the expression above can be calculated. It therefore follows that the maximum likelihood mapping, given two description, is found by maximizing the mutual information between the descriptions over all possible mappings.

$$h_{opt} : \max_h I_h(D_1; D_2) \qquad (6\text{-}27)$$

The strategy of Boyer and Kak, which minimizes the conditional information, in fact maximizes the conditional probability of description D_2, given description D_1 and the mapping function h and so obtain a mapping h'_{opt}.

$$h'_{opt} : \max_h P(D_2|D_1, h) \tag{6-28}$$

Using

$$P(h|D_1, D_2) \cdot P(D_1, D_2) = P(D_1, D_2, h) = P(D_2|D_1, h) \cdot P(D_1, h) \tag{6-29}$$

it is clear that

$$P(h|D_1, D_2) = P(D_2|D_1, h) \cdot \frac{P(D_1, h)}{P(D_1, D_2)} \tag{6-30}$$

Without knowing description D_2, description D_1 and mapping h are independent and since both $P(D_1)$ and $P(h)$ are constant, $P(D_1, h)$ is a constant too. As already used above, the assumption that the attributes show a large variety of values allows us to consider D_1 and D_2 to be independent, so that $P(D_1, D_2) = P(D_1) \cdot P(D_2)$. Because both descriptions are given, $P(D_1, D_2)$ also evaluates to a constant. This implies that the mapping with the smallest conditional information also is equivalent to the maximum likelihood solution, i.e.

$$h'_{opt} = h_{opt} \tag{6-31}$$

6.4.2 Advantages of the mutual information

From the information-theoretic side it is easy to see that the minimization of the conditional information and the maximization of the mutual information should lead to the same solution. Remember that the mutual information was defined as the difference between the self-information and the conditional information (equation 5-6).

$$I_h(D_1; D_2) = I(D_1) - I_h(D_1|D_2) \tag{6-32}$$

Because the message that is sent over the communication system is known (namely description D_1) and is independent of the mapping function h, the information of D_1 is merely a constant. From the above equation it then is clear that minimizing the conditional information is equivalent to maximizing the mutual information.

Thus, the two information-theoretic measures, the conditional information and the mutual information, only differ by a constant $I(D_1)$, but this simple constant allows us to eliminate many of the disadvantages of the conditional information.

- As shown in paragraph 5.1 (equation 5-7), the mutual information is a symmetric measure. This assures that matching description D_1 to description D_2 results in the same mapping as mapped in the reversed direction.

$$
\begin{aligned}
I_h(D_1; D_2) &= I(D_1) - I_h(D_1|D_2) \\
&= I(D_2) - I_h(D_2|D_1)
\end{aligned}
\tag{6-33}
$$

The conditional information, as follows from the above equation, is only a symmetric function for pairs of descriptions with the same information content (i.e. $I(D_1) = I(D_2)$).

- The differential mutual information is equivalent to the mutual information so that we now can freely combine discrete attributes with their probability distributions and continuous attributes with their probability density functions.

- If desired, one can discretize the probability density functions without losing too much of the mutual information. In paragraph 5.4 this has been shown for equally distributed functions. By approximating probability density functions by piecewise equal distributions this proof may be extended to all continuous density functions.

- The mutual information offers a very simple way to include the effects of wildcard assignments into the evaluation function. The mutual information between two primitives measures the information that one primitive contains about the other primitive. In principle, any primitive can be mapped to a wildcard. So, intuitively, the wildcard contains no information about the primitive it is mapped by and hence the mutual information between the a primitive and a wildcard should be zero.

From a probabilistic view one may say that any primitive (p_i) and the wildcard $(*)$ are independent. Since

$$
I(a; b) = \log \frac{P(a, b)}{P(a) \cdot P(b)}
\tag{6-34}
$$

indeed

$$
\begin{aligned}
I(p_i; *) &= \log \frac{P(p_i, *)}{P(p_i) \cdot P(*)} \\
&= \log \frac{P(p_i) \cdot P(*)}{P(p_i) \cdot P(*)} \\
&= 0
\end{aligned}
\tag{6-35}
$$

From the information-theoretic view we can apply the description length interpretation of the information. The mutual information between two primitives p_i and q_j can be regarded to be the number of bits that can be saved in describing p_i when it is known that q_j is the corresponding primitive. Knowing that a wildcard is the corresponding primitive of p_i it still takes the full effort of describing the attributes of p_i and therefore the mutual information between a primitive and a wildcard should be zero also.

Hence, the instantiation of a primitive with a wildcard doesn't support a mapping. It would be better if one could find a corresponding primitive with similar attribute values. But a wildcard assignment also doesn't contradict with the mapping. It may very well be a better solution to map a primitive to a wildcard than to map the primitive to a primitive which has completely different attribute values. Such two primitives would have a negative mutual information.

The same reasoning can be used for the attributes of the relation tuples that do not have corresponding attributes because the composed tuple has a membership value "false". The mutual information between the membership values of the corresponding tuples is added to the evaluation measure, but the other attributes of the relation can not be used for comparison if the corresponding tuple doesn't have these attributes. Hence, these attributes neither support nor contradict the mapping and, therefore, do not contribute to the evaluation measure.

6.4.3 Mutual information of uncertain attributes

The mutual information between attribute values measures the support that two attributes give to a mapping and comprises a term for the uncertainty of the transfer of the attribute over its channel. The measure as discussed above does not yet reflect the uncertainty of the determination of the attribute values. If attribute a takes value v_i in description D_1 and value v_j in description D_2, its contribution to the evaluation measure is the mutual information between these two values. But how sure are we that v_i, resp. v_j, indeed are the correct values for that attribute?

Suppose, we want to match two grey value images using the texture of regions that have been detected. Let it be given that there can only be three different types of texture in the image (v_1, v_2, v_3). It may well be that a texture classification algorithm can't exactly determine the texture of a region but outputs that there is a 70% chance that it will be texture v_1 and gives 20%, resp. 10% for textures v_2 resp. v_3. These probabilities are the a posteriori probabilities of this specific region given the image from which it is extracted and should not be confused with the a priori probabilities that give the probability that a texture will appear for some region in some image. Let these a posteriori probabilities be determined for a pair of corresponding regions from image G_1 and image G_2

and let $P(a(p_k) = v_i | G_1)$ denote the probability that the texture attribute a of region primitive p_k takes value v_i given the grey value image G_1.

Usually one considers a region to have the texture attribute value that has the highest probability. The contribution of the texture attribute of two corresponding regions then is the mutual information between the most likely values of both regions.

$$I(a(p_k); a(q_l)) = I(a(p_k) = v_i; a(q_l) = v_j) \qquad (6\text{-}36)$$

It would, however, be better to use the mutual information of all texture values weighted by the a posteriori probabilities of the texture classification.

$$I(a(p_k); a(q_l)) = \sum_{i=1}^{3} \sum_{j=1}^{3} P(a(p_k) = v_i | G_1) \cdot P(a(q_l) = v_j | G_2) \cdot$$
$$I(a(p_k) = v_i; a(q_l) = v_j) \qquad (6\text{-}37)$$

This sum reflects the uncertainty of the texture classification and therefore gives a better description of the support the texture of the regions gives to the mapping.

The same approach also might be used to take into account the accuracy of the measurement of a continuous attribute variable. Let the a posteriori probability density functions $p(a(p_k) = v_i | G_1)$ and $p(a(q_l) = v_j | G_1)$ be given. The contribution of this attribute to the evaluation function then is

$$I(a(p_k); a(q_l)) = \int_{-\infty}^{\infty} \int_{-\infty}^{\infty} p(a(p_k) = v_i | G_1) \cdot p(a(q_l) = v_j | G_2) \cdot$$
$$I(a(p_k) = v_i; a(q_l) = v_j) \ dv_i \ dv_j \qquad (6\text{-}38)$$

Matching a model with an image, usually there will be no uncertainties in the attribute values of the model. In this case, one of the two summations resp. integrations has to be omitted in the above two formulas.

6.4.4 Mutual information as a compatibility function for relaxation processes

The mutual information between attributes can also be used as compatibility coefficients for continuous relaxation processes. The compatibility of the assignment of label q_j to primitive p_i with the assignment of label q'_j to the neighbouring primitive p'_i is calculated by the sum of the mutual information of all attributes of the relations between p_i and p_i' and the relations between q_j and q_j'.

$$r(p_i, q_j, p_i', q_j') = \sum_{k=1}^{K} \sum_{i=1}^{N_k} \sum_{l=1}^{L_k} I(a(r_{k_i}); a(s_{k_j})) \tag{6-39}$$

Using the weights for the possible assignments, which represent a kind of likelihood, the support $S_{p_i}(q_j)$ that the assignments in the neighbourhood of p_i give to the assignment of q_j to p_i can be defined again (e.g. confirm equation 2-16).

Already in 1978, Peleg and Rosenfeld suggested the use of mutual information for continuous relaxation processes. They applied this method to the problem of curve enhancement and derived the compatibility coefficients from the initial weights (probabilities). These probabilities were obtained from the line detector. The weights calculated by the update formula should not be negative, since they are interpreted as probabilities. In order to obtain this, the events having a very high or a very low mutual information were ignored. Only extreme mutual information cause their update formula to produce negative weights. But, unfortunately, the events with a very high or a very low mutual information also are the events that are most valuable to the relaxation process (since they contain much information). Using an update function with the expression $e^{S_{p_i}(q_j)}$ instead of formula 2-16 with the expression $[1 + S_{p_i}(q_j)]$ would eliminate this problem. This update formula indeed has been proposed by Hummel and Rosenfeld [1977].

7 Tree search methods and heuristics

Many problems in language understanding, automatic programming, robotics, scene analysis, game playing, expert systems, and theorem proving have search spaces that can be represented in a graph or a tree. The search space of the relational matching problem is also represented in a tree. Solutions to these problems can be found by tree search methods. A variety of search methods already has been developed in the domain of artificial intelligence [Barr and Feigenbaum 1981, Nilsson 1982].

Several characteristics of problem representation and tree search methods are easily demonstrated by two well-known problems: the N-queens problem and the traveling salesman problem. Throughout this chapter we will therefore compare the methods for solving these puzzles with the methods used for solving the correspondence problem.

First we describe how these puzzles and the correspondence problem are represented in trees and show that the N-queens problem is very similar to the correspondence problem.

The next paragraph describes the standard search methods. The so-called *informed* search methods use a cost function to guide the search to the best solution. The new evaluation function, however, is a merit function. We will analyze if and how the behaviour of the tree search methods changes if they are to maximize instead of minimize the function value.

Apart from the evaluation function, there are some other strategies to minimize the search space, and thereby the search effort. These strategies are proce dures that perform extra consistency checks to avoid running into dead-end tree branches and rules of thumb that determine the order in which the nodes of the search tree are visited. They usually lead to a shorter search time, but may occasionally lead to an increased search time. We will describe both strategies and show that they can be effectively combined with the calculation of the evaluation function.

Despite the use of these strategies, the search space of many correspondence problems still will be too large to find the best mapping in a reasonable time. In the last paragraph two methods will be discussed that can find a non-optimal solution in a shorter time. Both methods, however, require a criterion to determine whether the suggested solution is good enough to be accepted. Such a criterion could not be defined in a manner valid for all kinds of matching problems. As shown later, such criteria can be defined for the object location problem.

7.1 Problem representations in a tree

The N-queens problem is the problem of how to place N queens on an $N \times N$ checkerboard so that no queen can take another [Haralick and Elliott 1980]. I.e. two queens may not be in the same row, the same column or on the same diagonal. The best way to solve this problem is to incrementally build up the solution, row after row. For each new row, one can only put a queen at the columns which are not under attack of the queens on the rows already done. Figure 7.1 shows half the search tree representation of the 4-queens problem. At each level in the tree one queen is added to the checkerboard. As soon as a

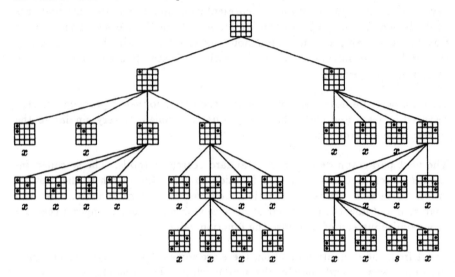

Figure 7.1: Half the search space of the 4-queen puzzle

partial solution (a configuration with less than 4 queens) is invalid, there is no use in placing another queen in the next row. The configuration of the nodes below and arising from a node with an invalid configuration will always be invalid too. All (partial) solutions marked with x are invalid. In this part of the tree there only is one solution, marked with s. The other half of the 4-queens search tree is completely symmetrical to the first half, so the 4-queens problem has two solutions.

The traveling salesman problem is a route planning problem [Barr and Feigenbaum 1981]. Given the number of cities to be visited and the distances between the cities, find the shortest route that visits all cities once and returns to the first city. An example for four cities is given in table 7.1 and figure 7.2. Starting in city A the next city to visit can be city B, C, or D. Choosing, for instance, city C (straight down in the search tree), city B and D are being left to visit. Denoted

cities	A	B	C	D
A	-	5	8	10
B		-	15	15
C			-	3
D				-

Table 7.1: Distance between the 4 cities

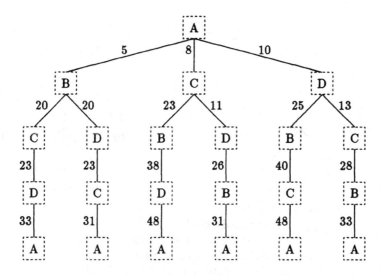

Figure 7.2: Search space of the traveling salesman problem with 4 cities

along the branches of the tree are the sums of the distances from the route node A to the node below. Two routes appear to be optimal: route ABDCA and route ACDBA. Of course, these are just the same routes taken in the opposite direction. All routes are represented twice in the search tree. The number of different routes for visiting N cities therefore is $(N$-1$)!/2$.

The tree representing the search space of the correspondence problem between a set of unit primitives and a set of label primitives uses one level for each unit and uses the branches for the selection of different labels for the units. While searching for a solution in an incremental way, adding one unit-label pair to the partial mapping of a node at each of its successors, several conditions may arise which lead to an invalid mapping. A mapping is invalid if the attributes of the primitive pairs or the attributes of the corresponding relation tuples are inconsistent. When the mapping is required to be one-to-one even more branches of the tree will have a dead end. The best mapping is represented by the path from the root node to one of the leaf nodes that optimizes the value of an evaluation function.

Suppose three units, 1, 2, and 3, are to be matched with three labels, A, B, and C. Further suppose that the attributes of unit 1, resp. unit 2 are inconsistent with the attributes of label B, resp. label A and that the attributes of the relations of unit pair 1-3, resp. unit pair 1-2 are inconsistent with the attributes of the relations of label pair C-B, resp. label pair A-C. Figure 7.3 then represents the search space for the one-to-one mapping from the units to the labels. Only

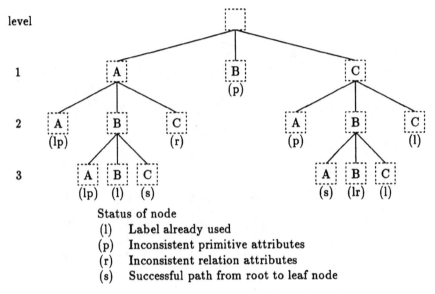

Status of node
(l)   Label already used
(p)   Inconsistent primitive attributes
(r)   Inconsistent relation attributes
(s)   Successful path from root to leaf node

Figure 7.3: Search space of an one-to-one mapping with 3 units and 3 labels

2 out of the maximum possible 27 (3^3) paths successfully reach a leaf node. The best mapping of these two has to be found by a mapping evaluation function.

The N-queens problem can also be envisaged as a matching problem. Considering the rows as the units and the columns as the labels, the solution to the N-queens problem is a one-to-one mapping from the rows to the columns, satisfying relational constraints. The definition of a one-to-one mapping already excludes the configurations that have two or more queens on a row or a column. The relational constraints are necessary to exclude configurations with two or more queens on a diagonal. The formulation of the relational constraint is straightforward. Let there be a binary relation tuple for each pair of rows, as well as for each pair of labels. Assign one attribute to each tuple, which is the absolute difference between the row-, resp. column-coordinates. The configurations with two queens on a diagonal can be excluded by requiring that the attributes of the corresponding relation tuples must not be the same.

7.2 Tree search methods

Tree search methods are to find solutions to problems which have their search space represented in a tree. All tree search methods start at the root node of the tree and proceed along the branches until a leaf node representing a solution has been found. They differ, however, in the order in which the nodes of a tree are visited. This order highly determines the efficiency of the tree search [Barr and Feigenbaum 1981, Nilsson 1982, Pearl 1984].

Tree search methods can be roughly divided into two categories: the blind methods and the informed methods. The blind methods have no information about where to look for the solution. All leaf nodes are equally likely to be the solution and all paths are equally likely to lead to it. The informed methods, on the contrary, have a function by which the nodes of the trees can be evaluated. This evaluation function gives a measure for the quality of the path from the root node to the current node or an indication about the likelihood that a node will be a node on the path leading to the solution.

The evaluation functions used in the classical tree search applications are cost functions. The costs of the path from the root node to the solution leaf node are to be minimized. Since the evaluation function developed in the previous paragraph is a merit function that is to be maximized and may take positive as well as negative values, we will slightly adapt the informed search methods and will describe the (small) changes that can be noticed in the tree search behaviour of some of these methods when using a merit function.

7.2.1 Blind search methods

In the paragraph on the problem representations several search trees were shown. Search trees are generated incrementally by the tree search methods. At each node several tests have to be performed, e.g. check if a label has been used before or attribute comparison. If these tests can be completed successfully the successor nodes of the next lower level are generated, i.e. the node is expanded. All search methods start with expanding the root node, but the order in which the other nodes are expanded is different from method to method. For the blind search there only are two basic concepts: the depth-first tree search and the breadth-first tree search.

The depth-first tree search, as already indicated in the name, always expands the node with the deepest level [Barr and Feigenbaum 1981, Nilsson 1982]. This is the node that was most recently generated. At each node it tries to expand this node immediately and to move down to one of its successors (figure 7.4). The search keeps going down until it reaches the lowest level of the tree or finds a dead end in the tree. It then moves up to the predecessor node and moves down again along the other branches of this node. This moving up to the next higher node which has some unexplored branches left is called *backtracking*.

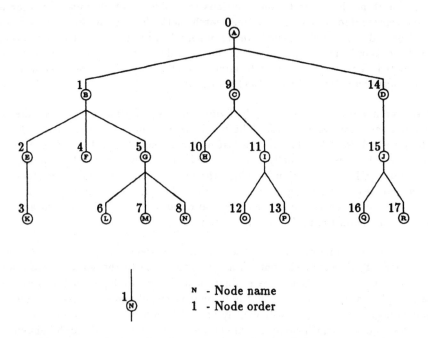

Figure 7.4: Order of node processing of a depth-first tree search

The breadth-first search always expands the (yet unexpanded) node at the highest level in the tree [Barr and Feigenbaum 1981, Nilsson 1982]. This is the node that was generated first of all unexpanded nodes (figure 7.5). Thus the breadth-first search only moves down to the next level after all nodes on the current level have been expanded.

Both the depth-first and the breadth-first search method are often described using a stack of the generated but still unexpanded nodes. This stack is initialized by putting the root node on the stack. Until the stack is empty or until a solution has been found a node is taken from the top of the stack and is expanded. Whereas the depth-first search method puts the generated successor nodes at the top of the stack, the breadth-first search method puts them at the end of the stack. Hence, the depth-first search selects the latest generated node and the breadth-first search selects the first generated unexpanded node to be expanded.

Both the depth-first and the breadth-first search methods have their specific applications. The N-queens problem, for instance, is usually faster solved with a depth-first than with a breadth-first search. Because the nodes representing the solutions of the N-queens problem all are situated on lowest level in the

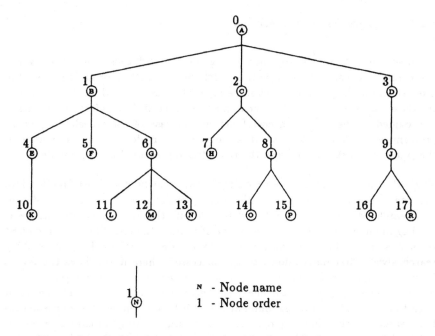

Figure 7.5: Order of node processing of a breadth-first tree search

tree (N), a breadth-first search will only find a solution after having scanned all higher levels whereas a depth-first search may encounter a solution after only expanding N nodes. For some other problems the breadth-first search may be preferred however. Consider, for example, the problem of finding the shortest path in terms of the number of edges in a graph from vertex A to vertex B. Each move from a vertex to another vertex is represented in the search tree by a move from a node to one of its successor nodes. Thus, the nodes on level 1 in the search tree represent the vertices that are joined by an edge to vertex A (which is represented by the root node). The nodes on level N represent the vertices that can be reached from vertex A within N edges. The problem of finding the shortest route from vertex A to vertex B thus is equivalent to finding vertex B on the highest possible level in the search tree. Since the breadth-first search scans the search tree level by level, it usually will find a solution faster than the depth-first search. The depth-first search is not even guaranteed to find a solution at all.

A general advantage of the depth-first search is the limited memory requirement. For a regular tree, where each node can be expanded to N successors, the length of the stack of unexpanded nodes at level k is always smaller than $(N-1)*k+1$: there may be N unexpanded nodes at level k and at most $N-1$ at the $k-1$ levels above (one of the nodes at the first $k-1$ levels is always expanded, otherwise the search could not have proceeded to level k). The stack of the breadth-first search, however, may have up to N^k unexpanded nodes when starting with level k.

7.2.2 Informed search methods

Blind search methods usually take a long time to find a solution. Wherever it is possible, is it useful to provide the search method with information about the prospects of finding a solution at some node. The search method then may first try those paths where it will be most likely to succeed. The information usually is provided in the form of a cost function. In case of the traveling salesman problem, for example, the costs of a move from a node to a successor node in the tree is the distance between the two cities represented by these nodes.

The *hill-climbing* strategy is a very simple way to include the cost function into the tree search [Pearl 1984]. The hill-climbing search is a variation on the depth-first search. Whereas the depth-first search puts the newly generated nodes at the beginning of the node stack in no specific order, the hill-climbing search first sorts these nodes after the costs a move to a node will incur. The hill-climbing search always first moves down to the successor where it will have the fewest costs. At node B in figure 7.6, e.g., three nodes are generated: node E, F and G. Since the edge to node G is the cheapest, this node is visited first. The cheapest path to a leaf node is already found at the eighth node (node L). Like the depth-first search hill-climbing employs the backtracking strategy in case a path does not lead to a solution. The memory requirements for the hill-climbing also are the same as for the depth-first search.

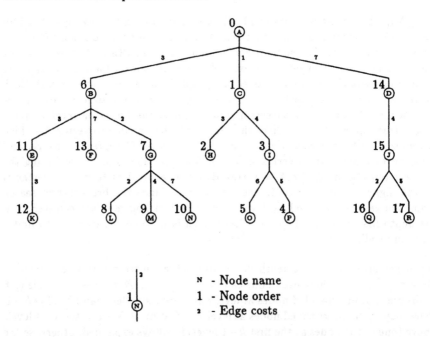

Figure 7.6: Order of node processing of a hill-climbing tree search

The hill-climbing search only uses the costs of the edges from a node to its successors. It decides locally which node will be the next to expand. The *best-first* search takes this decision more globally [Pearl 1984]. Instead of using the costs of one edge, for each unexpanded node it calculates the costs of the path from the root node to that node by summing up the costs of the edges that are a part of that path. The stack of the unexpanded nodes is sorted after these cost sums and the node with the cheapest path leading to it from the root node is expanded first. Figure 7.7 illustrates the order of node processing for the example search tree. Searching for the cheapest path from the root node to a leaf node the best solution is found at the seventh node. Note that the best-first search does not need to expand node J since the costs of the path from the root node to that node already exceed the costs of the path to the leaf node L that has been found before. The best-first search may jump from one node to a node at a completely different location in the tree. It therefore usually has more unexpanded nodes on the stack than the hill-climbing, and thus requires more memory to keep track of all nodes.

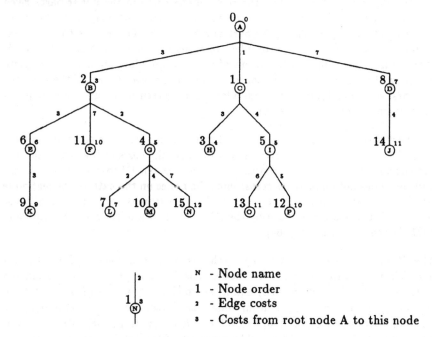

Figure 7.7: Order of node processing of a best-first tree search

The best-first search expands the node that has the cheapest path from the root node leading to it. The costs of this path are calculated by the sum of the costs of the edges building up the path. An edge on a good path will have lower costs than an edge on a bad path. But the costs of a long good path often exceed the costs of a short bad path, since the many small edge costs of the good path still may result in a large cost sum. As a consequence, bad nodes at high levels in the tree will be expanded although good nodes at low levels may be available. Preferring to expand nodes at high levels, the best-first search, like the breadth-first search, requires a large memory for the node stack.

Unfortunately, this undesired characteristic of the best-first search is especially true for the correspondence problem. On level one of the tree, the only costs arise from the attribute differences between the unit and the label primitive that are instantiated. On level two, one has to add not only the costs of the primitive attribute comparison of the primitives instantiated at this level, but also the costs arising from the attribute differences between the corresponding (binary) relation tuples. In general, on level k of the tree the additional costs are the sum of the costs of the primitive attribute differences between unit primitive k and its label and the costs of attribute differences between the corresponding tuples of $k - 1$ tuple pairs. Since the number of attribute comparisons one can make increases with the level in the tree, the costs of the edges in the lower part of the tree usually will be higher than the costs of the edges in the upper part. Even the costs of a single edge in the lower part of a good path may be higher than the costs of an edge in the upper part of a bad path. This causes the best-first search for the correspondence problem to focus very much on the higher levels of the search tree. Since the solutions of the corresponding problem (a complete mapping of all primitives) only can be found at the lowest level of the tree, the best-first search method often needs a long time to return a solution and requires much memory for the node stack.

The best-first search can be improved if one not only uses the costs of the path from the root node to the current node, but also the costs of the path from the current node to the leaf node representing the solution. Of course, at the current node one does not know these costs, since the nodes on the path to the leaf node still have to be generated, but one may be able to make an estimate of these costs. This is the strategy used by the A^* search method [Barr and Feigenbaum 1981, Nilsson 1982, Pearl 1984].

The A^* search uses a cost function $f(n)$ that is the costs of the path from the root node via node n to a solution leaf node. The function $f(n)$ can be considered as the sum of two functions $g(n)$ and $h(n)$ which are the costs of the path from the root node to node n, resp. from node n to the solution node. At node n the value of $g(n)$ can be calculated, the value of $h(n)$ has to be estimated however. This estimate is denoted $h^*(n)$. The estimate of the total costs from the root node to the solution node via node n, $f^*(n)$, is found by

$$f^*(n) = g(n) + h^*(n) \qquad (7\text{-}1)$$

The A^* algorithm always expands the node with the lowest value of the expected total costs $f^*(n)$. In the example of figure 7.8 the estimated total costs of a solution including the current node are written below the node order number. The solution is already found after examining four nodes.

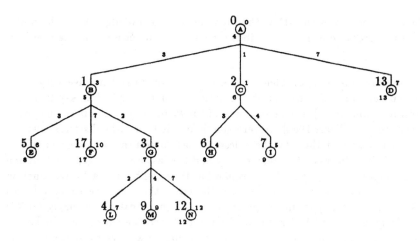

N - Node name
1 - Node order
2 - Edge costs
3 - Costs from root node A to this node
4 - Estimated total costs

Figure 7.8: Order of node processing of a A^* tree search

An important property of the A^* search method is that it does not have to expand the nodes that have a higher value of $f^*(n)$ than the best path to a leaf node found so far, as long as it is ensured that the costs of the path from node n to the solution node are never overestimated, i.e. $h^*(n)$ is always less or equal to the actual costs $h(n)$. The condition

$$h^*(n) \leq h(n) \qquad (7-2)$$

is called the admissibility condition. If it is fulfilled, the A^* search is admissible and will never miss the best solution by not expanding nodes that have a higher value of $f^*(n)$ than a solution that has already been found. In the example of figure 7.8 the nodes D, E and I do not have to be expanded because the estimated costs of the optimal path via these nodes exceed the costs of the solution found at node L.

The best-first method is a special case of the A^* method, namely with $h^*(n) = 0$ for all nodes. It only uses the costs of the path to the current node ($f^*(n) = g(n)$). For an A^* algorithm with a good estimate function $h^*(n)$ the values of this function will decrease with the depth of the tree. The differences between the values of the evaluation function $f^*(n)$ of nodes at different levels will therefore be smaller than for the best-first search method. Hence, the search of the A^* requires less memory for the node stack than the best-first method. Since the evaluation function of the A^* method also includes knowledge about the nodes below the current node, it usually finds the best solution faster than the best-first method.

The traveling salesman problem is one of the problems that have very large search spaces as soon as the number of cities becomes larger than say 20 or 25. Several functions $h^*(n)$ for the estimate of the future costs have been suggested for this problem [Pearl 1984]. A very simple one is to use the distance between the current city and the city the salesman has to return to. However, if the number of cities between the current city and the last one is large, this function underestimates the distance the salesman has to travel by far. A better function is the minimum spanning tree between the cities that still are to visit [Pearl 1984]. A minimum spanning tree for N cities can be calculated using $O(N^2)$ steps. It gives a good lower bound for the distance the salesman still has to travel. The minimum spanning tree never leads to an overestimation of the future distance, so that the A^* method remains admissible.

For many search problems, however, it is difficult to find a function that gives a good estimate of the future costs, while obeying the admissibility condition. Because this function also has to fulfil the admissibility condition in the most extreme cases, it usually underestimates the future costs in the average case. This causes the A^* algorithm to expand many nodes not leading to the solution. The ε-A^* algorithm offers an alternative by relaxing the admissibility condition [Barr and Feigenbaum 1981, Pearl 1984]. Instead of the evaluation function

$$f^*(n) = g(n) + h^*(n) \tag{7-3}$$

the ε-A^* algorithm uses

$$f^*(n) = g(n) + (1 + \varepsilon)h^*(n) \tag{7-4}$$

where ε is a small factor and $h^*(n)$ is an admissible function. Clearly $f^*(n)$ may now overestimate the total costs and therefore one may miss the optimal solution when using this function. However, the loss of optimality is bounded. When a solution is found with costs $f_{sol.}$, the nodes left on the stack of the unexpanded nodes only can lead to a solution with at least $\frac{1}{1+\varepsilon} f_{sol.}$ costs. Thus, in the most unfortunate case, the ε-A^* algorithm loses $\frac{\varepsilon}{1+\varepsilon}$ percent of the optimal solution. The ε-A^* method is therefore called ε-admissible [Pearl 1984]. In return for the relaxation of the optimality requirement, the ε-A^* algorithm will find a good solution in a shorter time, since the evaluation function now contains a better estimate of the future costs.

For some problems, however, even the use of the ε-A^* algorithm will not prevent the node stack from becoming very large. If the memory requirements exceed the available space, search methods that need a large stack (in the order of decreasing average stack length: breadth-first, best-first, A^* and ε-A^*) should be combined with methods that only require a small stack (depth-first and hill-climbing).

For instance, one can start to search a solution with the A^* algorithm until the available memory is nearly exhausted and then continue the search by exploring the sub-trees below each of the unexpanded nodes with the hill-climbing strategy. The use of such *mixed* or *hybrid strategies* of course leads to an increase in the number of nodes that need to be explored, but keeps the memory requirements within limits.

7.2.3 Informed search with a merit function

Unlike the functions commonly used for evaluation in search trees, the evaluation function for relational matching as developed in the previous chapter is a merit function. This function may take positive as well as negative values. Some of the search methods therefore require a small adaption in the definition and show a different behaviour.

The hill-climbing strategy remains unaffected from this change in the type of evaluation function. Instead of moving to the successor adding the lowest costs, it now moves to the successor that adds the highest support. Like for the cost function, the hill-climbing approach only differs from the depth-first search in that it sorts the newly generated nodes before it puts them on the node stack.

The best-first search, however, shows a different behaviour with a merit function as with a cost function. The best-first search expands the node with the highest merit of the path from the root node to the node. If some node is expanded, the best-first search will only track back from this node, if the paths to the successors below give a negative support to the state of this node. If this paths have a positive merit, the best-first will continue to move down in the tree. As long as a confirmation of a state of a node can be found at a lower level, the best-first with a merit function will process the tree in a depth-first manner. The explanation for this is plain. The node that is expanded has the highest merit of the path from the root node leading to it. If the merit of the edge to one of this node's successors is positive, the merit of the path from the root node to this successor will even be a little higher. Sorting the node stack after these merits, this node will be put on the top of the stack and will be expanded first. An example of the order of node processing of the best-first search for tree with a merit function is given in figure 7.9. Note that for this tree, the order is exactly the same as for the hill-climbing strategy.

For the correspondence problem of relational descriptions the depth-first-like scanning of the tree is even more striking when using wildcard assignments. As argued in the previous chapter, the support a wildcard assignment gives to a mapping is nil. Suppose the node, i.e. the partial mapping, that currently has the highest merit is completely wrong and therefore will have no successor nodes that positively support it. Leaving the possibility of a wildcard assignment there will, however, be an edge to a successor with merit zero. Hence, as long as there

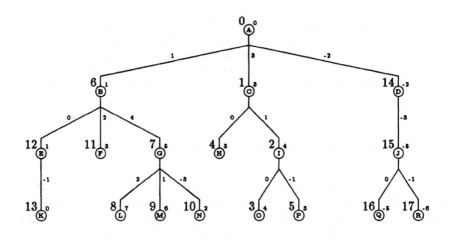

Figure 7.9: Order of node processing of a best-first tree search with a merit function.

is no limit on the number of allowed wildcards, the best-first search continues to assign wildcards until it reaches the bottom of the tree.

Another undesired feature of the best-first search with a merit function is that there is no possibility of not expanding all nodes without turning the risk of missing the best solution. The best-first search with a cost function does not have to expand a node that has a path from the root node that is more expensive than the path of a solution that has already been found. The best-first search with a merit function, however, even has to expand the nodes with a very negative merit, since it never knows if the future nodes will have a positive support that compensates for this negative merit.

Both above problems can be resolved for the largest part by including an estimate of the future merit into the evaluation function. This leads us to the A^* algorithm with a merit function. The stack of the unexpanded nodes is sorted after the expected merit of the path from the root node via the still unexpanded but already generated node to the node representing the solution. The node with the highest expected total merit is expanded first. The search is completed if the merit of a solution that has been found is larger than the expected merits of the paths via the nodes on the stack. For the A^* search with a merit function to be admissible, one has to require that the future merit may never be underestimated, i.e.:

$$h^*(n) \geq h(n) \tag{7-5}$$

The search is only admissible if it is guaranteed that the paths via the unexpanded nodes will have no more merit than the path of the solution that has been found.

Like for the A^* with the cost function, one may relax the admissibility condition if a small search time is more important than the optimality of the solution. The evaluation function $f^*(n)$ is then composed by

$$f^*(n) = g(n) + (1 - \varepsilon)h^*(n) \tag{7-6}$$

Note the minus sign. If the function $h^*(n)$ is admissible, it will probably overestimate the future merit in the average case. The above evaluation function gives a better estimate of the future merit at the risk of missing the best solution. The loss of optimality, however, is limited to $\frac{\varepsilon}{1-\varepsilon}$ percent of the merit of the best solution.

7.3 Checking consistency of future instantiations

Tree search methods, as described above, often are inefficient. They have some rule which determines which node is to be expanded next. This rule is applied until the search tree has been examined. While scanning the tree, the search often runs into dead end branches. The dead end is observed and the search backtracks. However, the reason why this branch had a dead end isn't memorized. It therefore happens that the search runs into other branches that have a dead end for the same reason. In order to avoid repeating the same mistakes the search has to remember these reasons.

Another reason for this inefficiency is that most search methods do not look ahead to the nodes on the path from the current node to the solution. Especially for matching problems an instantiation at level i in the tree may cancel out all possible labels for a unit at level $i+k$. A simple tree search method won't notice this until it arrives at level $i + k$.

Several strategies have been devised to improve the efficiency of tree search methods [Waltz 1972, Ullman 1976, Haralick and Shapiro 1979, 1980, Haralick and Elliott 1980]. In this paragraph we will illustrate the principles of two of them (called forward checking and looking ahead) by the example of the N-queens problem. We then show how the forward checking can be applied to the relational matching problem with an evaluation function.

Strategies like forward checking and looking ahead are often referred to as heuristics. Literally heuristic means "serving to discover". A heuristic is a rule of thumb or trick that should help to speed up the search. Usually it does, but sometimes a heuristic may be counter-productive. Some authors limit the term heuristic to those strategies that do not guarantee to find the best solution and in the worst case may not find a solution at all [Barr and Feigenbaum 1981], i.e. strategies that affect the admissibility of the search method. In this thesis, however, we will use the term heuristic in the broader sense of a method that in the average case improves the search characteristics. Admissible search methods that apply forward checking or looking ahead remain admissible.

7.3.1 Forward checking and looking ahead

Solving a matching problem, or a constraint satisfaction problem, like the N-queens problem, a search method puts a newly generated node onto the stack of unexpanded nodes after it has been checked that the instantiation at the current node is consistent with the instantiations that have been done at the higher levels in the tree (the past instantiations). E.g. in case of the N-queens problem, it has to verify that the proposed column (= label) in the current row (= unit) can not be taken by one of the queens in the past rows.

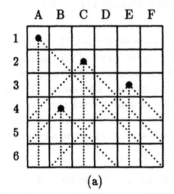 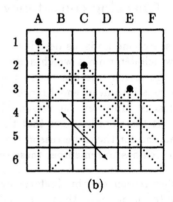

(a)   (b)

Figure 7.10: Forward checking (a) and looking ahead (b) in the 6-queens problem (from Haralick and Elliot [1980])

Proceeding this way, it may occur that an instantiation at the current unit eliminates all possible labels for a future unit. In the configuration of the 6-queens problem of figure 7.10a the instantiation of unit 4 with label B eliminates the last possible labels of unit 6. In a tree search without any extra checks this is only noticed at level 6. Every time the search method will explore a node on level 6 it will backtrack to level 5 and try another label for unit 5, not noticing that the true reason for the failure at level 6 isn't the instantiation at level 5 but the instantiation at level 4.

The *forward checking* strategy avoids such repetition of errors by checking the consistency of the current unit-label pair with the labels that are still available for the future units. If, for some future unit, all labels that are still available are inconsistent with the current instantiation, the search is sure to fail at that future unit and may as well backtrack immediately. After 3 instantiations in figure 7.10a, the only label that is still possible for unit 6 is label D. However, the unit-label pair (4,B) instantiated at the current level is inconsistent with the unit-label pair (6,D).

The forward checking is easily organized by registering the available labels in a two dimensional table (one dimension for the units, one dimension for the labels, figure 7.11). The search starts at the root node with an empty table, since all unit-label pairs are still possible. After the instantiation of unit 1 with label A, some of the labels can be ruled out for the future units. These labels are marked by an x in the table. The successors of the node representing the unit-label pair (1,A) inherit this table and can only select the labels that have not been marked (e.g. label C through F for unit 2). Choosing label C for unit 2 again some labels are ruled out for the units 3 through 6. These unit-label pairs are also marked in the table. This procedure is continued until, at the instantiation of unit 4 with label B, it is noticed that there are no more possible labels for unit 6. All columns in row 6 have been marked with an x.

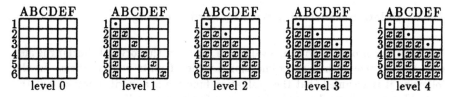

Figure 7.11: Registration of inconsistent labels

The number of tables needed for forward checking depends on the search method. One table is needed for each node that has one or more unexpanded successors, since these successors still have to inherit the table. Because the depth-first and the hill-climbing method first expand the successors of a node before searching elsewhere in the tree, the number of tables for these methods equals the depth of the search tree. Generally this number can be approximated by the quotient of the number of unexpanded nodes (= the stack length) and the average number of successors per node (the so-called branching factor). Of all search methods the breadth-first methods requires the most tables.

The *looking ahead* strategy performs even more consistency tests before putting a node on the stack. Whereas the forward checking only checks the consistencies of the current instantiation with the possible future instantiations, the looking ahead also verifies that each combination of the future unit and label is consistent with at least one label for each of the other future units. If it is not, this combination can not be a part of the solution and is ruled out.

After the instantiation of unit 3 with label E in the 6-queens problem of figure 7.10b the looking ahead method already notices that the future unit-label pair (4,B) is inconsistent with the future unit-label pair (6,D). Since label D is the only possible label for unit 6, this inconsistency rules out the label B for unit 4. And, since label B was the only label that was still available for unit 4, the looking ahead method knows that the instantiation of unit 3 with label E will not lead to a solution.

All consistency checks performed by forward checking are also performed by looking ahead. Since the looking ahead method also checks future unit-label pairs against other future unit-label pairs, looking ahead usually faster recognizes branches that do not lead to a solution and therefore has to expand fewer nodes. Exploring a smaller part of the tree saves search time, but it also takes time to perform the consistency checks. Haralick and Elliot [1980] investigated the efficiency of several heuristics like forward checking and looking ahead and concluded that the forward checking performs best. Apparently, it takes less time to expand a few more nodes, like the forward checking does, than to perform the extensive checks of the looking ahead. In the next paragraph we therefore will only consider the forward checking heuristic.

7.3.2 Relational matching with forward checking

For matching problems with an evaluation function, the forward checking is also easy to organize with a two-dimensional table of units versus labels. In the following it is assumed that the evaluation function is a merit function, but the method described can be applied to a cost function as well.

At the root level of the tree, the table of the merits is initialized with the merits of the primitive attribute comparisons. These are calculated for each entry of a unit (p_i) and a label (q_j) by summing up the merits of the corresponding L attribute values.

$$\text{merit-table}(p_i, q_j) = \sum_{l=1}^{L} I(a(p_i); a(q_j)) \tag{7-7}$$

Each node that is generated inherits the table from its predecessor. For each of the entries of a future unit and a label it adds to the table the merits that arise from the relations between the current instantiation, the past instantiations and that unit-label pair. More formally, let P^{past} be the set of past units and p_{cur} be the current newly instantiated unit. Further, let h be the partial mapping function that maps the past units and the current unit to their labels and let the unit-label pair (p_i, q_j) be an entry to the merit table. In case of N-ary relations all tuples consisting of the unit p_i, the current unit p_{cur} and $N - 2$ units from the set of past units are generated. Every tuple has its composed tuple

$$\{p_i \ p_{cur} \ p_1^{past} \cdots p_{N-2}^{past}\} \circ h = \{q_j \ h(p_{cur}) \ h(p_1^{past}) \cdots h(p_{N-2}^{past})\} \tag{7-8}$$

For each relation type, the merits of these tuple correspondences are added to the entry of future unit p_i and label q_j. Note that the past units are not involved in the binary relations. Proceeding this way for each unit-label pair, the merit table contains the merits of all primitive and relation tuple comparisons involving that unit and label up until the current level (or, in case the unit-label pair is already instantiated, up until the level of its predecessor).

The forward checking can use this table to rule out the labels of the future units that have become inconsistent by checking for which entries the merits have become infinitely negative. Besides, this merit table is very useful in calculating the values of the evaluation function. For each of the past nodes and the current node the table contains the merits of that node and the merits of that node in combination with the previous nodes. Hence the sum of the entries of the past nodes and the current node is the merit of the path from the root node to the current node, i.e. the value of $g(n)$.

The A^* algorithm also needs an estimate for the future merit $h(n)$. The function $h(n)$, which is also called the heuristic function, contains the merits of all comparisons involving future units: (1) the primitive comparisons of the future unit-label pairs, (2) the relation tuple comparisons of tuples with past, current and future units and their composed tuples, and (3) the relation tuple comparisons of tuples with future units only and their composed tuples. The merit table can provide good estimates for the first two terms by maximizing the table entries for each future unit over the available labels for that unit. This maximum is guaranteed to be no underestimation of the merit between the best future instantiation of that unit and the past and current instantiations. The third part of the heuristic function $h(n)$ can not be obtained from the merit table and must be estimated in another manner.

7.4 Unit ordering

The above heuristics perform some extra checks in order to determine dead end branches faster. Another heuristic that can be used to speed up the search is derived from the so-called *fail first principle*. This principle states that in order to succeed fast you should try first where you are most likely to fail [Haralick and Elliott 1980]. This seems in contradiction with the search methods like best-first. However, whereas the best-first applies the ordering to the merits of the generated nodes, the fail first principle is applied to the selection of the unit for which the nodes are to be generated next.

For the matching problem and most other constraint satisfaction problem, there is no need for processing the units in a fixed order. The unit order 3, N-1, 1, 5, N, ..., 4, 2 may do as well as the order 1, 2, 3, ..., N-1, N. This selection of the next unit even may be done locally, i.e. at the node that is to be expanded. Thus, the unit order may differ from branch to branch in the search tree.

If a unit is likely to fail, i.e. is likely to have no consistent labels, this is favourable for the search since it can backtrack fast and save exploring the part of the tree below the nodes of this unit. The search will encounter this unit anyway, so it is better to check its labels first as to check them after checking a lot of other nodes that are likely to be consistent.

For search problems without an evaluation function a straightforward implementation of this fail first principle is to select the unit with the lowest number of available labels. In the example of figure 7.12 three units, 1, 2 and 3 are to be matched that have 6, 3, and 1 possible labels respectively. If the units are matched in the order 1, 2, 3, the search tree has 42 nodes at which consistency checks have to be performed. Since all unit-label pairs are equally likely, the application of the fail first principle will sort the units after their number of possible labels, i.e. 3, 2, 1. The tree generated in this way only contains 22 nodes, thereby saving a lot of consistency checks.

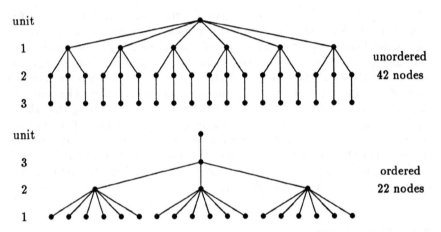

Figure 7.12: Unit ordering for a blind search

This strategy of selecting the unit with the fewest available labels can also be used for search problems with an evaluation function. For the matching problem, however, other selection criteria may also be useful. For instance, unit primitives that will be difficult to match, in a sense that on the average there only are a few possible label primitives for them, are primitives that have seldom attributes. This seldomness of a primitive can be measured by the self-information of the attributes of that primitive.

Interestingly, this seldomness of a primitive is also part of the mutual information that is used as the evaluation function. The mutual information is the difference between the self-information and the conditional information. Maximizing the mutual information implies maximizing the seldomness and optimizing the similarity between the attribute values. Considered over all primitives, the seldomness of the primitive set is constant. But using the high mutual information between a unit and a label primitive as a selection criterion for the next unit, also implies that a preference is given to the seldom primitive, i.e. the seldom primitives will be matched first. The advantage of using the mutual information to select the next unit is that the required values are obtainable from the merit table. One simply has to maximize over all possible labels of all future units to find the next unit primitive. A drawback, however, is that the other part of the merit function, i.e. the conditional information, may lead the selection too much away from the seldomness criterion.

7.5 The necessity of stop criteria for the correspondence problem

The search space of the correspondence problem is usually very large. Hidden in this space is the best solution to the problem. Usually there will be many solutions that are fairly good, i.e. that have a merit that is close to the merit of the best solution. For most tasks it is sufficient to find one of these solutions. Two approaches can be taken to find a solution faster: inadmissible search and perceptual grouping. Both approaches, however, require a test to verify that the selected solution is good enough.

7.5.1 Inadmissible search in large trees

The fact that the search space of correspondence problems is often very large is mainly due to the wildcards. Some unit primitives won't have corresponding label primitives and have to be assigned a wildcard. Since it is not known in advance which units have to be mapped to a wildcard, a wildcard assignment has to be considered for each unit. Thus, even the worst path in the tree can be continued down simply by assigning a wildcard at every level. This problem can only be resolved by putting a threshold on the number of allowed wildcards a path may contain, or, to some extent, by the use of the A^* algorithm. The A^* algorithm with a good heuristic function will notice a low future merit of such paths and therefore is unlikely to further extend them. If the future merit can not be estimated accurately, however, the A^* algorithm will further expand such paths as well.

To many correspondence problems the determination of the parameters of the geometrical transformation between the two primitive sets is an important task. For most applications like object recognition and surface reconstruction, only a few instantiations are needed to determine these parameters. The object recognition only needs three corresponding point-pairs to calculate the spatial resection and the surface reconstruction requires five instantiations for an iterative or eight for a direct solution of the relative orientation problem. The knowledge of the transformation parameters very much constrains the search space. After a transformation calculation only a few number of labels will be possible for the future units. Several authors therefore argue that the first few levels of the search tree until the level of transformation calculation mainly determine the width of the tree [Brooks 1981, Lowe 1985].

Most times this is true. Even if wildcards are allowed the merits of the correct instantiations will be higher than those of all other possibilities, so the A^*, best-first and even the hill-climbing algorithm will be able to find the solution fast. Despite the knowledge of the transformation parameters there still may remain some ambiguities to solve. For instance, a one-to-one mapping is to be found between two sets of lines. Due to noise or segmentation errors two small lines in a set correspond to one larger line in the other set. Since the mapping is required to be one-to-one one of these lines must be mapped to a wildcard. If the two small lines are about equally long, the merit of assigning them to the large line will be the same for both lines. Hence the tree search will have to consider both mappings, although the transformation parameters and the merit of the final result hardly will be influenced by the decision which of the two lines is to be assigned a wildcard. If such decisions have to be made for several lines in the data set, the problem of how to distribute the wildcards over the units leads to an exponential explosion of the search tree.

Since most of the solutions that will be found in this tree are about equally good and have about the same transformation parameters, it is a waste of search time to look for the very best solution. A better strategy would be to take just one of these solutions and check if this one is good enough.

Searching with the A^* strategy leads to a very large node stack because the A^* algorithm considers every possible wildcard assignment and hardly proceeds to the lower levels of the tree. To force the search to pick one of the solutions, i.e. to continue going down in the tree until a leaf node has been found, one has to apply mixed strategies. For example one can use the A^* algorithm until a certain level in the tree or until a certain amount of merit has been found and then continue the search with the hill-climbing algorithm. Another, more elegant method would be to combine the A^* algorithm with the ε-A^* algorithm, using a high value for ε in the lower parts of the tree.

The use of the hill-climbing or the ε-A^* strategy without backtracking clearly leads to an inadmissible search. Most of the solutions found by the mixed strategy will be good enough, but to be sure of a solution it should be tested. If the test is successful the search can be stopped and the solution is returned. If the test fails the search must backtrack. Such a test is required as a stop criterion.

7.5.2 Perceptual grouping of primitives

As already noted by people in the field of artificial intelligence: "the real trick in designing an efficient automatic problem solver is to search at the highest level permitted by the available information about the problem and about how it might be solved" [Nilsson 1971]. The word "level" is used in the meaning of level of data description. At a high level a data set can be described in terms of a few abstract units. The fewer units are to match, the smaller the search tree, and, consequently, the smaller the search effort will be.

Perceptual grouping is a useful tool to reach a higher level of data abstraction. The theory of perceptual grouping was initiated by the *Gestalt* school that claimed that "perception was something that happened as a whole rather than as a combination of individual primitive features" [Lowe 1985]. The Gestaltists described a number of phenomena that led to the grouping of individual primitives, like there are proximity, similarity, continuation, closure, symmetry and familiarity [Wertheimer 1958]. They further observed that people seem to perceive the simplest possible interpretation for any given data, although they (the Gestaltists) did not have a quantity to measure this simplicity. Interestingly, the minimum description length theory, as discussed in chapter 5, uses the same idea of simplicity. So one can say that it may be useful to group those primitives that have a smaller description as a group than when considered individually. For example, when matching line drawings of a blocks world, four lines in a rectangular configuration should be considered to represent a rectangular surface, and, on a higher level, a set of surfaces can be grouped to a polyhedron. Matching surfaces is faster than matching lines, since there will be less units to match. Matching polyhedra is even faster. When grouping lines to higher level units, all lines of the group become labeled at the level this unit is matched.

However, a grouping can not be considered as a certain interpretation of its elements. A minimal description length doesn't imply that the corresponding interpretation is known to be true but implies that it is the most likely interpretation. Clearly, four lines that make up a rectangle do not have to be the contours of a rectangular area. Thus, when using groupings of primitives in a tree search one always has to leave open the possibility that the grouping is wrong. The search tree as used without groupings can be extended with branches that use groupings but can never be reduced because one doesn't know if the groupings are correct. Consequently, a grouping of primitives in a search tree only makes sense if there is a stop criterion which prevents the search from exploring the whole tree. Without a stop criterion, perceptual grouping only increases the search effort as extra nodes have to be examined for the groupings without being able to cut on other branches.

Unfortunately there is no generally applicable criterion for all kinds of relational matching problems. For instance for the image-to-image matching problem one can not say that a mapping is good enough if the mutual information exceeds a certain threshold, if one doesn't know to which extent the images overlap, i.e. to which extent they may have information in common. The formulation of this stop criterion depends on the kind of problem. As will be shown in chapter 9 it is possible to define stop criteria for the object location problem.

The object location problem will be used to exemplify the possible applications of the theories that have been developed in part II. The new evaluation function will be specified for the attributes that are useful for the object location. For the attribute "angle" between two lines we will take advantage of the property that the attribute values may be discretized without significantly deteriorating the accuracy of the evaluation. The ε-A^* strategy will be guided by the new merit function and will use the forward checking and unit ordering heuristics to solve the object location problems.

Part III

Object location by relational matching

In the last part of this thesis we will apply the developed theory of relational matching to the problem of object location. *Object location* is the problem of finding the parameters that describe the transformation between the coordinate system of an object model and the coordinate system of the sensor that recorded the object. This general definition doesn't say anything about the dimensions of the object or the kind of data the sensor acquires. In the following, however, we will consider three-dimensional objects only and assume that the sensor is a CCD-camera sensing grey values. Thus, we will consider the problem of determining the position and orientation of an object in the coordinate system of the camera that recorded it by matching the 3-D object description with the 2-D image description. The orientation parameters then can be calculated by spatial resection.

As an introduction to the object location problem, we first make a comparison between this problem and the problem of object recognition. Although these problems have much in common, several differences have to be regarded.

Object recognition is the problem of detecting and classifying objects in an image. Whereas for the object location problem the object to be located is known to have been recorded in the image, an image given to an object recognition system may contain one or more objects but may also contain no objects at all. Furthermore the objects visible in the image have to be classified by comparing them to a library of specific or generic object models. In the case of the object location problem it is known which object is depicted in the image and how it looks like.

Thus an object recognition system is primarily interested in the classification of the objects detected in the image, whereas an object location system focuses on the determination of the position and orientation of the object. The determination of the object poses by an object recognition system is often only a by-product. The chief interest of a system should be reflected in the evaluation function for self-diagnosis. The main objective of an object recognition system should be the reliable detection and classification of the objects whereas the main objective of an object location system should be the reliable determination of the orientation parameters.

Applying the relational matching theory to the object location problem, we again will separate between the data that is matched, the evaluation function and the search method. In the next chapter we describe how the relational descriptions were extracted from the images of the recorded objects. In chapter 9 the evaluation function is specified for the object location problem and in chapter 10 several search strategies for and their performance in locating objects in digital images are presented.

8 Relational image and model description

The relational matching method compares relational descriptions. Therefore, the raw image and model data one wants to match have to be converted to relational descriptions.

The object models may be available in a CAD database. Gmür and Bunke [1988b, 1989] showed that such CAD models automatically can be converted into 3-D relational model descriptions. The attributes of primitives and their relations that are important for the relational matching are often implicitly stored in the CAD models. These attributes and relations have to be extracted and should be stored explicitly in the relational model descriptions. In absence of a CAD model conversion program the relational model descriptions of objects can also be made by hand or constructed from multiple object views [Helmke *et al.* 1990]. The model descriptions used in the next chapters were made by hand.

The extraction of a relational description from the raw image data (the grey value images) is a far more difficult task. A grey value image has to be segmented into features that can be matched, like points, lines and regions. Once these primitives have been extracted, the acquisition of the relations between them is usually straightforward. In the past few decades quite some image segmentation techniques have been developed. They can be separated into two groups: the gradient based methods and the region based methods. In the next paragraph we will shortly discuss the characteristics of these methods in order to determine the type of segmentation method that is most suitable for extracting features that can be used for matching purposes.

Then it will be described how the relational image descriptions that were used in this thesis have been extracted (paragraph 8.2) and which attributes were used for the relational matching (paragraph 8.3).

8.1 Image segmentation techniques

The main difference between the gradient based segmentation methods and the region based segmentation methods is the order in which they extract the two complementary features: lines and regions. The gradient based methods extract lines by linking the image pixels that show high grey value differences or differences in texture. The regions arise as the connected components of pixels surrounded by pixels with high gradient values. Surveys about gradient based segmentation methods can be found in [Davis 1975, Peli and Malah 1982].

The region based methods, on the contrary, first extract the regions by linking the image pixels that show similar grey or texture values. The lines then are defined by the boundaries of these regions. Usually the image is completely divided into regions so that the lines can also be said to separate the regions. Surveys about region based segmentation methods can be found in [Kanade 1980, Haralick and Shapiro 1985, Zucker 1976].

Regarding the matching of an image to a model the segmentation method should extract those primitives that are likely to be an image of physical object features like an object boundary or contrasting spots on the object's surface. I.e. the extracted primitives should contain information about the object. A pixel that contains an above average amount of information, in the sense of the information theory, is a pixel that has a high gradient value, since the probability that a pixel will have a high gradient value is low. Such information containing pixels are linked to lines by gradient based segmentation methods.

The region based methods, like region growing or histogram segmentation, merge the pixels with a low information content. The region growing algorithm expands an initial region pixel by pixel until the (grey) value of the region differs too much from the value of the surrounding pixels or until the region is completely surrounded by other regions and can not be expanded any further. The region boundaries often are pixels with high gradient values but may also very well be pixels with low gradient values. In the first case the region boundaries will contain information and probably give an accurate description of the projected model primitives, but in the second case the location of these boundaries depends on factors like the order in which the regions were expanded, or the threshold used for the merging criterion. The location of such boundaries is very uncertain and can not be used for matching purposes. The histogram segmentation method also may result in region boundaries that have no physical interpretation. Figure 8.1 shows an example of how a region based segmentation method (in this case region growing) extracts such unmatchable lines in case of weak contrast. The gradient based method can't extract a perfect description either, but the edges that are extracted at least have the correct shape and position, and thus could be matched to model edges.

Another disadvantage of the region based methods is their limited function of the lines in an image description. These methods only consider the lines as the boundaries of the regions. Images with lines that are not a part of a boundary of an homogeneous region can not be segmented properly, as shown in figure 8.2. Smooth grey value changes like in this figure also often result from a change of light reflexion on curved surfaces. Such changes mislead the region based segmentation methods [Vosselman 1989].

Hence, features that are extracted by a gradient based segmentation method are

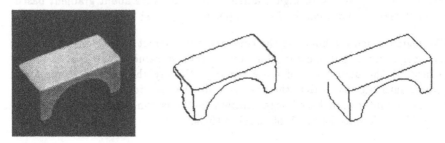

Figure 8.1: (a) Image with weak contrast. (b) Region based segmentation. (c) Gradient based segmentation.

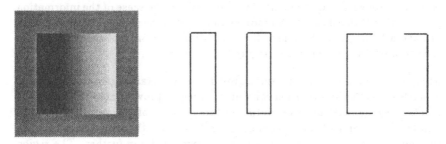

Figure 8.2: Wedge in a medium grey level background. (b) Region based segmentation. (c) Gradient based segmentation.

more reliable in a sense that they are more likely to arise from a physical phenomenon than features extracted by a region based segmentation method. The relational descriptions that were used in this thesis are obtained by a gradient based segmentation method. This method is described in the next paragraphs and was developed a few years ago.

In the meanwhile, research in image segmentation has continued and some new ideas were presented. An interesting new approach to image segmentation was formulated by Leclerc [1988] who defined the best image description as the description with a minimal length. The best segmentation in piecewise smooth patches and breaklines is found by the application of a continuation method. This method has a sound theoretical background and, in contrast to the gradient and region based methods, needs no thresholds to control the segmentation process.

8.2 Extraction of image features

The elementary image features one can extract from an image are points, lines and regions. These features will be used as the primitives for the object location.

- Points are those spots in the image that show a significant change of grey value in several directions. Points are found at corners of surfaces, but may also represent blobs.

- Lines are sequences of eight-connected pixels that show a significant grey value gradient in one direction. The line pixels are connected to lines in the direction perpendicular to the grey value gradient direction.

- Regions are four-connected components of pixels that are bounded by points and lines, i.e. by pixels with strong gradients. One may also define the lines as four-connected sequences of pixels. Since the regions are the complements of lines, the regions then are eight-connected.

The features as extracted by local gradient operators are often noisy and not suitable to be directly compared to a relational description of an object model. Therefore, these feature data were postprocessed to eliminate those features that are probably due to noise. So, the image segmentation consisted of four parts: point extraction, line extraction, region extraction and a cleaning step.

8.2.1 Point extraction

Many interest operators have been developed to extract significant points from grey value images [Moravec 1977, Dreschler 1981]. We used the interest operator first published by Paderes *et al.* [1984] and later improved by Förstner and Gülch [1987]. This operator can be used for point extraction as well as for line extraction and can determine point and line locations with sub-pixel accuracy. Like most other operators, this operator is gradient based. From the row- and column gradients, g_r and g_c, the following matrix can be composed by summing the products over the pixels of a window.

$$N = \begin{pmatrix} \sum g_r^2 & \sum g_r g_c \\ \sum g_r g_c & \sum g_c^2 \end{pmatrix} \qquad (8\text{-}1)$$

The summation can be performed by calculating the products for each pixel and then convolving the products with a 4×4 or 6×6 box (thus involving the grey values of the pixels in a 5×5 or 7×7 box). The trace of this matrix can be used as the interest value. The higher the trace, the more remarkable the pixel is. A threshold has to be used to select the pixel with strong gradients.

Interest points have strong gradients, but pixels on grey value edges have strong gradients too. The points are moreover characterized by their isotropic grey value distribution. Analogous to covariance matrices describing error ellipses, the matrix defined above also may be thought of as a matrix describing an ellipse. The roundness of this ellipse is given by:

$$q = \frac{4 \cdot |N|}{\mathrm{tr}^2(N)} \qquad (8\text{-}2)$$

The value of q is always between 0 and 1. If it is high, the ellipse is circular which implies that the gradient strength is about the same in all directions. This occurs at corners of grey value edges and at blobs. A threshold of 0.5 to 0.75 has proven to be appropriate for the point extraction in most applications.

Usually several adjacent pixels will have similar gradient strength and roundness values. The pixel with the highest gradient strength is filtered out by a non-maximum suppression and taken to be the interest point. Sub-pixel coordinates of the interest point can be obtained by determining the centre of gravity of all pixels within a window of the interest point using the matrix

$$\begin{pmatrix} g_{ri}^2 & g_{ri}g_{ci} \\ g_{ri}g_{ci} & g_{ci}^2 \end{pmatrix} \qquad (8\text{-}3)$$

as the weight matrix for each pixel i within this window.

8.2.2 Line extraction

Lines are sequences of pixels with strong gradients. The selection of those pixels again can be done with the interest operator described above. But now, unlike in the point extraction procedure, there is no restriction on the roundness value of the ellipse. All pixels which have a strong gradient are candidate line pixels. The size of the interest operator for this application is usually 3×3.

The direction of the gradient can be calculated from the elements of the same matrix N:

$$\phi = 0.5 \arctan\left(\frac{\sum g_r g_c}{\sum g_c^2 - \sum g_r^2}\right) \qquad (8\text{-}4)$$

Two candidate line pixels can be linked if the gradient directions of the pixels are about the same and the normal to the gradient direction of the first pixel points towards the second pixel. In this way a graph of possible links can be constructed (figure 8.3).

The costs of a link between two pixels is a fixed value minus the gradient strength of the second pixel. The candidate pixel with the strongest gradient is assumed to be part of a line and is taken as the first point for the line following. Starting

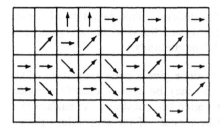 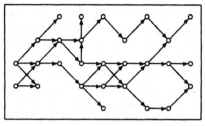

Figure 8.3: Edge directions and the constructed graph of possible lines. (adopted from Ballard and Brown [1982])

at this point, all paths of a certain length, i.e. a certain number of links, are evaluated. After selecting the combination of links with the lowest sum of link costs, the first part of that path, say half the path, is fixed and its pixels are classified as line pixels. Starting at the last fixed pixel, again all paths of a certain length are evaluated and the first part of the best path is fixed. Not fixing the best path over the complete length which has been evaluated, accomplishes that the selection of a pixel is influenced by the preceding pixels as well as by the following pixels. To avoid the extraction of many small parallel branches of a line, the pixels on the evaluated but not optimal paths may not be taken as start points for a new line. The line following terminates when:

- there are no more candidate line pixels to continue, or

- the line following finds a pixel classified as a point primitive, in which case this point becomes the end node of the line, or

- the line following finds a pixel that is already classified as a line pixel. This either is a pixel of an old line, in which case the old line is split into two lines, or it is a pixel of the line currently being followed, in which case a closed polygon has been found.

When the line following has terminated, the algorithm returns to the selected start pixel and traces the line in the opposite direction until one of the above conditions is met. After finishing the second direction a new pixel is selected as the starting point for the following of the next line. This process is repeated until there are no candidate line pixels left that can be used for a start point of a new line.

8.2.3 Region extraction

Once the point and line pixels have been labeled by the above extraction methods, the regions are the four-connected components of the remaining unlabeled pixels. The regions extracted by a gradient based segmentation technique are completely bounded by pixels with strong gradients. This definition of regions allows the presence of other primitives (points and lines) within a region. This is not possible with region based segmentation methods.

The grey value distributions within the regions give a good indication of the usefulness of a region for the matching and may be used to classify a region. If the grey values of the pixels within a region are constant, the surface that is represented by this region is likely to be planar. If the grey values show a gradual change depending on the pixel coordinates that can be modeled by a planar or a low order polynomial surface (using the pixel coordinates as the first two dimensions and the grey value as the third dimension), the region probably represents a curved object surface. If the grey values are not easily modeled, the region either represents a complex object surface or the region does not represent one object surface but represents several surfaces that could not be segmented properly. If the last interpretation is correct, such a region can not be used in a search process looking for a 1-1 mapping between image regions and object surfaces.

8.2.4 Symbolic post-processing

Gradient based segmentation methods extract the points and lines with local operators. The fewer the number of pixels that are involved, the noisier the extracted features will be. The line extraction, for example, uses a 3×3 mask. Using a larger mask reduces the influence of noise but will decrease the resolution that can be obtained. Instead of reducing the noise by using large edge detection masks, one can also extract the features with a small mask and try to remove the features that may be due to noise afterwards.

The post-processing of the features we applied also contained some other procedures that should simplify the raw description, assuming that a simple description is a better description. Some of these procedures are heuristic in a sense that they will usually improve the description but may sometimes deteriorate it. The five procedures that were applied are illustrated in figure 8.4. Each column (a) till (e) refers to the intended improvement of the procedures described below. The upper figure in each column gives an example of how the raw data may look like and the lower figure gives the output of the post-processing phase.

(a) Each pixel only has eight neighbour pixels. The directional resolution of pixel links is therefore very limited. Suppose that two lines intersect in a point that has been detected by the interest operator under an angle of 15 degrees and that one line already has been found by the line following algorithm. Tracing the second line, the line follower will encounter pixels that are already classified as line pixels before reaching the interest point and thus will create a line junction point and terminate the line following. The interest point and this line junction will be only a few pixels apart.

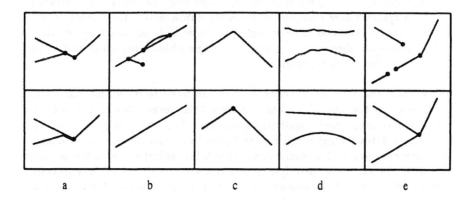

Figure 8.4: Post-processing of extracted features (see text)

They are likely to be due to the same underlying physical event. Hence, the first post-processing step merges all junction points that are connected by short (1-5 pixel) lines to an interest point to a single point. The short lines connecting the points are deleted and the other lines involved are extended to the new point. The new point is generated at the location of the interest point since it is assumed that the coordinates of this point will be the most precise. If there is no interest point in such a cluster of points, the point with the highest gradient value is taken.

(b) All pixels on paths that have been examined by the line following are marked so that they can not be taken as a start pixel for a next line. This is to prevent the extraction of many small lines and parallel lines. This strategy usually works quite well but may sometimes fail when the grey value edge is smooth. Small lines that are only connected to other lines at one of its endpoints are eliminated as they are unlikely to correspond to a line in the object model. Pairs of parallel lines are merged to one line. The line junction points that connect the two parallel lines or link the small lines to other lines are also eliminated.

(c) The interest operator detects points at grey value corners and blobs. It fails to recognize corners of lines that intersect under a large angle. In order to detect corners that were missed by the interest operator, the curvatures of each line are analyzed and a point is inserted at the locations of a sudden change in the direction of a line.

(d) The line following algorithm outputs the lines as sequences of pixel coordinates. As the lines of the used objects are all straight or circular, many of the extracted lines are shorter described by the parameters of a straight or an elliptic line than by lists of pixel coordinates. Besides, the classification of a line is a useful attribute for the relational matching. All extracted lines are therefore classified in straight, elliptic and "other" lines. A line can not be classified to be straight or elliptic if it only has a few pixels or if it does not directly correspond to a single object line, which may occur due to a wrong segmentation.

(e) Finally, the contrast of edges is often too weak to detect all pixels that belong to the line. The line following then terminates as it can't find anymore pixels with significant gradients. The last post-processing step extrapolates the extracted line and tries to extend the line to an already extracted point. The decision whether a line is indeed extended is taken with the minimum description length theory as discussed in paragraph 5.3. Especially if the line extension splits a region in two, the description of these two regions is often much shorter than the description of the original region. The grey values in the two regions can be modeled well by planar surfaces if they correspond to object regions. The grey values of the original regions usually will deviate from a planar surface to a larger extent and therefore will require a longer description.

Steps (a) and (e) can be considered as perceptual groupings. Step (a) uses the proximity of points, whereas step (e) uses the continuity of lines to obtain a better description.

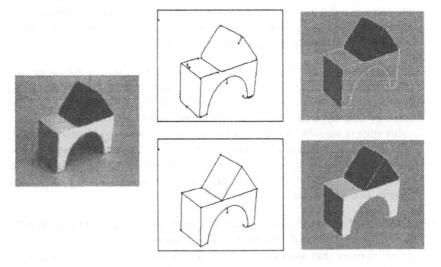

Figure 8.5: Example of points, lines and regions before and after the post-processing.

An example of the post-processing is given in figure 8.5. A grey value image is segmented into points, lines (upper middle image) and regions (upper right image, regions depicted in average grey value). The topological relations between the primitives were also acquired. The five steps described above resulted in the points, lines and regions showed at the bottom of the figure. Features due to noise were removed, lines were segmented and classified and some of the gaps were closed.

8.3   Used primitives and relations and their attributes

Both the relational image and model descriptions had three different types of primitives.

1. Point primitives. No attributes were used to describe the point primitives.

2. Line primitives. The line primitives were described by two attributes:

   - Length of the line primitives.

   - Type class of the line primitives. The shape of each line is classified in "straight", "elliptic" or "other".

3. Region primitives. No attributes were used to describe the region primitives.

The relational part of both descriptions consisted of three binary relations.

1. Relation "connected" between point and line primitives. This relation has one attribute which is a predicate. Its value is "true" if a point is the begin- or end-point of the line and "false" otherwise.

2. Relation "angle" between two line primitives. This relation has one numerical attribute which is the angle between the two lines. The direction of a line is defined by is begin- and end-point.

3. Relation "contour" between line and region primitives. This relation has one attribute which is a predicate. Its value is "true" if a line is part of the contour of a region and "false" otherwise.

9 Evaluation functions for object location

In chapter 6 it has been shown that the maximization of the mutual information between the corresponding attributes of two descriptions gives the maximum likelihood estimation of the mapping. The mutual information can be used to select the best mapping out of a group of mappings. This *relative* evaluation can be used for all kinds of matching problems, not only for object location, but also for object recognition and image matching.

Once a mapping has been found, one has to determine whether this mapping is good enough or not. Such a self-diagnosis, which can also serve as a stop criterion for the tree search, could not be defined in a general way valid for all kinds of matching problems. For particular problems, however, it may be possible to specify such criteria. Above we argued that in case of object location the reliability of the determination of the transformation parameters should be used for self-diagnosis. Later on in this chapter we will show that it is also possible to define a statistical test on the minimum amount of mutual information needed for a successful object location.

In order to calculate the mutual information between two descriptions one needs the probabilities of the attribute appearances and the conditional probabilities of the attribute correspondences, i.e. the transfer probabilities of the attribute correspondence channels. Furthermore one has to describe the support of the assumed transformation to the mapping in terms of mutual information. The mutual information of the corresponding attributes and of the spatial resection together constitute the evaluation function for the object location.

9.1 Composing the mutual information tables

There are many ways to calculate the mutual information between a model attribute value and an image attribute value:

$$
\begin{aligned}
I(a_m; a_i) &= \log \frac{P(a_i|a_m)}{P(a_i)} \\[2mm]
&= \log \frac{P(a_m|a_i)}{P(a_m)} \\[2mm]
&= \log \frac{P(a_i|a_m)}{\sum\limits_{a_m} P(a_i|a_m) \cdot P(a_m)} \\[2mm]
&= \log \frac{P(a_m|a_i)}{\sum\limits_{a_i} P(a_m|a_i) \cdot P(a_i)} \\[2mm]
&= \cdots
\end{aligned}
\tag{9-1}
$$

The best way is to use the probability of the model attribute value and the conditional probability of the image attribute value given the model attribute value, i.e.:

$$I(a_m; a_i) = \log \frac{P(a_i | a_m)}{\sum_{a_m} P(a_i | a_m) \cdot P(a_m)} \tag{9-2}$$

Since only one object is involved in the object location, the probabilities of the model attribute values are constants. If the conditions under which the object is recorded (camera, exposure) are the same for all images that are matched to the model, the conditional probabilities used in the expression above are constants too.

The probabilities of the model attribute values can be directly obtained from the object model. What is being left to determine are the conditional probabilities. There are three ways to determine the conditional probability function. One may be able to derive it analytically (1). Often the function will be too complex for this. If, however, one can model the transformation of the model value into the image value by a few stochastic parameters and one can describe the probability functions of these transformation parameters it becomes possible to determine the conditional probability function by numerical methods (2). Still many functions will be too complex to be determined this way. These functions can only be found by analyzing the probabilities of attribute correspondences in training matches, i.e. matches that were done by hand, guaranteeing the correctness of them (3).

All three methods have been applied to determine the conditional probabilities of the attributes that have been used for the object location (paragraph 8.3): the mutual information of line length attributes has been derived analytically (1), the mutual information of angle attributes was determined by numerical simulation of many correspondences (2), and the mutual information of the line type attributes and the membership values of the point-line connection relation and the line-region contour relation were determined by training matches (3).

9.1.1 Mutual information of line length measurements

The length of an image line is a continuous variable. To calculate the mutual information between an image line length and a model line length, we therefore have to derive the conditional probability density function of the image line length given the model line length. For simplicity of the derivation, let us assume that a 3-D model line with length l_m lies on the X-axis of the model coordinate system with the middle of the line at the coordinate system's origin (figure 9.1). Since we do not have any information about the orientation of the camera all positions on a unit sphere around the origin are equally likely. For the moment we assume that the image scale is known to be 1, so that the maximum length of the projected line, l_i, is l_m. The length of the line in the image taken from a point on the sphere can be calculated from the projection of the model line onto the tangent plane of the sphere in that point.

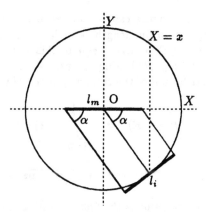

Figure 9.1: Derivation of the line length density function.

Figure 9.1 depicts the XOY plane of the line and the sphere. Let there be a plane $X = x$. The length of the projected line in all points on the intersection of this plane with the sphere will be $l_i = l_m \cdot \sin(\alpha) = l_m \cdot \sqrt{1 - x^2}$. Figure 9.2a shows the length ratio $r = \frac{l_i}{l_m}$ as a function of the coordinate x.

If a set of points is equally distributed on the surface of the unit sphere, the x-coordinates of those points is equally distributed on the interval [-1,1]. This is shown in appendix B. The probability that the camera position will be in the plane $X = x$ thus is a constant. In order to simplify the derivation below, we will assume that the x-coordinate can only be positive. Because of the symmetry of

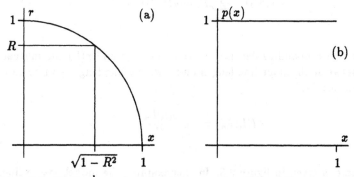

Figure 9.2: Ratio $\frac{l_i}{l_m}$ and probability as a function of the x-coordinate

the sphere, this is allowed. The probability density function of the x-coordinate therefore is (figure 9.2b):

$$p(x) = 1 \qquad \text{on } [0,1] \tag{9-3}$$

The two functions in this figure can be combined into the distribution of the image line length. A certain line length ratio R occurs if $x = \sqrt{1 - R^2}$. At all positions of the camera with a larger value of this x, the projected line length will be smaller than $R \cdot l_m$. Reflecting the probability density function of the x-coordinate, the distribution of the ratio r is defined by

$$P(r \leq R) \quad = \quad \int_{\sqrt{1-R^2}}^{1} p(x) \; dx$$

$$= \quad 1 - \sqrt{1 - R^2} \tag{9-4}$$

The probability density function is the first derivative of this distribution. Elaborating the expression of the derivative, one obtains:

$$p(r) = \frac{dP(r \leq R)}{dR} = \frac{r}{\sqrt{1 - r^2}} \tag{9-5}$$

Substituting r by the ratio $\frac{l_i}{l_m}$ and scaling with $\frac{1}{l_m}$ the conditional probability density function of the image line length l_i given the model line length l_m is

$$p(l_i|l_m) = \begin{cases} \dfrac{1}{l_m} \dfrac{\frac{l_i}{l_m}}{\sqrt{1 - \left(\frac{l_i}{l_m}\right)^2}} & \text{for } 0 \leq l_i \leq l_m \\ 0 & \text{else} \end{cases} \tag{9-6}$$

Since the probabilities of the line lengths in the model are known, the probability density function of the image line length can be calculated by

$$p(l_i) = \sum_{l_m} p(l_i|l_m) \cdot P(l_m) \tag{9-7}$$

With the two probability density functions $p(l_i|l_m)$ and $p(l_i)$ the mutual information between an image line length and a model line length can be calculated (from equation 5-15)

$$I(l_i; l_m) = \log \frac{p(l_i|l_m)}{p(l_i)} \tag{9-8}$$

An example is given in figure 9.3. In this example the model has 18 lines with line length distribution of table 9.1.

class	length	frequency
1	8.0	4
2	28.0	4
3	40.0	6
4	60.0	2
5	69.0	2

Table 9.1: Example of a model line length distribution.

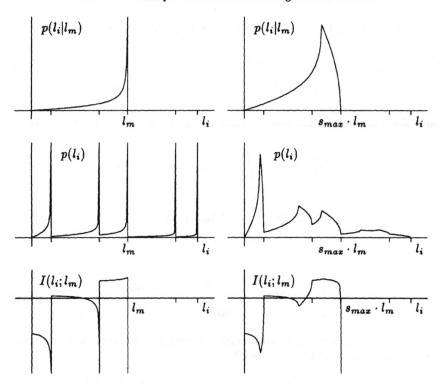

Figure 9.3: Conditional density $p(l_i|l_m)$, density $p(l_i)$ and mutual information $I(l_i; l_m)$ functions with (left) and without (right) the knowledge of the scale parameter for the example of table 9.1.

The left side of the figure shows three graphs. The first graph is the conditional probability density of the image line length given that the length of the model line $l_m = 40$ (and the image scale is 1). The length of the image line can be at most 40. The probability density asymptotically moves to infinite as l_i approaches l_m. The second graph shows the probability density function of the image line length, without the knowledge of the length of the projected line. The third graph shows the mutual information between an image line length and a model line with length 40.0 as a function of the image line length. For the graphs on the left side, the scale parameter was known to be 1.

Usually the image scale is not known. In many object location problems, however, the distance between the camera and the object is approximately known, so that the scale parameter s is known to lie within an interval $[s_{min}, s_{max}]$. For this case we will now derive the conditional probability density function, assuming that the probability of the scale parameter is equally distributed on the interval $[s_{min}, s_{max}]$ and zero outside this interval.

Knowing the scale parameter s we derived that (compare to equation 9-6)

$$p(l_i|l_m, s) = \begin{cases} \dfrac{1}{l_m \cdot s} \dfrac{\frac{l_i}{l_m \cdot s}}{\sqrt{1 - \left(\frac{l_i}{l_m \cdot s}\right)^2}} & \text{for } 0 \le l_i \le l_m \cdot s \\ 0 & \text{else} \end{cases} \tag{9-9}$$

Since the model line length and the scale parameter are independent, we have

$$\begin{aligned} p(l_i|l_m) &= \int_{s_{min}}^{s_{max}} p(l_i|l_m, s) \cdot p(s|l_m) \; ds \\ &= \int_{s_{min}}^{s_{max}} p(l_i|l_m, s) \cdot p(s) \; ds \end{aligned} \tag{9-10}$$

with

$$p(s) = \begin{cases} \dfrac{1}{s_{max} - s_{min}} & \text{for } s_{min} \le s \le s_{max} \\ 0 & \text{else} \end{cases} \tag{9-11}$$

This results in the following conditional probability density function of the image line length given the model line length:

$$p(l_i|l_m) = \begin{cases} \dfrac{1}{l_m} \dfrac{1}{s_{max} - s_{min}} \left\{ \arcsin\left(\frac{l_i}{l_m \cdot s_{min}}\right) - \arcsin\left(\frac{l_i}{l_m \cdot s_{max}}\right) \right\} \\ \qquad\qquad \text{for } 0 \le l_i \le s_{min} \cdot l_m \\ \dfrac{1}{l_m} \dfrac{1}{s_{max} - s_{min}} \left\{ \frac{\pi}{2} - \arcsin\left(\frac{l_i}{l_m \cdot s_{max}}\right) \right\} \\ \qquad\qquad \text{for } s_{min} \cdot l_m < l_i \le s_{max} \cdot l_m \\ 0 \qquad\qquad \text{else} \end{cases} \tag{9-12}$$

The proof is given in appendix C.

In the example of figure 9.3 the graph at the top right side shows the conditional probability density function of the image line length given that the model line length is 40.0 and that the scale parameter is equally distributed on the interval [0.8, 1.0]. The graph in the middle on the right shows the probability density function of the image line length, without knowing the model line length. This function is again calculated with equation 9-7. The last graph in this figure shows the mutual information between the image line length and the model line length $l_m = 40.0$ as a function of the image line length reflecting the scale uncertainty. For image lines larger that 40, the mutual information is minus infinite, because the projection of the model line can not be longer than 40 (with $s_{max} = 1$).

9.1.2 Mutual information of angle measurements

The angle between two lines is a relation attribute. Although small model line angles may be projected as large image line angles and large model line angles may be projected as small image line angles, this attribute still contains information since, for instance, small model line angles will be more likely to correspond to small image line angles than to large line angles. Like the line length attribute the angle attribute is a continuous variable. The attribute transition therefore should be modeled by a conditional density function. Given a model line angle, what is the probability density function of the angle between the lines projected in the image? Given two model lines and the orientation of the camera it is easy to calculate the image angle between the two projected lines. It is, however, difficult to analytically derive the conditional probability density function when not knowing the camera position.

It is far more easier to generate a large number of random camera orientations, to calculate the corresponding image line angles and to analyze the distribution of these angles. For the last step one needs to discretize the range of the image angle values, i.e. to make angle value classes and for each class to calculate the frequency of the calculated image angles belonging to it. So, instead of calculating the mutual information between continuous angle values, we calculate the mutual information between discrete classes of angle values. And thus, instead of probability density functions we are using probability functions. As shown in paragraph 5.2 the mutual information has the same form for both probability density and probability functions. We also proved that the loss of information caused by the discretization is expected to be small when using a small discretization interval (paragraph 5.4).

For the line angle attribute which has a value range from 0 to 90 degrees we chose a discretization interval of 1 degree. Furthermore, we assumed a measurement noise of the image angle of 5 degrees. For each of the angles that could occur in the model (0, 45 and 90 degrees) 1.000.000 randomly distributed points on a unit sphere were generated, in such a way that the density of the points on the sphere was expected to be homogeneous. The two model lines were assumed to intersect in the centre of the sphere and each generated point is the position of an imaginary camera looking at the centre of the sphere. The model lines were projected into each image plane and the corresponding image angles were overlayed with noise and tabulated. Figure 9.4 shows the conditional

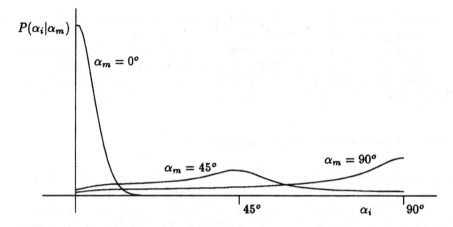

Figure 9.4: Conditional probabilities of image angle classes given model angles of 0, 45 and 90 degrees.

probabilities as a function of the image angle given for model angle for the model angles 0, 45 and 90 degrees. The conditional probability given a model angle of 0 degrees of course is completely shaped by the noise addition since the angle between the projected model lines will always be 0 degrees too. For each of the three model values the graph shows the probabilities of the 90 image angle classes. The probabilities of the neighbouring classes are connected by a straight line which thus gives a good impression of how the probability density functions must look like. The conditional probability functions only depend on the amount of noise and the model angle. They do not depend on the frequencies of the angles in the model, so that they can be used for all models that have to be located.

angle	frequency
0	81
45	56
90	188

Table 9.2: Example of a model angle distribution.

For the model angle distribution of table 9.2 the derived conditional angle probabilities resulted in the mutual information functions depicted in figure 9.5. Small image angle values are highly supported by the model angle of 0 degrees, but as soon as the image values become larger, the model angles 45 and 90 degrees give a stronger support. The mutual information functions are independent of the distribution of the image angles. They only have to be calculated once for each model.

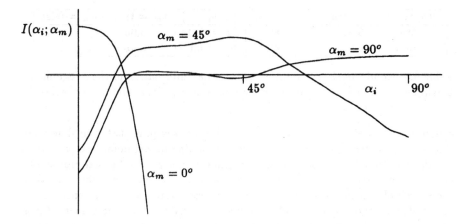

Figure 9.5: Mutual information between image angle classes and model angles of 0, 45 and 90 degrees for the example of table 9.2.

9.1.3 Mutual information determined from training matches

The fact whether the projections of a model point and a model line that are connected in the model again are connected in the image depends on a lot of factors like recording circumstances, image resolution, image noise and the method used for feature extraction. It would be very difficult to describe the transition of a model membership value of such a topological relation by one of the two methods described above.

The easiest way to determine the conditional probability tables of the membership values is by taking a lot of images of the object to be located that are characteristic for the kind of images the future object location system may expect. These images then have to be matched to the object model, either by hand or by a matching procedure that uses provisional roughly estimated transition probabilities. In the latter case the resulting mapping should be verified by hand to ensure that it is correct. The conditional probabilities can be acquired by simply counting the correspondences of the membership values in the correct mappings.

From a series of 50 training matches the conditional probabilities were obtained for the membership values of the relation "connected" between point and line primitives. These probabilities are shown on the left side in table 9.3. For a model with 52 connected point-line pairs and 364 not connected pairs this resulted in the mutual information of relation "connected" shown on the right side in the table.

In the set of test matches it did not occur that the projections of a point and a line that were not connected in the model were connected in the image. As a

$P(v_i\|v_m)$	$v_m = \text{true}$	$v_m = \text{false}$
$v_i = \text{true}$	0.92	0.00
$v_i = \text{false}$	0.08	1.00

$I(v_i; v_m)$	$v_m = \text{true}$	$v_m = \text{false}$
$v_i = \text{true}$	3.00	$-\infty$
$v_i = \text{false}$	-3.49	0.18

Table 9.3: Conditional probabilities and mutual information of the image membership value v_i and the model membership value v_m of the relation "connected".

consequence the object location program will always require that point-line pairs that are connected in the image have corresponding model point-line pairs that are also connected. It makes a large difference whether a conditional probability is zero or very small. If it is small the value transition is possible and thus the search algorithm may generate new successor nodes and may continue the search down although these nodes are very unlikely to be the best ones. If it is zero, however, the combination of attributes of the primitives or relation tuples that were compared is impossible, and, hence, the mapping that is currently investigated is impossible. This implies that the search may backtrack at this node without generating successor nodes. Thus, conditional probabilities that are zero help to limit the search space.

$P(v_i\|v_m)$	$v_m = \text{true}$	$v_m = \text{false}$
$v_i = \text{true}$	0.98	0.00
$v_i = \text{false}$	0.02	1.00

$I(v_i; v_m)$	$v_m = \text{true}$	$v_m = \text{false}$
$v_i = \text{true}$	2.59	$-\infty$
$v_i = \text{false}$	-5.80	0.26

Table 9.4: Conditional probabilities and mutual information of the image membership value v_i and the model membership value v_m of the relation "contour".

Using the same method, the mutual information tables for the membership value of the relation "contour" and for the line type attribute were determined. The results for the contour relations are shown in table 9.4. The mutual information table is for a model with 12 surfaces and 26 lines. As all lines are part of the contour of two surfaces, there are $26 \cdot 2 = 54$ membership values "true" and $26 \cdot 10 = 260$ membership values "false".

The transition probabilities of the line type attribute can not be described by a single table. The results of the algorithm that classified the image lines in straight, elliptic and "other" lines, heavily depended on the length of the line. The shape of long lines is much easier to be classified than the shape of short lines. Many short lines could not be classified and were labeled "other". For the matching problems that will be described in the next chapter, the mutual information tables were derived for three different classes of line lengths (lines shorter than 25 pixels, shorter than 100 pixels, and longer than 100 pixels, table 9.5). Although many of the training images did contain short elliptic lines, none of these lines were classified elliptic. The mutual information between model lines and short elliptic image lines could therefore not be calculated.

The mutual information of the entries in table 9.5 change quite a lot from line

$P(v_i|v_m)$	$v_m = $ straight	$v_m = $ elliptic
$v_i = $ straight	0.81	0.35
$v_i = $ elliptic	0.00	0.00
$v_i = $ other	0.19	0.65

$I(v_i; v_m)$	$v_m = $ straight	$v_m = $ elliptic
$v_i = $ straight	0.07	-1.15
$v_i = $ elliptic	undef.	undef.
$v_i = $ other	-0.24	1.52

Tables for image lines shorter than 25 pixels.

$P(v_i|v_m)$	$v_m = $ straight	$v_m = $ elliptic
$v_i = $ straight	0.99	0.03
$v_i = $ elliptic	0.00	0.78
$v_i = $ other	0.01	0.19

$I(v_i; v_m)$	$v_m = $ straight	$v_m = $ elliptic
$v_i = $ straight	0.11	-5.08
$v_i = $ elliptic	$-\infty$	3.70
$v_i = $ other	-1.02	2.83

Tables for image lines shorter than 100 pixels.

$P(v_i|v_m)$	$v_m = $ straight	$v_m = $ elliptic
$v_i = $ straight	0.95	0.00
$v_i = $ elliptic	0.00	1.00
$v_i = $ other	0.05	0.00

$I(v_i; v_m)$	$v_m = $ straight	$v_m = $ elliptic
$v_i = $ straight	0.12	$-\infty$
$v_i = $ elliptic	$-\infty$	3.70
$v_i = $ other	0.12	$-\infty$

Tables for image lines longer than 100 pixels.

Table 9.5: Conditional probabilities and mutual information of the image line type v_i and the model line type v_m

length class to line length class. In order to acquire the mutual information of the line type classification properly, one would have to use many more line length classes. This would, however, involve too much training matches to be performed within the scope of this thesis.

9.2   The mutual information of the spatial resection

Not only attributes of primitives and relations contain information about the mapping but also the parameters of the spatial resection. Without knowing the transformation parameters the coordinates of the image primitives and the coordinates of the model primitives are independent. To describe the image coordinates with a resolution of ε pixels it takes

$$I(c_i|c_m) = I(c_i) = \log \frac{R}{\varepsilon} \text{ bits} \tag{9-13}$$

for each coordinate c_i when the image size is R pixels. For n coordinate pairs it thus takes

$$2n \log \frac{R}{\varepsilon} \text{ bits.} \tag{9-14}$$

Knowing the transformation parameters, the image coordinates can be described by the deviations from the corresponding model coordinates projected into the image. Like for the line fitting example in paragraph 5.3.2, it takes n bits to classify a coordinate pair as outlier or not. The n_{out} outliers again are described by

$$2n_{out} \log \frac{R}{\varepsilon} \text{ bits.} \tag{9-15}$$

The other n_{good} coordinate pairs are modeled by the deviation from the transformed model coordinates $c_{m,proj}$ which requires

$$\sum_{k=1}^{2n_{good}} \frac{1}{2 \log_e 2} \left(\frac{c_i^k - c_{m,proj}^k}{\sigma} \right)^2 + n_{good} \log 2\pi \left(\frac{\sigma}{\varepsilon} \right)^2 \text{ bits.} \tag{9-16}$$

Furthermore n bits are needed to separate the outliers from the other coordinate pairs. Given the transformation parameters t and the model coordinates the description of the image coordinates has a length of

$$I(c_i^k, k = 1, 2, \ldots, 2n|c_m^k, k = 1, 2, \ldots, 2n, \ t) = \tag{9-17}$$

$$n + 2n_{out} \log \frac{R}{\varepsilon} + \sum_{k=1}^{2n_{good}} \frac{1}{2 \log_e 2} \left(\frac{c_i^k - c_{m,proj}^k}{\sigma} \right)^2 + n_{good} \tfrac{1}{2} \log 2\pi \left(\frac{\sigma}{\varepsilon} \right)^2 \text{ bits.}$$

The mutual information between the coordinates of the image and the model, as a function of the transformation parameters t, therefore is

$$I_t(c_i^k, k = 1, 2, \ldots, 2n; c_m^k, k = 1, 2, \ldots, 2n) = \tag{9-18}$$

$$n_{good} \log \tfrac{1}{2\pi} \left(\frac{R}{\sigma} \right)^2 - n - \sum_{k=1}^{2n_{good}} \frac{1}{2 \log_e 2} \left(\frac{c_i^k - c_{m,proj}^k}{\sigma} \right)^2 \text{ bits.}$$

Note that this support is independent of the coordinate resolution ε.

9.3 Construction of the evaluation function for object location

The mapping evaluation function is the mutual information between the attributes of all primitives and relation tuples that are corresponding according to the mapping plus the support given by the transformation parameters. As described in paragraph 8.3, for the object location we use two line attributes (line length and line type) and three relations with one attribute each ("connected" between points and lines, "angle" between line pairs, and "contour" between lines and regions). Let p_p, p_l and p_r denote a point, line and region primitive respectively. The support two relational descriptions D_1 and D_2 give to a mapping h is then defined by

$$
\begin{aligned}
I_h(D_1; D_2) \;=\; & \sum_{p_l} I(\text{linelength}(p_l); \text{linelength}(h(p_l))) + \\
& \sum_{p_l} I(\text{linetype}(p_l); \text{linetype}(h(p_l))) + \\
& \sum_{p_p} \sum_{p_l} I(\text{connected}(p_p, p_l); \text{connected}(h(p_p), h(p_l))) + \\
& \sum_{p_l^i} \sum_{p_l^j}^{p_l^{i+1}} I(\text{angle}(p_l^i, p_l^j); \text{angle}(h(p_l^i), h(p_l^j))) + \\
& \sum_{p_l} \sum_{p_r} I(\text{contour}(p_l, p_r); \text{contour}(h(p_l), h(p_r))) + \\
& I_t(c_i^k, k = 1, 2, \ldots, 2n; c_m^k, k = 1, 2, \ldots, 2n)
\end{aligned}
\tag{9-19}
$$

This function is the merit function used for the object location with the informed search strategies presented in the next chapter. Optimizing this function leads to the maximum likelihood mapping between the two descriptions D_1 and D_2.

9.4 Functions for the self-diagnosis of object location

A maximum likelihood estimator determines the parameter, vector or mapping that is the likeliest among all possibilities, but the estimated quantity is not guaranteed to be good. For instance, for any group of two or more points one can calculate the maximum likelihood fit of a line through these points. However, this doesn't imply that the points indeed are situated on a line. They may have any distribution. Similarly, the maximization of the mutual information will lead to the maximum likelihood mapping, but under circumstances even this mapping may be a very bad one. Hence, one needs to verify whether a mapping that has been estimated is good enough or not, i.e. one needs a measure for the self-diagnosis of the object location.

A successful self-diagnosis can also be used as a stop criterion for the tree search. In paragraph 7.5 we showed that stop criteria are required if one wants to reduce the search effort with inadmissible search methods or perceptual grouping. For the general formulated relational matching problem we could not define such criteria. In this paragraph we will define two criteria for the specific problem of object location.

Above we argued that the estimation of the transformation is the most important part of the object location problem and that the reliability of the transformation parameters should therefore be used as a function for self-diagnosis. Reliability analysis alone, however, can not discover all gross errors, as will be illustrated below.

As a second criterion we will define a statistical test on the amount of mutual information that is required for a successful object location. This criterion partly complements the reliability analysis.

9.4.1 Reliability of transformation parameters

The reliability of parameters estimated with the least squares method has been extensively researched in the field of adjustment theory for geodetic networks [Baarda 1968, Förstner 1983, 1987]. It is beyond the scope of this thesis to give a full description of the obtained results. Instead we will describe the computational flow from the observations and the observation equations to the measures for reliability.

The spatial resection determining the transformation parameters is performed with all image and model points that are mapped to each other by the suggested mapping. For each pair of an image and a model point two equations can be formulated. Linearizing these equations results in the linear model [Koch 1988]

$$E(x) = Ay \qquad (9\text{-}20)$$

where x is the vector of the observations, y the vector of the unknowns, i.e. the 6 orientation parameters, and A is the design matrix with the coefficients of the observation equations. It is assumed that all observations are independent and all have a Gaussian distribution $N \sim (Ay, \sigma_x^2)$, so that the covariance matrix C_{xx} of the observation is

$$C_{xx} = diag(\sigma_x^2, \sigma_x^2, \ldots, \sigma_x^2) = \sigma_0^2 I \qquad (9\text{-}21)$$

The transformation parameters and their precisions are estimated by [Koch 1988]

$$\hat{y} = (A^T A)^{-1} A x \qquad (9\text{-}22)$$
$$C_{\hat{y}\hat{y}} = \sigma_0^2 (A^T A)^{-1} \qquad (9\text{-}23)$$

The corrections to the observed values (residuals) and their precisions are

$$\hat{e} = A\hat{y} - x = \hat{x} - x \tag{9-24}$$
$$C_{\hat{e}\hat{e}} = (C_{xx} - AC_{\hat{y}\hat{y}}A^T) = C_{xx} - C_{\hat{x}\hat{x}} \tag{9-25}$$

The variance factor σ_0^2 can be estimated by

$$\hat{\sigma}_0^2 = \frac{e^T e}{r} \tag{9-26}$$

with r being the redundancy of the parameter determination, i.e. the number of independent observations minus the number of orientation parameters (6). A statistical test can determine whether the value of $\hat{\sigma}_0$ is acceptable or not.

The normalized residuals are tested with a significance level α_0 (usually 0.01 or 0.001), such that, on the average, only $\alpha_0 \times 100\%$ of the good observations are rejected (data snooping). Despite such tests an erroneous observation may remain undetected. It is desired that such errors only have a small influence onto the parameter determination. This influence is described by the so-called *external reliability*. The external reliability is a function of the *redundancy number* of an observation and the *non-centrality parameter*.

A redundancy number r_i describes the relative effect an error in the observation x_i has onto its residual $\hat{e}_i$. The redundancy matrix R is defined by

$$R = C_{\hat{e}\hat{e}}C_{xx}^{-1} \tag{9-27}$$

The redundancy number r_i of observation x_i is the ith element of the diagonal of the redundancy matrix, $r_i = R_{ii}$.

The non-centrality parameter δ_0 is a function of the test significance (α_0) and the power of the test β_0 (usually 80%). When testing the normalized residual with a significance level α_0 an error can be detected with a probability higher than β_0 if the error exceeds the boundary value $\nabla_0 x_i$ which is calculated by

$$\nabla_0 x_i = \sigma_{x_i} \frac{\delta_0(\alpha_0, \beta_0)}{\sqrt{r_i}} \tag{9-28}$$

The external reliability $\bar{\delta}_{0i}$ of observation x_i is defined by (cf. [Förstner 1987])

$$\bar{\delta}_{0i} = \delta_0 \sqrt{\frac{1 - r_i}{r_i}} \tag{9-29}$$

The influence of an undetected erroneous observation onto an estimated parameter $\nabla_{0i} y_k$ can be no more than $\bar{\delta}_{0i}$ times the standard deviation of this parameter σ_{y_k}

$$\nabla_{0i} y_k \leq \bar{\delta}_{0i} \sigma_{y_k} \tag{9-30}$$

When all values $\bar{\delta}_{0i}$ are below 4 or 5 (empirical values) the orientation parameters can be determined reliably.

One aspect that is hard to control is the partial symmetry of an object. If an object is completely rotational symmetric one can not discern whether the object is viewed from one side or the other side. The precision and the reliability of the transformation parameters will be the same for both views. If the object is only partial symmetric there will be a perfect fit to the model when the correct mapping is tested. But also if the wrong mapping is suggested many points may fit well and only a few image points will have no well corresponding model point. In such cases it is possible that the data snooping filters out the bad point correspondences but that still enough correspondences are left to reliably determine the transformation parameters.

 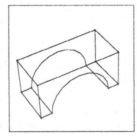 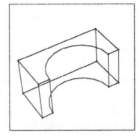

Figure 9.6: Points of partial symmetric models may fit well

An example is given in figure 9.6. The left picture shows the grey value image of a simple toy block. The middle picture shows the model projected with the correct orientation parameters. The right picture shows the model rotated by 90 degrees. Also for this model viewpoint all corners of the object that can be detected in the image will have coordinates similar to those of the projected points of the model. The only image primitive that does not fit is the arc. But since all other primitives fit perfectly, this arc is likely to be thrown out by a data snooping procedure. The question rises whether one line that doesn't fit gives enough support to the suggestion that a transformation may not be correct.

An object location system should therefore analyze the symmetries of the object model before matching it to the image data. If a transformation has been found it should automatically also consider the orientations giving a similar view onto the object and select the best transformation out of this group.

9.4.2 A statistical test on the amount of support

A proper analysis of the reliability of the transformation parameters can only be performed after all image primitives have been matched, i.e. at the leaf nodes of the search tree. However, as soon as a transformation has been proposed, using the correspondences of three image and model points, one can calculate a threshold for the amount of mutual information that a mapping with this transformation should have. If the maximum expected total amount of mutual information as estimated by the A^* algorithm is below this threshold the suggested path can be abandoned earlier, thereby saving search time. It is therefore very useful to not only check the reliability of the transformation parameters but also to check the amount of mutual information of a mapping in an earlier stage. To a part these two criteria also complement one another.

When a transformation has been proposed, one can calculate which parts of the model will be visible in the image. A very simple test may check for the percentage of visible model primitives that are indeed mapped to by an image primitive [Grimson and Huttenlocher 1990]. It would, however, be better to involve the mutual information between these primitives into this test.

Assuming that the image segmentation is good, each visible model primitive can be mapped to an image primitive. For each attribute of a visible model primitive and each attribute of a relation between visible model primitives this involves a comparison to the corresponding image attribute that contributes the mutual information to the support of the mapping. Let us consider the attribute "linetype" in case of an elliptic model line. The conditional probabilities and the mutual information between the types of image and model lines are given. Let table 9.6 give their values. Combining the conditional probabilities and the

v_i	$I(v_i; v_m = \text{elliptic})$	$p(v_i \mid v_m = \text{elliptic})$	$\sum p(v_i \mid v_m = \text{elliptic})$
straight	-2.3 bit	0.14	0.14
other	1.4 bit	0.18	0.32
elliptic	3.7 bit	0.68	1.00

Table 9.6: Conditional probabilities and mutual information between an elliptic model line and image line types

mutual information one can say that a visible elliptic model line contributes -2.3 bits to the mapping support with a probability of 0.14, 1.4 bits with a probability of 0.18 and 3.7 bits with a probability of 0.68. The entries in this table are sorted after the mutual information. By accumulating the conditional probabilities in the last column, the cumulative distribution of the mutual information can be constructed (figure 9.7). The second entry in table 9.6 for instance reveals that there is a probability of 32% that the mutual information between an elliptic model line and the line type attribute of the corresponding image line will not exceed 1.4 bits.

Table 9.7 shows the cumulative distribution of the mutual information for two elliptic model lines. Again, the entries are sorted after their mutual information. The distribution is visualized in figure 9.8. The underlined values in the table 9.7 are shown in this figure.

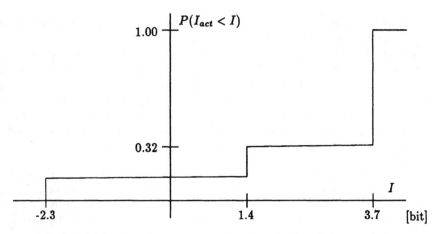

Figure 9.7: Mutual information distribution given an elliptic model line

v_{i_1}	v_{i_2}	$I(v_{i_1}, v_{i_2}; v_{m_1}, v_{m_2})$	$p(v_{i_1}, v_{i_2} \mid v_{m_1}, v_{m_2})$	$\sum p(\ldots)$
straight	straight	-2.3 + -2.3 = -4.6 bit	0.14 · 0.14 = 0.0196	0.0196
straight	other	-2.3 + 1.4 = -0.9 bit	0.14 · 0.18 = 0.0252	0.0448
other	straight	1.4 + -2.3 = -0.9 bit	0.18 · 0.14 = 0.0252	0.0700
straight	elliptic	-2.3 + 3.7 = 1.4 bit	0.14 · 0.68 = 0.0952	0.1652
elliptic	straight	3.7 + -2.3 = <u>1.4 bit</u>	0.68 · 0.14 = 0.0952	<u>0.2604</u>
other	other	1.4 + 1.4 = 2.8 bit	0.18 · 0.18 = 0.0324	0.2928
elliptic	other	3.7 + 1.4 = 5.1 bit	0.68 · 0.18 = 0.1224	0.4152
other	elliptic	1.4 + 3.7 = 5.1 bit	0.18 · 0.68 = 0.1224	0.5376
elliptic	elliptic	3.7 + 3.7 = 7.4 bit	0.68 · 0.68 = 0.4624	1.0000

Table 9.7: Distribution of mutual information given two elliptic model lines

By combining the distribution of the mutual information of all attributes of all primitives and relation tuples given the values of the model attributes we obtain the distribution of the support the two descriptions will give to the mapping *if* the assumed transformation is correct.

Since some of the attributes have continuous value ranges this distribution has to be calculated by numerical methods. For each model attribute value we therefore defined the mutual information I as a function of the probability that the image attribute value tells less than I bits about the model attribute value, i.e. the actual mutual information I_{act} is less than I bits. These functions were quantized in small probability intervals of say 1%. Combining two function with 100 values gives a function with 10000 probability intervals. These intervals were sorted after their mutual information and the average value over each group of 100 intervals was calculated so that the combined distribution function again had 100 intervals. For the two elliptical model lines this resulted in the distribution of figure 9.8. For some model with a total of 209 attributes of 9 visible points,

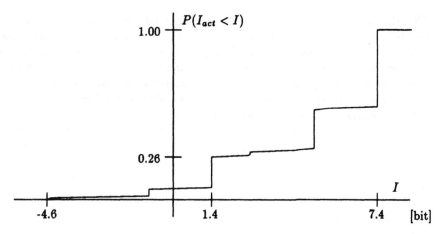

Figure 9.8: Mutual information distribution given two elliptic model lines

11 visible lines and 3 visible regions for some transformation this resulted in the distribution of the mapping support shown in figure 9.9. By allowing a type I

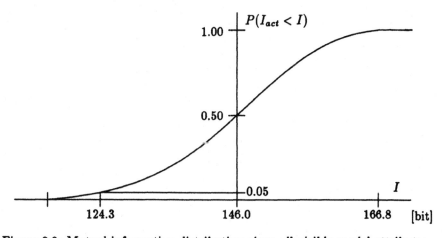

Figure 9.9: Mutual information distribution given all visible model attributes

error (rejection of correct mapping) of for instance 5% a threshold of 124.3 bits results for nodes with these transformation parameters. All nodes that can not reach this support do not have to be explored any further.

Due to the averaging over 100 probability intervals each time a new distribution is added to the total distribution the total distribution will be smoothed. Especially in the probability ranges close to 0.0 and 1.0 this will filter out the extreme values of the mutual information. Consequently, the smaller the type I error should be, the higher the resolution has to be with which the distribution functions are quantized.

This threshold estimation method assumes that all model primitives that are visible in the image indeed are mapped to by an image primitive. This is not necessarily true. In case of image segmentation errors such a perfect mapping will not be possible. Some of the visible model primitives will then remain unused as some image primitives will be mapped to a wildcard. In order to reflect this in the support threshold the probability of a wildcard assignment has to be acquired, for instance by training matches.

10   Strategy and performance of the tree search for object location

In this chapter we will match relational image and model descriptions with a tree search method using the evaluation function that has been developed above. We will make the following assumptions:

- The object that is to be located is completely depicted in the image. When a transformation has been calculated (after three point instantiations) a simple test whether all model points are projected within the image can eliminate most of the incorrect transformations.

- The object that is to be located is the only object depicted in the image. There are no other objects in the background.

- The object is untransparent. This poses a constraint on the search space. If an image point that is connected to three or more lines is mapped onto a model point that is connected to three or more lines, the order of the image lines (e.g. clockwise) must be the same as the order of the model lines they are mapped to. Two model lines can not be interchanged, or, alternatively formulated, the lines can not be viewed from the inside of the object.

- The illumination of the object is such that the feature extraction algorithm can find the major part of the object features that are visible from the camera viewpoint. Thus the descriptions will give a good support to the correct mapping.

- The best mapping between the image and the model features is a one-to-one mapping. On the one hand this restriction limits the search space as no two image primitives can map to one model primitive and an image primitive can not be mapped to two different model primitives. On the other hand, however, the search sometimes is forced to assign a wildcard to image primitives when the image is not properly segmented or when the image description contains T-junctions caused by occlusions. These wildcards may increase the complexity of the search tree. On the whole this restriction will reduce the search space.

- A maximum of 30% of all image primitives can be matched to a wildcard. Nodes in the search tree related to partial mappings that already use more wildcards are considered to lie on unsuccessful paths and are not expanded.

The tree search method we will use basicly is the A^* algorithm with the forward checking heuristic. A few other heuristics and variations on the A^* algorithm to optimize the search speed will be discussed and compared to each other.

The A^* algorithm calculates the merit of the path from the root node to the current node and estimates the merit of the path from the current node to the best leaf node. A part of this estimate can be obtained from the merit table used for forward checking as described in paragraph 7.3.2. We will now complete this estimation of the future merit.

10.1 Estimation of the future merit

We will again discern between past, current and future unit primitives, denoted p_{past}, p_{cur} and p_{fut}, respectively. The past units and the current unit are already instantiated with a label. For each of the past unit-label pairs and the current unit-label pair the merit table contains the merit of that unit-label pair (due to primitive attributes) and the merits of that pair in combination with the prior unit-label pairs (due to relation attributes). The sum of the table entries of the instantiated unit-label pairs gives the merit of the path from the root node to the current node, i.e. the value of the function $g(n)$ (paragraph 7.3.2). Let P_{past} be the set of all past units p_{past} and h the partial mapping function of the current node that maps the past and the current units to their labels. Then, $g(n)$ is defined by

$$g(n) = \sum_{p \in P_{past} \cup \{p_{cur}\}} \text{merit-table}(p, h(p)) \qquad (10\text{-}1)$$

The other part of the evaluation function of the A^* algorithm $f^*(n)$ estimates the merit of the path from the current node to the solution node $h^*(n)$. This estimate involves the merits from the future unit-label pairs in combination with the past unit-label pairs, the current unit-label pair and the future unit-label pairs. For each of the future unit-label pairs the merit table contains the merit due to the primitive attributes and due to the attributes of the relations with the already instantiated unit-label pairs, i.e. the past and current unit-label pairs. Let this part of $h^*(n)$ be denoted $h_1^*(n)$ and let P_{fut} be the set of future units and L_{free} be the set of unused labels. The maximum contribution of a future unit in combination with instantiated unit-label pairs to the mapping support is well approximated by the table entry of this unit and the label $l \in L_{free}$ with the highest merit. Thus $h_1^*(n)$ can be defined as

$$h_1^*(n) = \sum_{p \in P_{fut}} \max_{l \in L_{free}} \text{merit-table}(p, l) \qquad (10\text{-}2)$$

If the maximum contribution of a future primitive is negative it has to be corrected to zero since for this primitive the wildcard label will be the best one. Especially in the lower levels of the search tree the correct label of the next future unit has the highest merit of all possible labels for this unit. In this case the function $h_1^*(n)$ is a perfect estimator.

What is left to be estimated is the merit $h_2^*(n)$ of the attributes of the relations tuples of future units and their composed tuples. Whereas the computation of $h_1^*(n)$ involved one summation and one maximization, that of $h_2^*(n)$ needs two of both in case of binary relations, three of both in case of ternary relations, and so on. The contribution of a binary relation $R_k(p_1, p_2)$ between future units and their labels to $h_2^*(n)$, denoted $h_{2,R_k}^*(n)$, can be estimated by

$$h_{2,R_k}^*(n) = \sum_{p_1 \in P_{fut}} \sum_{p_2 \in P_{fut} \setminus \{p_1\}} \max_{l_1 \in L_{free}} \max_{l_2 \in L_{free} \setminus \{l_1\}} I(R_k(p_1, p_2); R_k(l_1, l_2))$$

(10-3)

with $I(R_k(\ldots); R_k(\ldots))$ being the mutual information between the two tuples of the kth relation. Again all maxima that are negative must be corrected to zero because of possible wildcard instantiations.

The summation of $h_{2,R_k}^*(n)$ over all relations in R then results in the estimation of contribution of the future relations $h_2^*(n)$ so that the maximum merit of a path through node n is given by

$$f^*(n) = g(n) + h_1^*(n) + h_2^*(n)$$

(10-4)

Although the computation of the last part $h_2^*(n)$ has a polynomial complexity of order four (two summations over the future units and two maximizations over their labels) its computation still requires a lot of time as it has to be performed at every node in the search tree.

We therefore applied another strategy which is much faster but, consequently, also gives a worse estimate of the future merit. Instead of summing up the merits found by maximization of the support over the labels, all maxima are stored in a *future support table* sorted after their support. This is only done for the root node where all units are future units. Each time some node in the tree needs an estimate for the support between future unit-label pairs one only has to derive the number of relations between the future units NR_{fut} from the number of future units (e.g. there are $\frac{n(n-1)}{2}$ angle relations between n future line units) and to sum up the first NR_{fut} maxima of the future support table of this relation.

The accuracy of this estimation method decreases with the depth of the node in the tree. Usually the units and labels that give a high support to a mapping will be instantiated on the first few levels of the tree. The relations between them often also give a high support. These supports are likely to be tabulated at the top of the future support table. Hence the nodes on the lower levels will use these supports in their future merit estimation whereas the true future merit will be smaller.

An optimum between accuracy and speed of the estimate may be found in the combination of the two estimation methods. One can use the last described method for the estimates on the higher levels in the tree and use the more accurate estimate on the lower levels. For the nodes on the high levels in the tree the method using the future support tables gives a fairly good estimate. The nodes on the lower levels have a smaller number of future units. Hence, for those nodes it becomes feasible to use the method with a higher computational complexity. The benefits of this combined estimation method have not been analyzed in this thesis. All future merit estimates were calculated from the future support tables.

10.2 Heuristics for object location

In the paragraph on unit ordering (7.4) we described the fail first principle as a strategy to organize the search such that the tree has a minimum number of nodes. The simplest implementation of this heuristic was to take the unit with the smallest number of possible labels to be the next unit to be mapped. In the following paragraphs a few other heuristics will be described. For a part they are also based on the fail first principle.

10.2.1 Grouping of primitives

The frequencies of the transition of the membership values of the relations "connected" and "contour" have been derived from training matches. In these matches all points and lines that were connected in the image also were connected in the model and all lines that were (a part of) a region contour in the image corresponded to model lines bounding the corresponding model region. This resulted in transitions that always must be true (probability 1) and transitions that never can be correct (probability 0). The derived probabilities are of course estimates. One can think of views onto a model where points are connected to lines in the image but not in the model.

We will, however, assume that the transition probabilities really are 0 or 1, because, as argued before, impossible attribute transitions (conditional probability 0) constrain the search space. Consequently, if in some image a point will be connected to a line whereas they are not connected in the model, either the point or the line must be mapped to a wildcard, as the instantiation of both would violate the relational constraint. The same holds for the contour relation between lines and regions. These constraints lead to a faster match. As a consequence, the cardinality of the match (i.e. the number of image primitives that are mapped onto a model primitive) may be a little smaller.

As we now have such tight constraints between neighbouring points, lines and regions, this should be utilized to consider a neighbourhood of primitives as a whole and to find the labels for all primitives in a neighbourhood at a single node in the search tree. This has already been suggested by Shapiro [1985]. We excluded the point primitives from the neighbourhoods and defined the neighbourhood of a point to be the set of the line primitives that are connected to that point and of the region primitives that are bounded by these lines. Given that an image point matches to some model point the primitives in the neighbourhood of the image point are known to match to the primitives in the neighbourhood of the model point.

Further constraints follow from the contour relation and the untransparent object assumption. Let, for example, model point p_a represent an object corner with lines l_a, l_b, and l_c and regions r_a, r_b, and r_c in its neighbourhood (figure 10.1 left). When this point is matched to an image point p_1 with three lines, the model lines l_a, l_b, and l_c can only match to l_1, l_2, resp. l_3, or to, l_2, l_3, resp. l_1, or, l_3, l_1, resp. l_2 and not to e.g. l_3, l_2, l_1 as this would only be possible if we would look onto the model point from the inside of the object. Such consistency checks are most efficiently performed if the primitives of a neighbourhood are mapped in one step, i.e. at one node.

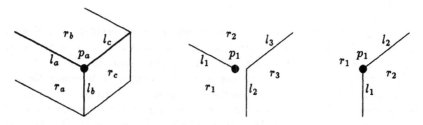

Model neighbourhood   Image neighbourhood 1   Image neighbourhood 2

Figure 10.1: Model and image neighbourhoods (see text)

If one of the model lines is not visible, due to segmentation errors or occlusion the model neighbourhood must be mapped to an image neighbourhood with less primitives (e.g. neighbourhood 2 in figure 10.1). At least one of the primitives in the image neighbourhood must be mapped to a wildcard, because the relation constraints would be violated otherwise. If e.g. in neighbourhood 2 line l_1 is mapped to model line l_b and line l_2 is mapped to model line l_c, the image region r_1 neither can be mapped to r_a because r_a is not bounded by l_c, nor to r_b because r_b is not bounded by l_b.

Although the primitives in a neighbourhood are tightly constrained, the possibility of a wildcard label for each of the primitives still leaves a lot of assignment combinations. In case an image neighbourhood with three lines and three regions is mapped to a model neighbourhood with three lines and three regions there are 228 (!) possible combinations. In case of 4 lines and regions in the image and in the model there already are 1789 combinations. If one or more primitives in the neighbourhood are already mapped to labels on a node at a higher level in the tree, this number decreases substantially. The node instantiating the first neighbourhood, however, has a large number of successor nodes.

Another type of primitive grouping can be obtained by perceptual grouping, making use of symmetries, continuation and other striking properties of the primitives. We only mention it here as a possibility. The only groups we use are the neighbourhoods described above.

10.2.2   The usefulness of a known transformation

The knowledge of the transformation parameters puts an important constraint onto the search space. If the transformation is known the model point primitives can be projected into the image and their coordinates can be compared to those of the image points. This usually leaves only one or two possible model points for each image point. This constraint is rapidly propagated onto the line and region primitives by the connectivity and contour relations in the neighbourhoods of the points.

Figure 10.2 shows the search tree of an object location problem solved with an A^* search. The image of this problem had one point that was connected to four lines. In the model there only were four points with four lines, whereas all other model points (12) were connected to three lines. So, following the fail first principle, the search method selected this image point to be the primitive to be mapped at the first level of the tree resulting in five successor nodes of the root node (four for the model points and one for a wildcard). On the next level of the search tree each of the instantiations with a model point results in a matching of the neighbourhoods of these points. Because all primitives in the neighbourhoods are still unlabeled at this level of the search, the second level of the tree shows a very large number of nodes. Only a small number could be eliminated because of inconsistent attributes of the angle relation between the lines in the neighbourhood. The tree becomes so dense that the branches of the tree merge in figure 10.2. The total number of nodes in this tree was 1826.

Another important parameter of search methods is the maximum length of the stack of unexpanded nodes. This not only gives an indication of the required storage space but since this stack has to be updated after each node expansion it also has a large influence on the search time. Due to the large number of nodes at the second level of the tree in figure 10.2 the node stack became very large and contained a maximum of 1361 nodes.

The instantiation of a neighbourhood only constrains the adjacent primitives. The knowledge of a transformation, however, gives a global constraint and therefore may prune the search tree much better. Again after the fail first principle, it would be better to seek a fast determination of the transformation parameters than a fast instantiation of neighbourhoods.

Figure 10.2: A search tree matching large neighbourhoods at the top of the tree

Figure 10.3 shows another search tree of the same object location problem. This time the search was focussed on a fast instantiation of three points[6]. Until the transformation could be calculated only a minimum number of lines was instantiated in order to constrain the search for the corresponding points with the connectivity relation. No image region primitives were used before the transformation calculation. The figure shows the resulting much sparser tree which had 594 nodes. An even stronger reduction was obtained for the stack length. It contained at most 143 unexpanded nodes.

The discriminating power of the transformation can clearly be observed in the tree. It takes two lines to connect three points. Hence, a transformation can be calculated at the fifth level in the tree. Quite some nodes at this level can not be expanded any further. Others expand to level six or seven. This is due to wildcard instantiations or a failure in the transformation calculation in case of a collinear point triple. As soon as a transformation can be calculated the wrong

[6]We only used matched points to determine the transformation with the algorithm described by [Fischler and Bolles 1981], although it is also possible to use the lines for this purpose [Huang and Netravali 1990].

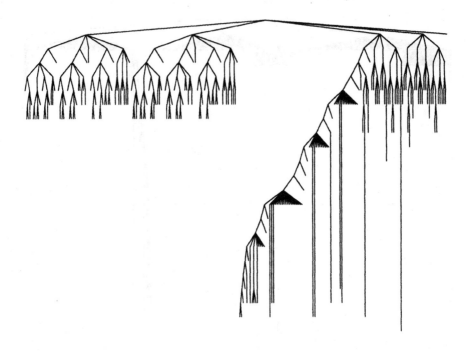

Figure 10.3: A search tree seeking a fast transformation determination

mappings are filtered out. Only a few branches can be continued to the lower levels of the tree. In fact, all nodes on these lower levels represent the same transformation. The only difference is in the distribution of a few wildcards over the image primitives.

10.2.3   Underestimation of future merit

An A^* algorithm with a perfect estimator for the future merit will only expand the nodes on the best path because it will correctly expect a smaller total merit for all other nodes. Overestimation of the future merit leads to the expansion of non-optimal nodes causing a higher search effort. Underestimation of the future merit may be faster than an admissible A^* method but turns the risk of missing the best path if the future merit of a node on the best path is estimated too pessimisticly. The ε-A^* algorithm slightly underestimates the future merit such that the loss of merit of the best solution that will be found is limited.

We tried to take advantage of the speed of the inadmissible ε-A^* search while guaranteeing that a good enough solution will be found. To this purpose we used two evaluation functions. The first function makes an admissible estimate of the total merit of a path through a node. The estimated merit of this function will not be smaller than the merit of the best path. For the second function we used the evaluation function of the ε-A^* algorithm. This function underestimates the total merit by multiplying the most optimistic estimate of the future merit with a factor smaller than one.

The search method employs the following strategy. The second, inadmissible, evaluation function is used to order the nodes on the stack. The order of node expansion therefore is the same as with the ε-A^* algorithm. The task of the first function is to decide whether the generated nodes are put on the stack or not. If a node has a function value that is smaller than the merit of a solution that already has been found there is no use in expanding it. Since this function is admissible no nodes on the best path will be lost. When the search reaches a leaf node, the related mapping is evaluated with the self-diagnosis functions described in the previous chapter. If the mapping is accepted it is saved. The search may stop at this stage if only a good enough mapping is required. If one wants to have the best mapping or in case the mapping is not accepted the search simply expands the next node on the stack.

At the first leaf node that is encountered an admissible A^* search would only have nodes on its stack that lead to worse solutions. But, due to the inadmissible ordering of the nodes by the first evaluation function our search method may have more successful nodes on its stack.

If the underestimation of the future merit misleads the search to expand nodes on non-optimal paths the number of expanded nodes may become larger than with the admissible A^* strategy. However, it was experienced that most of the times the search method decides correctly and finds a solution much faster. This is also due to the fact the an underestimation of the maximum expected future merit often gives a better estimate of the true future merit.

The stack ordering by the evaluation function of the ε-A^* method intends at reaching the lower levels of the search tree faster than the A^* method. It expands the nodes in a more depth-first-like manner. It thereby also keeps the node stack smaller, allowing a faster insertion of new nodes. Because of this advantage, even without terminating the search at a good enough leaf node this search method often is faster than the normal A^* method.

This advantage is even larger when using a heuristic suggested by Boyer and Kak [1988]. They scanned their search trees with the depth-first search method. Like our method, it does not guarantee that the first leaf node that is examined represents the best solution. Boyer and Kak required that, as soon as a solution using N_W wildcards has been found, only those nodes on the stack may be expanded that use less than N_W wildcards, because a better mapping than the one that has been found already is highly unlikely to use more than N_W wildcards. This heuristic allows us to considerably prune the search tree as soon as a solution has been found. It can, however, not be used with an admissible A^* search. The number of nodes expanded by the A^* search therefore is often larger than the number of nodes expanded by our method using this heuristic.

10.3   Description of the objects and their images

The performance of the evaluation functions and the search strategy was tested on 15 different object location problems. Three different objects (toy blocks A, B and C) were recorded in 5 images per object. Figure 10.4 shows the three object models in a wire-frame representation. Table 10.1 lists the number of points, lines and surfaces primitives in these models. The simplest object contained 32 primitives. The most complex object contained 66 primitives.

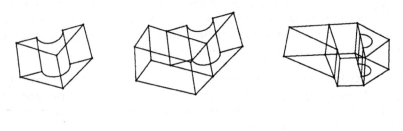

Model A   Model B   Model C

Figure 10.4: The three object models in wire-frame representation

Model	# Points	# Lines	# Surfaces	=	# Features
A	10	15	7	=	32
B	16	26	12	=	54
C	18	33	15	=	66

Table 10.1: Number of point, line and surface features per object model

The 15 images (figure 10.5) were segmented into points, lines and regions using the method described in chapter 8. The extracted points and lines are depicted in figure 10.6. We will denote the images with A1, A2, ..., C4, C5. Although the segmentation parameters were tuned optimally, some points and lines could not be extracted.

153

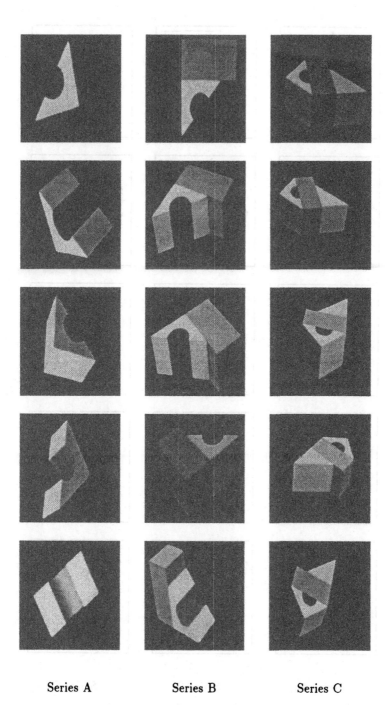

Series A   Series B   Series C

Figure 10.5: The recorded images

Series A   Series B   Series C

Figure 10.6: The points and lines of the segmented images

10.4   Performance of the object location

The objects were located with the modified ε-A^* algorithm described in paragraph 10.2.3. Every image was matched to its model 20 times while varying the three following parameters.

- The influence of the underestimation of the future merit was investigated by performing the tree search with 5 different values of ε, ranging from 0.1 to 0.5 (underestimation of 10 to 50%). A higher value of ε causes the search to focus on the lower nodes in the tree. It may therefore reach a solution node faster but also turns the risk of running into paths without acceptable solutions.

- All searches were performed in a "partial search" and a "full search" mode. In the partial search mode each leaf node that was encountered was subjected to a self-diagnosis. The search was terminated if the support of the model and the image description to the mapping was high enough, using the test on the amount of mutual information with a type I error of 5%. Otherwise the search continued. In the full search mode the self-diagnosis was only done for the best mapping found in the whole tree, i.e. the search was only terminated after all nodes on the node stack had been expanded.

- Underestimating the future merit, the expected total amount of mutual information of a path may increase with the depth of a node on that path. I.e. the mutual information of a node may be larger than that of its predecessor. So, if some primitive has several competitive candidate labels, the ε-A^* algorithm will search the sub-tree below one of them and, for the moment, will leave the other possible instantiations on the node stack. If the label primitives are completely competitive, like they often are in case of partial symmetric object models, the order in which these labels are considered solely depends on the enumeration of the model primitives. Especially for the higher values of ε the model primitive enumeration can have a large impact onto the order in which the nodes of the tree are processed and thus also onto the performance of the object location. In order to obtain a fairer statistic on the tree search performance, all objects were located twice while randomly changing the enumeration of the model primitives after the first search.

Tables 10.2, 10.3 and 10.4 show the average search tree characteristics and search times[7] of the locations of objects A, B, resp. C. For each combination of the search mode and the value of ε the average values are computed from 10 different matches, as there are 5 different images of each object and each image was located twice.

---

[7] The search times are in CPU seconds on a VAX Station 3500 on which the object location algorithm was implemented in the programming language POP-11 [Barrett et al. 1985]. POP-11 is embedded in the convenient program development environment POPLOG (together with

search mode	ε	number of nodes		node of best solution	number of transfor- mations	max. stack length	cpu time [s]
		visited	expanded				
partial	0.1	–	–	–	–	–	–
partial	0.2	530	530	530	70	671	353.1
partial	0.3	138	138	138	24	138	93.2
partial	0.4	92	92	92	18	85	65.0
partial	0.5	103	103	103	19	96	89.3
full	0.1	–	–	–	–	–	–
full	0.2	2597	1913	586	545	968	1545.1
full	0.3	511	392	146	98	149	270.1
full	0.4	1331	1266	100	339	219	827.5
full	0.5	1368	1290	109	343	200	852.1

Table 10.2: Average counters for the location of object A

search mode	ε	number of nodes		node of best solution	number of transfor- mations	max. stack length	cpu time [s]
		visited	expanded				
partial	0.1	–	–	–	–	–	–
partial	0.2	1067	1067	1067	84	2180	1790.7
partial	0.3	157	157	157	15	150	86.1
partial	0.4	246	246	246	22	218	120.0
partial	0.5	532	532	532	110	332	230.4
full	0.1	–	–	–	–	–	–
full	0.2	3502	1281	1298	126	2188	2272.0
full	0.3	586	430	331	85	164	285.7
full	0.4	731	539	436	102	201	319.8
full	0.5	1024	749	566	135	288	405.4

Table 10.3: Average counters for the location of object B

About half the images (A4, B3, B5 and C1 through C5) could not be matched with $\varepsilon = 0.1$ and images C2 and C3 could not be matched with $\varepsilon = 0.2$ either. In these cases the node stack became to large for the memory of the program

the languages LISP and PROLOG) originally designed for research and teaching in artificial intelligence. The convenience of programming in POP-11 of course has its price: matrix addition and matrix multiplication in POP-11, for example, take about 7 times resp. 8 times the time they need in FORTRAN.

The merit tables that have to be stored for each parent node of a node on the stack consume quite some space (up to 20-30 Mbyte). It is inconvenient to deal with such large amounts of data in the memory space of POP-11, because the built-in garbage collector would consume a lot of time for searching in the space allocated by the merit tables that hardly contains garbage (data structures that are not assigned to a variable). The merit tables were therefore written to disk in a direct access file. Implementing the matching program in a language like FORTRAN or PASCAL and managing the merit tables in the main memory would certainly decrease the search times substantially.

search mode	ε	number of nodes		node of best solution	number of transfor- mations	max. stack length	cpu time [s]
		visited	expanded				
partial	0.1	–	–	–	–	–	–
partial	0.2	–	–	–	–	–	–
partial	0.3	164	164	164	15	407	172.1
partial	0.4	227	221	227	36	401	333.3
partial	0.5	1587	1512	1587	77	1173	1595.6
full	0.1	–	–	–	–	–	–
full	0.2	–	–	–	–	–	–
full	0.3	1166	748	203	188	461	1016.5
full	0.4	1407	848	360	202	570	1184.5
full	0.5	6032	4965	1255	1325	1202	8319.5

Table 10.4: Average counters for the location of object C

environment which could contain up to about 15000 nodes. The average results could therefore not be calculated for $\varepsilon = 0.1$ for all objects and for $\varepsilon = 0.2$ for object C.

In all other cases where the memory was sufficient the matching algorithm found the correct transformation (figure 10.7). The differences between the first acceptable solution as returned in the partial search mode and the best solution as found in the full search mode were minor. Very often the first solution even was the best solution. In case it was not, only small differences could be noticed in the distribution of the required wildcards over the primitives. Especially for the images with segmentation errors (missing points or lines) a complete scan of the search tree may take up to 15 times the time needed to find the first acceptable solution. Here, searching the whole tree needs a lot of time to confirm that an already found solution indeed is (nearly) the best. Thus the termination of the search after a successful self-diagnosis of the found mapping proved to be a very helpful tool in reducing the search effort.

One may expect that the search effort to locate the objects A, B and C will increase with the number of primitives. The time needed to find object C indeed is larger than the time needed to locate one of the other two objects, but the effort to locate object A or B is approximately the same. The reason for this may be the symmetry of object A. Whereas there is only one solution to the spatial resection problem of object B and C, for each image of object A there are two views onto the object that can result into this image. Consequently there are two paths in the search tree that lead to a solution. As nodes on both paths can be expanded a larger effort is required to reach the first leaf node that can be tested.

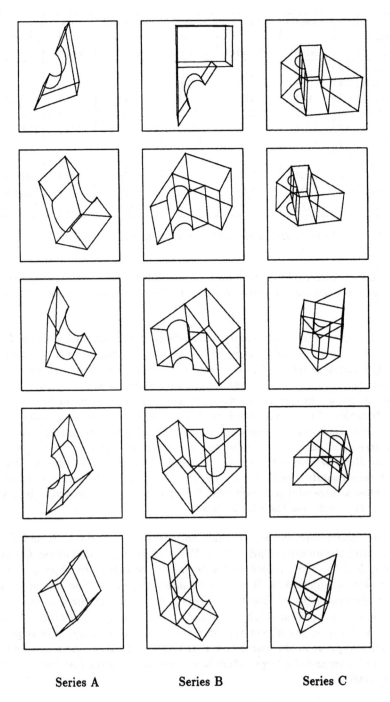

Series A   Series B   Series C

Figure 10.7: Object models in the recognized perspective

In case the search was terminated at a leaf node with a good enough mapping this leaf node was the last node that was taken from the stack in order to be investigated. This explains for the equality between the number of investigated nodes and the number of the solution node in the partial search mode. Usually in this mode, the number of expanded nodes was also equal to the number of investigated nodes, implying that all investigated nodes were expanded up to the point that the solution node was examined.

From the tables it can be seen that the fastest acceptable results were achieved with ε being 0.3 in the partial search mode. (Table 10.5 shows the results of the object location for each of the images obtained with these parameters. All search results are tabulated in appendix D.) Hence, the multiplication of the admissible estimate of the future merit by 0.7 ($= 1 - 0.3$) on the average yields the best estimate of the actual future merit. On the average, the admissible estimate overestimates the actual future merit by 40% ($\frac{1-0.3}{1} \times 100\%$).

image	number of nodes		number of transfor- mations	maximum stack length	cpu time [s]
	investigated	expanded			
A1	319	319	74	196	257.1
A2	20	20	2	29	12.2
A3	116	116	28	87	60.2
A4	127	127	4	239	67.4
A5	110	110	10	141	69.3
B1	457	457	28	291	144.7
B2	46	46	5	92	58.8
B3	62	62	14	111	70.1
B4	79	79	14	184	72.1
B5	141	117	13	74	85.0
C1	62	62	16	231	118.5
C2	123	123	15	257	172.5
C3	90	90	21	143	90.4
C4	95	95	14	188	116.7
C5	451	451	11	1218	362.4

Table 10.5: Search results per image for partial search with $\varepsilon = 0.3$

Although the search performs best with an ε value of 0.3, for some matching problems it still generates a considerable number of nodes and requires quite some time to find the solution. To a large part this performance can be explained by one of the problem sources described below.

- Considering the exponential nature of the tree search, the number of primitives to be matched (up to 43 for image B3) is quite high. The topological and geometrical constraints that are put upon the search space of course help to reduce the complexity, but even with a low average number of successor nodes per node, i.e. a low branching factor, a search tree of depth 43 already contains a large number of nodes. The only way to further reduce the search space is to aggregate the point, line and region primitives into larger, higher level primitives and to match these composed primitives. Aggregation and a hierarchical structure of the relational descriptions seems to be inevitable for matching more complex images and models.

- Some points and lines could not be extracted by the segmentation algorithm. A missing point causes two object lines to be projected onto one and the same image line. Requiring a one-to-one mapping the image line can not be mapped to a model line and has to be assigned to a wildcard. Similarly, a missing line causes two object surfaces to be projected onto one and the same image region. This region can't be mapped properly either. Such missing features increase the complexity of the search space.

- In the images A4 and B3 a curved surface is projected such that it is partially occluded by another surface. One of the curved boundary lines then intersects with the occluding surface. At this position the segmentation algorithm correctly extracts a point which is connected to the curved line and the two parts of the intersected line. This representation can not be directly mapped onto the three-dimensional model description. The intersection point has no physical interpretation. It can not be mapped onto a model point and thus has to be assigned to a wildcard. Requiring a one-to-one mapping the two parts of the intersected line can not be mapped to one and the same model line. So, again a wildcard is needed to solve this problem. The search algorithm now has to find out which distribution of the wildcards over the primitives in the vicinity of the intersection causes the smallest loss of information. This problem has a combinatorial complexity.

One may argue that such surface occlusions almost always results in the extraction of a T-junction in the image. A T-junction certainly indicates that the intersection point is more likely to be due to an occlusion than other points, but, since the model itself may also contain T-junctions (in fact, model B and C do), points at T-junctions can not be mapped to a wildcard automatically.

- Another problem occurred in images A1, A5 and B1. These images show perpendicular views onto surfaces of the object. The spatial resection is calculated after three points on these surfaces have been mapped to model points. For all combinations of three image points in these images the projection centre of the camera is very close to the dangerous cylinder through the image points. Therefore, the algorithm solving the spatial resection problem sometimes fails and often returns transformation parameters that differ considerably from the correct values. Due to these bad values of the transformation parameters

- the least squares determination of the spatial resection after the instantiation of all points often failed. The values given by the direct solution are used as approximate values for the least squares estimate. If they were not good enough, the least squares method was not able to converge to the correct solution and diverged.

- the self-diagnosis rejected correct mappings. When the camera would have had a slightly different position, some neighbouring surfaces would have been visible that are now occluded by the front surface. So, when the calculated transformation parameter values are not very good, the self-diagnosis assumes these side surfaces to be visible in the image whereas they are not. Because they are missing in the image, the mutual information between the image and the model is less than the expected amount. In case these side surfaces would have brought in a relatively large percentage of the expected support, the lack of this support leads to a rejection of the suggested mapping.

If the transformation fails one of the tree points will be assigned a wildcard. Together with the two other points the next point that is instantiated will again constitute a point triple that is used for the next attempt to solve the spatial resection problem. These tries are continued with new point triples until the approximate values calculated by the direct solution method are good enough to avoid both above problems. This explains for the large number of transformations that were calculated for the images A1, A5 and B1.

Table 10.6 gives an overview of the image characteristics that usually have a significant impact onto the search results. The images A2, B2, C1 and C3, that have no problem sources indicated in this table, indeed are the images that could be matched fastest in their series (compare with table 10.5). On the average, the characteristics of the images in the B and the C series are about the same. The worse search results of the images in series C are explained by the larger number of primitives in model C.

In the next chapter we will summarize the results that were obtained in this thesis and discuss some ideas for further improvement of the relational matching method.

image	image features			merged features		# T-junctions	dangerous cylinder
	# points	# lines	# regions	# lines	# regions		
A1	6	6	1	0	0	0	yes
A2	9	11	3	0	0	0	no
A3	7	8	2	2	2	0	no
A4	10	13	4	0	0	1	no
A5	8	10	3	0	0	0	yes
B1	8	9	2	0	0	0	yes
B2	13	17	5	0	0	0	no
B3	15	21	7	0	0	1	no
B4	12	16	5	0	0	0	no
B5	13	18	6	2	2	0	no
C1	13	19	7	0	0	0	no
C2	12	17	6	2	2	0	no
C3	12	17	6	0	0	0	no
C4	12	17	6	2	2	0	no
C5	10	15	6	4	0	0	no

Table 10.6: Image characteristics relevant to the search effort

11   Summary and discussion

Tasks like 3-D object recognition and 3-D object location can only be solved when the relations between the primitives are used to constrain the search space of the possible mappings. Up to now the relational matching method is the only method that can match relational descriptions unambiguously.

In this thesis we analyzed the relational matching method and discussed the developments that have been published in literature. We discerned between the description, evaluation function and search method of relational matching and compared the method to other matching techniques. Utilizing the probability and information theory, we presented a new function for the evaluation of relational mappings. This function was combined with the standard tree search methods. The new concepts were shown to be applicable by the example of the object location problem. In detail we achieved the following results:

- The mutual information between two relational descriptions was shown to be very well suited for the evaluation of mappings. Like the conditional information, as suggested by Boyer and Kak [1988], the mutual information has the following nice properties.

  - Both measures are based on the information theory. In contrast to older evaluation functions their calculation requires no thresholding or normalizations of the attribute values and does not need weights to combine different contributions into one measure.

  - Their optimization (minimization of the conditional information and maximization of the mutual information) leads to the maximum likelihood estimation of the mapping.

  - They both can combine numerical and symbolical attributes into one and the same measure, due to the fact that the similarity is judged by transition probabilities and not by differences in attribute values.

  Compared to the conditional information, the mutual information has several striking advantages.

  - The mutual information is a symmetric measure. I.e. bijective mapping h from primitives P to primitives Q has the same evaluation value as its inverted mapping h^{-1} from Q to P. Matching description D_1 with description D_2 therefore results in the same mapping as matching D_2 with D_1. The conditional information is not a symmetric measure, so that the mapping direction (which primitives are the units, which are the labels?) may influence the evaluation of the mapping when using this measure.

- Unlike the conditional information, the mutual information allows the combined use of discrete and continuous attributes. The differential mutual information (the information between continuous attributes) is equivalent to the mutual information (the information between discrete attributes). This equivalence doesn't hold for the conditional information.

- Transition probability density functions can not be learned in the training stage as this would involve an infinite number of training matches. When dividing the continuous attribute range into intervals the attribute transfer can be described by conditional probabilities. The amount of mutual information lost by this discretization (i.e. the inaccuracy in the evaluation) is a function of the interval size and therefore can be limited by choosing an appropriate discretization interval. The conditional information between continuous attributes, on the contrary, can not be obtained by a discretization, because the interval size then becomes the dominating factor in the evaluation.

- Since a wildcard doesn't contain information about primitives, the mutual information between a primitive that is mapped to a wildcard and that wildcard is zero. Thus, the mapping of a primitive to a wildcard is evaluated with the same function as the mappings of primitives to other primitives. Using the conditional information there is no such suitable evaluation of wildcard instantiations.

• The tree search uses the evaluation function to direct the search to the best mapping among all possible mappings. Even the best mapping, however, may not be a good one. Each mapping that is found by the search algorithm therefore needs to be subjected to an extra evaluation procedure in order to determine whether it can be accepted or not. For image-to-image matching such a diagnosis is difficult to define, because it is not known to what extent the objects in the images may be occluded.

In the case of object recognition and object location the suggested mappings can be analyzed easier. After an assumption has been made about the orientation of the camera (which is defined by three point instantiations), one can determine which part of the object should be visible in the image. Given the model primitives and their relations that should be visible, one can calculate the distribution of the mutual information between the model and an image taken from the assumed camera position. A threshold on the mutual information of a mapping is derived from this distribution by fixing the probability of a type I error. Thus the mutual information can also be used to verify the correctness of a mapping. This evaluation can also be used to decrease the search time, because the search can be terminated as soon as a leaf node (a full mapping) that is encountered is accepted. The differences between the mapping of the first acceptable leaf node and the best mapping are usually very small. Often the first solution also is the best solution.

- In order to avoid problems with the evaluation of wildcard instantiations, Boyer and Kak employ a depth-first search strategy that tries to find the best mapping that uses as few wildcards as possible. The depth-first search method, however, is a simple method that may take a very long time to find a solution that is good enough. Because the evaluation of wildcard instantiations is fully integrated into the mutual information, this new evaluation function can be used with all search methods, including the more sophisticated A^* and ε-A^* strategy that show a much better performance.

- The evaluation functions that are normally used to guide tree search methods are cost functions. The mutual information, on the contrary, is a support function. For the best-first method, the A^* and the ε-A^* algorithm this change had the following consequences.

  - The best-first method shows a different behaviour. When using a support function it tends to focus more on the lower levels of the tree.

  - The A^* strategy had to be slightly changed in its definition. The A^* strategy with a cost function is admissible when the future costs are not *overestimated*. An A^* algorithm with a support function is admissible when the future merit is never *underestimated*.

  - Similarly the ε-A^* strategy was adapted. With a cost function, the ε-A^* search purposely overestimates the future costs by multiplying the admissible estimate with a factor larger than one. With a support function the future merit is underestimated by multiplying the admissible estimate with a factor smaller than one.

With the above changes in the definitions of the A^* and the ε-A^* strategy, these methods show the same behaviour with a support function as they do with a cost function.

- The A^* and the ε-A^* algorithm were combined into a new admissible search strategy. The evaluation function of the A^* algorithm was used to decide whether a node was put onto the node stack or not. The evaluation function of the ε-A^* method was used to order this node stack. Thus the order of node expansion was determined by the ε-A^* strategy, aiming at reaching a leaf node fast, while the evaluation function of the A^* algorithm assured that the nodes on the path of the best solution were put onto the node stack. The new search strategy needs less storage space for its node stack than the A^* method and is therefore able to solve larger problems. Because it requires less time for the insertion of new nodes into the node stack, it is usually also faster.

- The heuristics of a search method have a large influence on its performance. We showed that it is more important to find the parameters of the transformation between the two descriptions as to have constraints that limit the possible number of instantiations in a cluster of neighbouring primitives. The geometric constraint of a known transformation is more important than the topological relations. The order of unit primitives in the tree was therefore determined such, that a minimum number of nodes had to be expanded in order to instantiate three unit-label pairs of point primitives that defined the spatial resection.

For the 15 object location problems that were solved with the modified ε-A^* algorithm, the search with an ε value of 0.3 showed the best results. However, even if the matching program would have been implemented in a faster language, it still would take about one minute to solve the most difficult problem of those 15 examples. This is mainly due to the large number of primitives in the tree search (31 image primitives versus 66 model primitives) and some errors in the image segmentation. It may be expected that the search effort can be significantly reduced by

- using fewer, higher level primitives,

- improving the image descriptions, and

- using better search heuristics.

Grouping primitives into higher level primitives will benefit the search in two ways. First, there will be less primitives to be matched and, hence, the search tree will be much smaller. Secondly, but certainly not less important, higher level primitives will contain more information, so that fewer label primitives will have to be considered for each unit primitive after comparing the primitive attributes. Perceptual grouping looking for proximity, similarity, continuation, closure, symmetry [Gool et al. 1990] and familiarity of primitives can be combined with the minimal description length theory in order to find the best description of high level primitives. Projective invariants [Forsyth et al. 1990] could also enrich the attribute descriptions of these composed primitives and further reduce the search space.

The image segmentations that were used in the object location problems were very much optimized by tuning the parameters of the segmentation algorithm for each image individually. This strategy is not feasible in an industrial environment. Using fixed parameters would, however, increase the number of errors in the image descriptions. These errors can only be handled by the matching algorithm by assigning a wildcard to primitives representing oversegmented model primitives and primitives due to image noise. The problem which primitives (in the area of the segmentation error) are to be assigned a wildcard has a combinatorial complexity. A reduction of segmentation errors may be obtained by supplying the image segmentation process with information about the recorded objects. Fua and Hanson [1987] e.g. demonstrated that houses could be extracted from digitized aerial photographs much better when generic house models were provided. For close range tasks, like object recognition in an industrial environment, the use of range images (possibly in combination with grey level images) may further help to improve the relational descriptions. As range images directly record the 3-D shape of the visible part of an object, they are easier to segment (no texture, no shadows) and are easier to match to the 3-D model description. The uncertainty in the attribute transition probabilities, when matching a grey value image to a 3-D object, is mainly caused by the projection of the object into the image. Because the recording of range images doesn't involve a projection, there will be a much clearer distinction between the mutual information of correct attribute correspondences and that of incorrect correspondences. The attributes will contain a much better indication of the correct mapping and, therefore, will direct the search algorithm to the solution faster.

The search method spent a lot of time to select which primitives around a segmentation error or a T-junction caused by occlusion were the best to instantiate with a wildcard. The different mappings that are considered in those neighbourhoods usually have about the same mutual information. The differences between their evaluation values are very small, the calculated transformations often are identical. So, the search wastes time, but gains almost nothing. An improved search heuristic should avoid this by just taking one of the possible wildcard instantiations and discouraging the expansion of the other nodes (e.g. by reducing the estimation of the future merit of these nodes by some amount). Another heuristic to be improved is the estimation of the merit of the relations between future primitives. In the 15 solved correspondence problems we used a look-up table that was calculated before the search started. For the nodes at the lower levels in the tree, i.e. the nodes with a small number of future units, a better estimate should be obtainable at a relatively small increase in computational costs.

With these improvements the performance of the tree search can be increased considerably. Combined with the new evaluation function and the diagnosis of the best mapping, relational matching will be a powerful method for matching tasks like object location and object recognition.

Literature

Ackermann, F. and P. Krzystek [1991]: MATCH-T: Automatic Mensuration of Digital Elevation Models. Presented paper to the 3rd Technical Seminar of the Sociedad Espanola de Cartografia Fotograrnetria y Teledeteccion, April, 12 1991.

Baarda, W. [1968]: A Testing Procedure for Use in Geodetic Networks. New Series, vol. 2, no. 5, Netherlands Geodetic Commission, Delft, 1968.

Ballard, D.H. and C.M. Brown [1982]: Computer Vision. Prentice-Hall, Englewood Cliffs, NJ, 1982.

Barnard, S.T. [1986]: A Stochastic Approach to Stereo Vision. Technical Note 373, SRI International, Artificial intelligence center, 1986.

Barnard, S.T. [1987]: Stereo Matching by Hierarchical Microcanonical Annealing. Technical Note 414, SRI International, Artificial intelligence center, 1987.

Barnard, S.T. and W.B. Thompson [1980]: Disparity Analysis of Images. *IEEE Transactions on Pattern Analysis and Machine Intelligence*, vol. 2, pp. 333-340, 1980.

Barr, A. and E. Feigenbaum [1981]: The Handbook of Artificial Intelligence. Kaufmann Inc., Los Altos, California, 1981.

Barrett, R., A. Ramsay and A. Sloman [1985]: POP-11, A Practical Language for Artificial Intelligence. Ellis Horwood Ltd., Chichester, West Sussex, England, 1985.

Ben-Arie, J. and A.Z. Meiri [1987]: 3D Objects Recognition by Optimal Matching Search of Multinary Relation Graphs. *Computer Vision, Graphics and Image Processing*, vol. 37, pp. 345-361, 1987.

Berzins, V. [1984]: Accuracy of Laplacian Edge Detectors. *Computer Vision, Graphics and Image Processing*, vol. 27, pp. 195-210, 1984.

Binford, T.O. [1982]: Survey of Model-Based Image Analysis. *International Journal of Robotics Research*, vol. 1, no. 1, pp. 18-64, 1982.

Blahut, R.E. [1987]: Principles and Practice of Information Theory. Addison-Wesley, Reading, MA, 1987.

Bobick, A. and R. Bolles [1989]: Representation Space: An Approach to the Integration of Visual Interpretation. In: *Proc. IEEE Computer Society Conference on Computer Vision and Pattern Recognition Conference*, San Diego, 1989, pp. 492-499.

Boyer, K.L. and A.C. Kak [1986]: Symbolic Stereo from Structural Descriptions. Technical Report TR-EE 86-12, School of Electrical Engineering, Purdue University, West Lafayette, Indiana, February 1986.

Boyer, K.L. and A.C. Kak [1988]: Structural Stereopsis for 3-D Vision. *IEEE Transactions on Pattern Analysis and Machine Intelligence*, vol. 10, no. 2, pp. 144-166, 1988.

Boyer, K.L., A.J. Vayda and A.C. Kak [1986]: Robotic Manipulation Experiments using Structural Stereopsis for 3D Vision. *IEEE Expert*, pp. 73-94, 1986.

Brooks, R.A. [1981]: Symbolic Reasoning Among 3-D Models and 2-D Images. In: *Computer Vision*, J.M. Brady (ed.), Elsevier Science Publishers B.V., 1981, pp. 285-348.

Brooks, R.A. [1983]: Model-Based Three-Dimensional Interpretations of Two-Dimensional Images. *IEEE Transactions on Pattern Analysis and Machine Intelligence*, vol. 5, no. 2, pp. 140-150, March 1983.

Carnevali, P., L. Coletti and S. Patarnello [1985]: Image Processing by Simulated Annealing. *IBM Journal of Research and Development*, vol. 29, no. 6, pp. 569-579, November 1985.

Castleman, K.R. [1979]: Digital Image Processing. Prentice-Hall, Englewood Cliffs, NJ, 1979.

Corneil, D.G. and C.G. Gottlieb [1970]: An Efficient Algorithm for Graph Isomorphism. *Journal of the Association of Computing Machinery*, vol. 17, pp. 51-64, 1970.

Davis, L.S. [1975]: A Survey of Edge Detection Techniques. *Computer Graphics and Image Processing*, vol. 4, pp. 248-270, 1975.

Davis, L.S. [1979]: Shape Matching using Relaxation Techniques. *IEEE Transactions on Pattern Analysis and Machine Intelligence*, vol. 1, pp. 60-72, 1979.

Dreschler, L. [1981]: Ermittlung markanter Punkte auf den Bildern bewegter Objekte und Berechnung einer 3D-Beschreibung auf dieser Grundlage, PhD thesis, Fachbereich Informatik, University of Hamburg, 1981.

Ebner, H., D. Fritsch, W. Gillessen and C. Heipke [1987]: Integration von Bildzuordnung und Objektrekonstruktion innerhalb der Digitalen Photogrammetrie. *Bildmessung und Luftbildwesen*, pp. 194-203, 1987.

ECCV1, First European Conference on Computer Vision [1990], O. Faugeras (ed.), Antibes, France, April 1990, Springer Verlag.

Fan, T.J. [1988]: Describing and Recognizing 3-D Objects using Surface Properties, PhD thesis, Institute for Robotics and Intelligent, Systems School of Engineering, University of Southern California, Los Angeles, California, August 1988.

Faugeras, O.D. and K. Price [1981]: Semantic Description of Aerial Images using Stochastic Labeling. *IEEE Transactions on Pattern Analysis and Machine Intelligence*, vol. 3, pp. 638-642, 1981.

Faugeras, O.D. and M. Hebert [1986]: The Representation, Recognition and Locating of 3-D Objects. *International Journal of Robotics Research*, vol. 5, no. 3, pp. 27-52, 1986.

Fischler, M.A. and R.C. Bolles [1981]: Random Sample Consensus: A Paradigm for Model Fitting with Applications to Image Analysis and Automated Cartography. *Communications of the Association of Computing Machinery*, vol. 24, no. 6, pp. 381-395, June 1981.

Förstner, W. [1983]: Reliability and Discernability of Extended Gauss-Markov Models. In: *Seminar on Mathematical Models of Geodetic/Photogrammetric Point Determination with Regard to Outliers and Systematic Errors*, Deutsche Geodätische Kommision, Series A, no. 98, Munich, 1983, pp. 79-103.

Förstner, W. [1986]: A Feature Based Correspondence Algorithm for Image Matching. In: *International Archives of Photogrammetry and Remote Sensing*, vol. 26-3/3, Rovaniemi, 1986.

Förstner, W. [1987]: Reliability Analysis of Parameter Estimation in Linear Models with Applications to Mensuration Problems in Computer Vision. *Computer Vision, Graphics and Image Processing*, vol. 40, pp. 273-310, 1987.

Förstner, W. [1989]: Image Analysis Techniques for Digital Photogrammetry. In: *Proceedings of the 42th Photogrammetric Week*, Series of the Institute of Photogrammetry, Stuttgart University, vol. 13, Stuttgart, September 1989, pp. 205-221.

Förstner, W. and E. Gülch [1987]: A Fast Operator for Detection and Precise Location of Distince Points, Corners and Centers of Circular Features. In: *Proc. ISPRS Intercommission Workshop on "Fast Processing of Photogrammetric Data"*, Interlaken, June 1987.

Förstner, W. and A. Pertl [1986]: Photogrammetric Standard Methods and Digital Image Matching Techniques for High Precision Surface Measurements. In: *Pattern Recognition in Practice II*, E.S. Gelsema and I.N. Kanal (eds.), Elsevier (North-Holland), 1986, pp. 57-72.

Forsyth, D., J.L. Mundy and A. Zisserman [1990]: Invariance - A New Framework for Vision. In: *Proc. ICCV3*, Osaka, 4-7 December 1990, pp. 598-605.

Fraser, C.S. and D.C. Brown [1986]: Industrial Photogrammetry: New Developments and Recent Applications. *Photogrammetric Record*, vol. 12, no. 68, pp. 197-217, 1986.

Fua, P. and A.J. Hanson [1987]: Resegmentation using Generic Shape: Locating General Cultural Objects. *Pattern Recognition Letters*, vol. 5, no. 3, pp. 243-252, March 1987.

Fua, P. and A.J. Hanson [1988]: Extracting Generic Shapes Using Model-Driven Optimization. In: *Proc. Image Understanding Workshop*, April 1988, pp. 994-1004.

Geman, S. and D. Geman [1984]: Stochastic Relaxation, Gibbs Distributions and Bayesian Restoration of Images. *IEEE Transactions on Pattern Analysis and Machine Intelligence*, vol. 6, no. 6, pp. 721-741, November 1984.

Gennery, D.B. [1977]: A Stereo Vision System for Autonomous Vehicle. In: *Proc. 5th International Joint Conference on Artificial Intelligence*, Cambridge, Mass., 1977.

Georgeff, M.P. and C.S. Wallace [1984]: A General Selection Criterion for Inductive Inference. In: *Proc. of Advances in Artificial Intelligence*, Amsterdam, September 1984, North Holland.

Gmür, E. and H. Bunke [1988a]: 3D Object Recognition Based on Subgraph Matching in Polynomial Time. In: *Proc. IAPR Workshop on Syntactical and Structural Pattern Recognition*, Pont-a-Mousson, France, September 12-14 1988.

Gmür, E. and H. Bunke [1988b]: PHI-1: Ein CAD-basiertes Roboter Sichtsystem. In: *Mustererkennung 1988*, Informatik Fachberichte, no. 180, Zürich, September 1988, Springer Verlag, pp. 240-247.

Gmür, E. [1989]: Ein Roboter-Sichtsystem basierend auf CAD-Modellen, PhD thesis, Universität Bern, 1989.

Gonzalez, R.C. and P. Wintz [1977]: Digital Image Processing. Addison-Wesley, Reading, MA, 1977.

Gool, L. van, J. Wagemans, J. Vandeneede and A. Oosterlinck [1990]: Similarity Extraction and Modelling. In: *Proc. ICCV3*, Osaka, 4-7 December 1990, pp. 530-534.

Grimson, W.E.L. [1981]: From Images To Surfaces: A Computational Study of the Human Early Vision System. M.I.T. Press, Cambridge, MA, 1981.

Grimson, W.E.L. [1985]: Computational Experiments with a Feature Based Stereo Algorithm. *IEEE Transactions on Pattern Analysis and Machine Intelligence*, vol. 7, pp. 17-34, 1985.

Grimson, W.E.L. [1988]: The Combinatorics of Object Recognition in Cluttered Environments using Constrained Search. In: *Proc. ICCV2*, Tarpon Springs, Florida, December 1988, pp. 218-227.

Grimson, W.E.L. and D.P. Huttenlocher [1990]: On the Verification of Hypothesized Matches in Model-Based Recognition. In: *Proc. First European Conference on Computer Vision*, Antibes, France, April 1990, Springer Verlag, pp. 489-498.

Grimson, W.E.L. and T. Lozano-Perez [1984]: Model-Based Recognition and Localization from Sparse Range or Tactile Data. *International Journal of Robotics Research*, vol. 3, no. 3, pp. 3-35, 1984.

Grün, A.W. [1985]: Adaptive Least Squares Correlation - A Powerful Image Matching Technique. *South African Journal of Photogrammetry, Remote Sensing and Cartography*, vol. 14, no. 3, pp. 175-187, 1985.

Hahn, M. [1989]: Automatic Measurement of Digital Terrain Models by Means of Image Matching Techniques. In: *Proceedings of the 42th Photogrammetric Week*, Series of the Institute of Photogrammetry, Stuttgart University, vol. 13, Stuttgart, September 1989, pp. 141-151.

Haralick, R.M. [1985]: Computer Vision Theory. The Lack Thereof. In: *Proc. Third Workshop on Computer Vision: Representation and Control*, Bellaire, Michigan, October 1985, pp. 113-121.

Haralick, R.M. and G.L. Elliott [1980]: Increasing Tree Search Efficiency for Constraint Satisfaction Problems. *Artificial Intelligence*, vol. 14, pp. 263-313, 1980.

Haralick, R.M. and J. Kartus [1978]: Arrangements, Homomorphisms and Discrete Relaxation. *IEEE Transactions on System, Man and Cybernetics*, vol. 8, pp. 600-612, 1978.

Haralick, R.M. and L.G. Shapiro [1979]: The Consistent Labeling Problem, Part I. *IEEE Transactions on Pattern Analysis and Machine Intelligence*, vol. 1, pp. 173-184, 1979.

Haralick, R.M. and L.G. Shapiro [1980]: The Consistent Labeling Problem, Part II. *IEEE Transactions on Pattern Analysis and Machine Intelligence*, vol. 2, pp. 193-203, 1980.

Haralick, R.M. and L.G. Shapiro [1985]: Image Segmentation Techniques, a Survey. *Computer Vision, Graphics and Image Processing*, vol. 29, pp. 100-132, 1985.

Harary, F. [1969]: Graph Theory. Addison-Wesley, Reading, MA, 1969.

Helava, U.V. [1976]: Digital Correlation in Photogrammetric Instruments. In: *International Archives of Photogrammetry and Remote Sensing*, vol. 20,2, Helsinki, 1976.

Helava, U.V. [1988]: Object Space Least Squares Correlation. In: *International Archives of Photogrammetry and Remote Sensing*, vol. 27, B3, Kyoto, 1988, pp. 321-331.

Helmke, H., R. Janssen and G. Saur [1990]: Automatische Erzeugung dreidimensionaler Kantenmodelle aus mehreren zweidimensionalen Objektansichten. In: *Mustererkennung 1990*, Informatik Fachberichte, no. 254, Oberkochen-Aalen, September 1990, Springer Verlag, pp. 617-624.

Hildreth, E.C. [1983]: The Detection of Intensity Changes by Computer and Biological Vision Systems. *Computer Vision, Graphics and Image Processing*, vol. 22, pp. 1-27, 1983.

Horaud, P. and R.C. Bolles [1984]: 3DPO's Strategy for Matching Three-Dimensional Objects in Range Data. In: *Proc. International Conference on Robotics*, Atlanta, Georgia, March 1984, pp. 78-85.

Hough, P.V.C. [1962]: Method and Means for Recognizing Complex Patterns. U.S. Patent 3.069.654, 1962.

Huang, T.S. and A.N. Netravali [1990]: Motion and Structure from Feature Correspondences: A Review. In: *Proc. Tutorial on Computer Vision and Dynamic Scene Analysis*, Zürich, September 1990, International Society of Photogrammetry and Remote Sensing, 55 p..

Huertas, A. and G. Medioni [1986]: Detection of Intensity Changes with Sub-pixel Accuracy using Laplacian-Gaussian Masks. *IEEE Transactions on Pattern Analysis and Machine Intelligence*, vol. 8, pp. 651-664, 1986.

Hummel, R.A. and A. Rosenfeld [1977]: Relaxation Processes for Scene Labeling. Technical Report TR-562, Computer Science Center, University of Maryland, College Park, August 1977.

Hummel, R. and S. Zucker [1983]: On the Foundations of Relaxation Labeling Processes. *IEEE Transactions on Pattern Analysis and Machine Intelligence*, vol. 5, pp. 267-287, 1983.

Ingels, F.M. [1971]: Information and Coding Theory. Intext Educational Publishers, Scranton, Pennsylvania, 1971.

ICCV1, First International Conference on Computer Vision [1987], J.M. Brady and A. Rosenfeld (eds.), London, 8-11 June 1987.

ICCV2, Second International Conference on Computer Vision [1988], R. Bajcsy and S. Ullman (eds.), Tampa, 5-8 December 1988.

ICCV3, Third International Conference on Computer Vision [1990], M. Nagao (ed.), Osaka, 4-7 December 1990.

Kanade, T. [1980]: Region Segmentation: Signal vs Semantics, Survey. *Computer Graphics and Image Processing*, vol. 13, pp. 279-297, 1980.

McKeown, D.M., W.A. Harvey and J. McDermott [1985]: Rule-Based Interpretation of Aerial Imagery. *IEEE Transactions on Pattern Analysis and Machine Intelligence*, vol. 7, no. 5, pp. 570-585, September 1985.

Koch, K.-R. [1988]: Parameter Estimation and Hypothesis Testing in Linear Models. Springer Verlag, Berlin, Heidelberg, 1988.

Koch, K.-R. [1990]: Bayesian Inference with Geodetic Applications. Lecture Notes in Earth Sciences, Springer Verlag, Berlin, Heidelberg, 1990.

Leclerc, Y.C. [1988]: Constructing Simple Stable Descriptions for Image Partitioning. In: *Proc. Image Understanding Workshop*, vol. 1, Cambridge, Mass., April 1988, pp. 365-382.

Lowe, D.G. [1985]: Perceptual Organization and Visual Recognition. Kluwer Academic Publishers, Boston, Mass., 1985.

Lynch, M.F. [1968]: Storage and Retrieval of Information on Chemical Structures by Computer. *Endeavour*, vol. 27, no. 101, pp. 68-73, May 1968.

Mayhew, J.E.W. and J.P. Frisby [1981]: Psychophysical and Computational Studies towards a Theory of Human Stereopsis. In: *Computer Vision*, J.M. Brady (ed.), Elsevier Science Publishers B.V., 1981, pp. 349-385.

Marr, D.C. and E.C. Hildreth [1980]: Theory of Edge Detection. In: *Proc. Roy. Soc. London*, Series B, vol. 207, 1980, pp. 187-217.

Marr, D.C. and T. Poggio [1979]: A Computational Theory of Human Stereo Vision. In: *Proc. Roy. Soc. London*, Series B, vol. 204, 1979, pp. 301-328.

Medioni, G. and R. Nevatia [1984]: Matching Images using Linear Features. *IEEE Transactions on Pattern Analysis and Machine Intelligence*, vol. 6, pp. 675-685, 1984.

Mohan, R. and R. Nevatia [1989]: Segmentation and Description Based on Perceptual Organization. In: *Proc. IEEE Computer Society Conference on Computer Vision and Pattern Recognition*, San Diego, CA, 1989, pp. 333-341.

Moravec, H.P. [1977]: Towards Automatic Visual Obstacle Avoidance. In: *Proc. 5th International Joint Conference on Artificial Intelligence*, 1977, pp. 584-.

Nagao, M., T. Matsuyama and H. Mori [1979]: Structural Analysis of Complex Photographs. In: *Proc. International Joint Conference on Artificial Intelligence*, Tokyo, August 1979, pp. 610-616.

Nevatia, R. and K.E. Price [1982]: Locating Structures in Aerial Images. *IEEE Transactions on Pattern Analysis and Machine Intelligence*, vol. 4, pp. 476-484, 1982.

Nilsson, N.J. [1971]: Problem-solving in Artificial Intelligence. McGraw-Hill, New York, 1971.

Nilsson, N.J. [1982]: Principles of Artificial Intelligence. Tioga Publishing Company, Palo Alto, CA, 1982.

Oshima, M. and Y. Shirai [1983]: Object Recognition Using Three-Dimensional Information. *IEEE Transactions on Pattern Analysis and Machine Intelligence*, vol. 5, no. 4, pp. 353-361, July 1983.

Paderes, F.C., E.M. Mikhail and W. Förstner [1984]: Rectification of Single and Multiple Frames of Satellite Scanner Imagery using Point and Edges as Control. In: *Proc. NASA Symposium on Mathematical Pattern Recognition and Image Analysis*, Houston, 1984.

Pearl, J. [1984]: Heuristics: Intelligent Search Strategies for Computer Problem Solving. Addison-Wesley, Reading, MA, 1984.

Peleg, S. [1980]: A New Probabilistic Relaxation Scheme. *IEEE Transactions on Pattern Analysis and Machine Intelligence*, vol. 2, no. 4, pp. 362-369, July 1980.

Peli, T. and D. Malah [1982]: A Study of Edge Detection Algorithms. *Computer Graphics and Image Processing*, vol. 20, pp. 1-21, 1982.

Pertl, A. [1985]: Digital Image Correlation with an Analytical Plotter. *Photogrammetria*, no. 40, pp. 9-19, 1985.

Pollard, S.B., J.E.W. Mayhew and J.P. Frisby [1985]: PMF: A Stereo Correspondence Algorithm Using a Disparity Gradient Limit. *Perception*, vol. 14, pp. 449-470, 1985.

Price, K.E. [1985]: Relaxation Matching Techniques - A Comparison. *IEEE Transactions on Pattern Analysis and Machine Intelligence*, vol. 7, pp. 617-623, 1985.

Price, K. [1985]: I've Seen Your Demo; So What?. In: *Proc. Third Workshop on Computer Vision: Representation and Control*, Bellaire, Michigan, October 1985, pp. 122-124.

Rissanen, J. [1978]: Modeling By Shortest Data Description. *Automatica*, vol. 14, pp. 465-471, 1978.

Rissanen, J. [1985]: Modeling by the Minimum Description Length Principle - A Survey. 1985.

Rissanen, J. [1987]: Minimum-Description-Length Principle. In: *Encyclopedia of Statistical Sciences*, Wiley and Sons, 1987, pp. 523-527.

Rosenfeld, A., R.A. Hummel and S.W. Zucker [1976]: Scene Labeling by Relaxation Operations. *IEEE Transactions on System, Man and Cybernetics*, vol. 6, pp. 420-433, 1976.

Rosenfeld, A. and A.C. Kak [1976]: Digital Picture Processing. Academic Press, New York, 1976.

Rosenholm, D. [1987]: Multi-point Matching using the Least-Squares Technique for Elevation of Three-Dimensional Models. *Photogrammetric Engineering and Remote Sensing*, vol. 53, no. 6, pp. 621-626, 1987.

Sanfeliu, A. and K.-S. Fu [1983]: A Distance Measure Between Attributed Relational Graphs for Pattern Recognition. *IEEE Transactions on System, Man and Cybernetics*, vol. 13, no. 3, pp. 353-362, May/June 1983.

Schek, H.-J. and M.H. Scholl [1986]: The Relational Model with Relation-Valued Attributes. *Information Systems*, vol. 11, no. 2, pp. 137-147, June 1986.

Schek, H.-J. and M.H. Scholl [1987]: The Two Roles of Nested Relations in the DASDBS Project. In: *Proc. Workshop on Theory and Applications of Nested Relations and Complex Objects*, S. Abiteboul, P.C. Fischer and H.-J. Schek (eds.), Lecture Notes in Computer Science, vol. 361, Heidelberg, 1987, Springer Verlag, pp. 50-68.

Schewe, H. and W. Förstner [1986]: The Program PALM for Automatic Line and Surface Measurement using Image Matching Techniques. In: *International Archives of Photogrammetry and Remote Sensing*, vol. 26, Rovaniemi, August 1986.

Sester, M. and W. Förstner [1989]: Object Location based on Uncertain Models. In: *Mustererkennung 1989*, Informatik Fachberichte, vol. 219, Hamburg, October 1989, Springer Verlag, pp. 457-464.

Shannon, C.E. and W. Weaver [1949]: The Mathematical Theory of Communication. University of Illinois Press, 1949.

Shapiro, L.G. [1985]: A Fast Structural Matching Algorithm with Applications in Stereo Vision. In: *Proc. 4th Scandinavian Conference on Image Analysis*, vol. 1, June 1985, pp. 159-166.

Shapiro, L.G. and R.M. Haralick [1981]: Structural Description and Inexact Matching. *IEEE Transactions on Pattern Analysis and Machine Intelligence*, vol. 3, pp. 504-519, 1981.

Shapiro, L.G. and R.M. Haralick [1985]: A Metric for Comparing Relational Structures. *IEEE Transactions on Pattern Analysis and Machine Intelligence*, vol. 7, pp. 90-94, 1985.

Shapiro, L.G. and R.M. Haralick [1987]: Relational Matching. *Applied Optics*, vol. 26, pp. 1845-1851, 1987.

Straforini, M., C. Coelho, M. Campani and V. Torre [1990]: On the Understanding of Indoor Scenes. In: *Proc. International Workshop on Robust Computer Vision*, Seattle, WA, October 1990, pp. 151-166.

Sussenguth, E.H. [1965]: A Graph-Theoretic Algorithm for Matching Chemical Structures. *Journal of Chemical Documentation*, vol. 5, pp. 36-43, 1965.

Unger, S.H. [1964]: GIT - A Heuristic Program for Testing Pairs of Directed Line Graphs for Isomorphism. *Communications of the Association of Computing Machinery*, vol. 7, no. 1, pp. 26-34, January 1964.

Ullman, J.R. [1976]: An Algorithm for Subgraph Isomorphism. *Journal of the Association of Computing Machinery*, vol. 23, pp. 31-42, 1976.

Vosselman, G. [1986]: The Precision of a Digital Camera, Master's thesis, Faculty of Geodesy, Technical University of Delft, November 1986.

Vosselman, G. and W. Förstner [1988]: The Precision of a Digital Camera. In: *International Archives of Photogrammetry and Remote Sensing*, vol. 27, Part B1, July 1988, pp. 148-157.

Vosselman, G. [1989]: Symbolic Image Descriptions for Relational Matching. In: *Proc. International Workshop on High Precision Navigation*, Stuttgart / Altensteig-Wart, May 1989, SFB Hochgenaue Navigation, Springer Verlag, pp. 378-391.

Wahl, F.M. [1984]: Digitale Bildsignalverarbeitung. Springer-Verlag, Berlin, Heidelberg, New York, 1984.

Wallace, R.S. and T. Kanade [1989]: Finding Hierarchical Clusters by Entropy Minimization. In: *Proc. Image Understanding Workshop*, Palo Alto, CA, 1989, pp. 1105-1116.

Waltz, D.L. [1972]: Generating Semantic Descriptions from Drawings of Scenes with Shadows. Technical Report 271, M.I.T. Artificial Intelligence Laboratory, Cambridge, MA, 1972.

Waltz, D.L. [1975]: Understanding Drawings of Scenes with Shadows. In: *The Psychology of Computer Vision*, P.H. Winston (ed.), McGraw-Hill, New York, 1975, pp. 19-91.

Wertheimer, M. [1958]: Principles of Perceptual Organization. In: *Readings in Perception*, D. Beardslee and M. Wertheimer (eds.), , Princeton, N.J., 1958, pp. 115-135.

Wilson, H.R. [1983]: Psychophysical Evidence for Spatial Channels. In: *Physical and Biological Processing of Images*, O.J. Braddick and A.C. Sleigh (eds.), 88-99, Springer Verlag, 1983.

Winston, P.H. [1977]: Artificial Intelligence. Addison-Wesley, Reading, MA, 1977.

Witkin, A. [1983]: Scale Space Filtering. In: *Proc. International Joint Conference on Artificial Intelligence*, Karlsruhe, 1983, pp. 1019-1021.

Witkin, A., D. Terzopoulos and M. Kass [1987]: Signal Matching Through Scale Space. *International Journal on Computer Vision*, pp. 133-144, 1987.

Wrobel, B. [1987a]: Digitale Bildzuordnung durch Facetten mit Hilfe von Objektraummodellen. *Zeitschrift für Bildmessung und Luftbildwesen*, vol. 55, no. 3, pp. 93-101, 1987.

Wrobel, B. [1987b]: Facet Stereo Vision (FAST Vision) - A New Approach to Computer Stereo Vision and to Digital Photogrammetry. In: *Proc. ISPRS Intercommission Workshop on "Fast Processing of Photogrammetric Data"*, Interlaken, June 1987, pp. 231-258.

Wrobel, B. [1989]: Geometrisch-physikalische Grundlagen der digitalen Bildmessung. In: *Proceedings of the 42th Photogrammetric Week*, Series of the Institute of Photogrammetry, Stuttgart University, vol. 13, Stuttgart, September 1989, pp. 223-241.

Yuille, A.L. and T.A. Poggio [1986]: Scaling Theorems for Zero Crossings. *IEEE Transactions on Pattern Analysis and Machine Intelligence*, vol. 8, pp. 15-25, 1986.

Zucker, S.W. [1976]: Region Growing: Childhood and Adolescence. *Computer Graphics and Image Processing*, vol. 5, pp. 382-399, 1976.

A Mutual information between a continuous signal and a discretized noisy observation

Given the continuous signal A with an equal distribution

$$p(a) = \frac{1}{x_2 - x_1} \quad \text{on } [x_1, x_2] \tag{A-1}$$

the noise source N with distribution

$$p(n) = \begin{cases} \frac{1}{\Delta n} & \text{on } [-\frac{1}{2}\Delta n, \frac{1}{2}\Delta n] \\ 0 & \text{elsewhere} \end{cases} \tag{A-2}$$

and the discretized noisy observation C which has an equal distribution over n intervals of width Δx

$$P(c_i) = \frac{\Delta x}{x_2 - x_1} \quad \text{for } i = 1, 2, \ldots, n \tag{A-3}$$

the conditional probability density of the original signal A given a discrete noisy observation c_i is

$$p(a|c_i) = \begin{cases} 0 & : a < c_i - \frac{1}{2}\Delta max - \frac{1}{2}\Delta min \\[2mm] \dfrac{a - c_i + \frac{1}{2}\Delta max + \frac{1}{2}\Delta min}{\Delta max \cdot \Delta min} & : \begin{array}{l} c_i - \frac{1}{2}\Delta max - \frac{1}{2}\Delta min \leq a \\ a < c_i - \frac{1}{2}\Delta max + \frac{1}{2}\Delta min \end{array} \\[4mm] \dfrac{1}{\Delta max} & : \begin{array}{l} c_i - \frac{1}{2}\Delta max + \frac{1}{2}\Delta min \leq a \\ a < c_i + \frac{1}{2}\Delta max - \frac{1}{2}\Delta min \end{array} \\[4mm] \dfrac{-a + c_i + \frac{1}{2}\Delta max + \frac{1}{2}\Delta min}{\Delta max \cdot \Delta min} & : \begin{array}{l} c_i + \frac{1}{2}\Delta max - \frac{1}{2}\Delta min \leq a \\ a < c_i + \frac{1}{2}\Delta max + \frac{1}{2}\Delta min \end{array} \\[4mm] 0 & : c_i + \frac{1}{2}\Delta max + \frac{1}{2}\Delta min \leq a \end{cases} \tag{A-4}$$

where Δmax is the maximum of Δn and Δx and Δmin is the minimum of them.

For these distributions the average mutual information between original signal and the discretized noisy observation is

$$H(A; C) = \log\left(\frac{x_2 - x_1}{\Delta max}\right) - \frac{1}{2}\frac{\Delta min}{\Delta max} \tag{A-5}$$

Proof:

$$H(A; C) = \sum_{i=1}^{n} P(c_i) \int_{x_1}^{x_2} p(a|c_i) \log \frac{p(a|c_i)}{p(a)} \, da$$

$$= \sum_{i=1}^{n} \frac{\Delta x}{x_2 - x_1}$$

$$\left[\int_{c_i - \frac{1}{2}\Delta max - \frac{1}{2}\Delta min}^{c_i - \frac{1}{2}\Delta max + \frac{1}{2}\Delta min} \frac{a - c_i + \frac{1}{2}\Delta max + \frac{1}{2}\Delta min}{\Delta max \ \Delta min} \log\left(\frac{a - c_i + \frac{1}{2}\Delta max + \frac{1}{2}\Delta min}{\Delta max \ \Delta min \ \frac{1}{x_2 - x_1}} \right) da \ + \right.$$

$$\int_{c_i - \frac{1}{2}\Delta max + \frac{1}{2}\Delta min}^{c_i + \frac{1}{2}\Delta max - \frac{1}{2}\Delta min} \frac{1}{\Delta max} \log\left(\frac{\frac{1}{\Delta max}}{\frac{1}{x_2 - x_1}} \right) da \ + \qquad \text{(A-6)}$$

$$\left. \int_{c_i + \frac{1}{2}\Delta max - \frac{1}{2}\Delta min}^{c_i + \frac{1}{2}\Delta max + \frac{1}{2}\Delta min} \frac{-a + c_i + \frac{1}{2}\Delta max + \frac{1}{2}\Delta min}{\Delta max \ \Delta min} \log\left(\frac{-a + c_i + \frac{1}{2}\Delta max + \frac{1}{2}\Delta min}{\Delta max \ \Delta min \ \frac{1}{x_2 - x_1}} \right) da \right]$$

Using the substitutions

$$\left. \begin{array}{rcl} t_i & = & \dfrac{a - c_i + \frac{1}{2}\Delta max + \frac{1}{2}\Delta min}{\Delta max \ \Delta min} \\[2mm] da & = & \Delta max \ \Delta min \ dt_i \end{array} \right\} \quad \text{for the first group of integrals} \quad \text{(A-7)}$$

$$\left. \begin{array}{rcl} t_i & = & \dfrac{-a + c_i + \frac{1}{2}\Delta max + \frac{1}{2}\Delta min}{\Delta max \ \Delta min} \\[2mm] da & = & -\Delta max \ \Delta min \ dt_i \end{array} \right\} \quad \text{for the third group of integrals} \quad \text{(A-8)}$$

one gets

$$H(A; C) = \sum_{i=1}^{n} \frac{1}{n}$$

$$\left[\int_{0}^{\frac{1}{\Delta max}} [t_i \log(t_i) + t_i \log(x_2 - x_1)] \ \Delta max \ \Delta min \ dt_i \ + \right.$$

$$\frac{1}{\Delta max} \log \frac{x_2 - x_1}{\Delta max} (\Delta max - \Delta min) \ - \qquad \text{(A-9)}$$

$$\left. \int_{\frac{1}{\Delta max}}^{0} [t_i \log(t_i) + t_i \log(x_2 - x_1)] \ \Delta max \ \Delta min \ dt_i \right]$$

Since the boundaries of the intervals over which the integrals are taken are now independent of the index i, we can write

$$H(A;C) \;=\; 2\,\Delta max\;\Delta min\int_0^{\frac{1}{\Delta max}} t\log(t)\;dt\;+$$

$$2\,\Delta max\;\Delta min\int_0^{\frac{1}{\Delta max}} t\log(x_2-x_1)\;dt\;+ \qquad \text{(A-10)}$$

$$\frac{\Delta max-\Delta min}{\Delta max}\log\left(\frac{x_2-x_1}{\Delta max}\right)$$

Using the partial integration

$$\int x\log x\;dx=\frac{1}{2}x^2\log x-\int\frac{1}{x}\frac{1}{2}x^2\;dx=\frac{1}{2}x^2\log x-\frac{1}{4}x^2 \qquad \text{(A-11)}$$

results in

$$H(A;C) \;=\; 2\,\Delta max\;\Delta min\left(\frac{1}{2}t^2\log(t)-\frac{1}{4}t^2\right)\Bigg|_0^{\frac{1}{\Delta max}}\;+$$

$$2\,\Delta max\;\Delta min\log(x_2-x_1)\,\frac{1}{2}\frac{1}{\Delta max^2}\;+$$

$$\frac{\Delta max-\Delta min}{\Delta max}\log\frac{x_2-x_1}{\Delta max}$$

$$=\;\Delta max\;\Delta min\,\frac{1}{\Delta max^2}\log\left(\frac{1}{\Delta max}\right)-$$

$$\frac{1}{2}\Delta max\;\Delta min\,\frac{1}{\Delta max^2}\;+$$

$$\Delta max\;\Delta min\,\frac{1}{\Delta max^2}\log(x_2-x_1)\;+$$

$$\frac{\Delta max-\Delta min}{\Delta max}\log\left(\frac{x_2-x_1}{\Delta max}\right)$$

$$=\;\frac{\Delta min}{\Delta max}\log\left(\frac{x_2-x_1}{\Delta max}\right)-\frac{1}{2}\frac{\Delta min}{\Delta max}\;+$$

$$\frac{\Delta max-\Delta min}{\Delta max}\log\left(\frac{x_2-x_1}{\Delta max}\right)$$

$$=\;\log\left(\frac{x_2-x_1}{\Delta max}\right)-\frac{1}{2}\frac{\Delta min}{\Delta max} \qquad \text{q.e.d.} \qquad \text{(A-12)}$$

B Distribution of the coordinates of points on a sphere

If a set of points with coordinates (x, y, z) is randomly distributed on the surface of a sphere with origin $(0,0,0)$ and radius 1, the x, y, and z coordinates of those points are equally distributed on the interval $[-1,1]$. Thus the density of the x, y, and z coordinates is a constant on that interval.

For the x-coordinate, this will be proven. Let us consider a half sphere that is parameterized by

$$\vec{x} = \begin{pmatrix} x \\ y \\ z \end{pmatrix} = \begin{pmatrix} \cos \phi \\ \sin \phi \sin \lambda \\ \sin \phi \cos \lambda \end{pmatrix} \tag{B-1}$$

with $0 < \phi \le \frac{\pi}{2}$ and $0 < \lambda \le 2\pi$. Thus, on this half sphere, the x-coordinate is always positive.

The two vectors $\vec{x}_\phi$ and $\vec{x}_\lambda$ are the derivatives of $\vec{x}$ to ϕ and λ. They are both tangent to the sphere surface.

$$\vec{x}_\phi = \begin{pmatrix} -\sin \phi \\ \cos \phi \sin \lambda \\ \cos \phi \cos \lambda \end{pmatrix} \quad \text{and} \quad \vec{x}_\lambda = \begin{pmatrix} 0 \\ \sin \phi \cos \lambda \\ -\sin \phi \sin \lambda \end{pmatrix} \tag{B-2}$$

Their outer product is the surface normal $\vec{n}$

$$\vec{n} - \begin{pmatrix} -\cos \phi \sin \phi \\ -\sin^2 \phi \sin \lambda \\ -\sin^2 \phi \cos \lambda \end{pmatrix} \tag{B-3}$$

with length $\sin \phi$. The size of a surface can be calculated by the integral of this length of the surface normal. Hence, the size of the half sphere is

$$\int_0^{2\pi} \int_0^{\frac{\pi}{2}} \sin \phi \; d\phi \; d\lambda = 2\pi \tag{B-4}$$

The probability that a point out of a set of points, that is equally distributed on the half sphere, has an x-coordinate smaller than X, is the ratio of the size of that part of the half sphere with $x \le X$, and the size of the half sphere. I.e.

$$P(x \le X) = \frac{1}{2\pi} \int_0^{2\pi} \int_{\arccos x}^{\frac{\pi}{2}} \sin \phi \; d\phi \; d\lambda$$

$$= -\cos \phi \Big|_{\arccos x}^{\frac{\pi}{2}} = x \tag{B-5}$$

The density of the x-coordinate therefore is

$$p(x) = \frac{P(x \leq X)}{dX} = 1 \qquad \text{(B-6)}$$

Hence, if a set of points is equally distributed on a sphere, the x-coordinates of these points also have an equal distribution.

C Conditional probability density function of the image line length

Given the conditional probability density function with known scale s

$$p(l_i|l_m, s) = \begin{cases} \dfrac{1}{l_m \cdot s} \dfrac{\frac{l_i}{l_m \cdot s}}{\sqrt{1 - \left(\frac{l_i}{l_m \cdot s}\right)^2}} & \text{for } 0 \leq l_i \leq l_m \cdot s \\ 0 & \text{else} \end{cases} \qquad \text{(C-1)}$$

the scale uncertainty is reflected by

$$\begin{aligned} p(l_i|l_m) &= \int_{s_{min}}^{s_{max}} p(l_i|l_m, s) \cdot p(s|l_m) \; ds \\ &= \int_{s_{min}}^{s_{max}} p(l_i|l_m, s) \cdot p(s) \; ds \end{aligned} \qquad \text{(C-2)}$$

with

$$p(s) = \begin{cases} \dfrac{1}{s_{max} - s_{min}} & \text{for } s_{min} \leq s \leq s_{max} \\ 0 & \text{else} \end{cases} \qquad \text{(C-3)}$$

so that

$$p(l_i|l_m) = \begin{cases} \dfrac{1}{l_m} \dfrac{1}{s_{max} - s_{min}} \left\{ \arcsin\left(\dfrac{l_i}{l_m \cdot s_{min}}\right) - \arcsin\left(\dfrac{l_i}{l_m \cdot s_{max}}\right) \right\} \\ \qquad\qquad\qquad\qquad \text{for } 0 \leq l_i \leq s_{min} \cdot l_m \\ \dfrac{1}{l_m} \dfrac{1}{s_{max} - s_{min}} \left\{ \dfrac{\pi}{2} - \arcsin\left(\dfrac{l_i}{l_m \cdot s_{max}}\right) \right\} \\ \qquad\qquad\qquad\qquad \text{for } s_{min} \cdot l_m < l_i \leq s_{max} \cdot l_m \\ 0 \qquad\qquad\qquad\qquad \text{else} \end{cases} \qquad \text{(C-4)}$$

Proof: for the image line lengths l_i smaller than $s_{min} \cdot l_m$ we have

$$p(l_i|l_m) = \int_{s_{min}}^{s_{max}} \dfrac{1}{l_m \cdot s} \dfrac{\frac{l_i}{l_m \cdot s}}{\sqrt{1 - \left(\frac{l_i}{l_m \cdot s}\right)^2}} \dfrac{1}{s_{max} - s_{min}} \; ds \qquad \text{(C-5)}$$

Using the substitutions

$$\sin \alpha = \dfrac{l_i}{l_m \cdot s} \qquad \text{and} \qquad ds = -\dfrac{l_i}{l_m} \dfrac{\cos \alpha}{\sin^2 \alpha} \; d\alpha \qquad \text{(C-6)}$$

it follows that

$$p(l_i|l_m) = \frac{-1}{l_m}\frac{1}{s_{max}-s_{min}}\int\limits_{\arcsin\left(\frac{l_i}{l_m\cdot s_{min}}\right)}^{\arcsin\left(\frac{l_i}{l_m\cdot s_{max}}\right)} d\alpha \qquad (C\text{-}7)$$

$$= \frac{1}{l_m}\frac{1}{s_{max}-s_{min}}\left\{\arcsin\left(\frac{l_i}{l_m\cdot s_{min}}\right) - \arcsin\left(\frac{l_i}{l_m\cdot s_{max}}\right)\right\}$$

For the image line length l_i between $s_{min}\cdot l_m$ and $s_{max}\cdot l_m$ the density $p(l_i|l_m, s)$ is zero if $l_i > s \cdot l_m$, so that the integral over the scale range is to be taken from $\frac{l_i}{l_m}$ to s_{max}:

$$p(l_i|l_m) = \int\limits_{\frac{l_i}{l_m}}^{s_{max}} \frac{1}{l_m\cdot s}\frac{\frac{l_i}{l_m\cdot s}}{\sqrt{1-\left(\frac{l_i}{l_m\cdot s}\right)^2}}\frac{1}{s_{max}-s_{min}}\,ds$$

$$= \frac{-1}{l_m}\frac{1}{s_{max}-s_{min}}\int\limits_{\frac{\pi}{2}}^{\arcsin\left(\frac{l_i}{l_m\cdot s_{max}}\right)} d\alpha$$

$$= \frac{1}{l_m}\frac{1}{s_{max}-s_{min}}\left\{\frac{\pi}{2} - \arcsin\left(\frac{l_i}{l_m\cdot s_{max}}\right)\right\} \qquad (C\text{-}8)$$

D   Tables with search results

For the five different values of the ε parameter of the ε-A^* search methods the results are given for the partial (left tables) and the full (right tables) search mode. Each table contains the following parameters:

The image name (image name)
The number of investigated nodes (inv.)
The number of expanded nodes (exp.)
The number of calculated transformations (# trafo)
The maximum length of the node stack (max. stack)
The CPU time in seconds (time [s])

The tables of the full tree searches also contain the number of the node at which the best solution was found (node sol.). In case of the partial search this always is the last investigated node.

image name	# nodes inv.	exp.	# trafo	max. stack	time [s]	# nodes inv.	exp.	node sol.	# trafo	max. stack	time [s]
A1	466	466	114	349	325.5	809	470	470	115	349	343.6
A2	28	28	3	36	18.4	75	44	25	4	34	25.1
A3	918	918	228	827	718.8	7280	6788	1371	3216	1796	5944.8
A4	–	–	–	–	–	–	–	–	–	–	–
A5	614	614	62	746	471.6	564	289	222	40	303	245.2
B1	2925	2925	746	2922	1772.2	6700	4237	3082	1236	2922	2592.0
B2	444	444	14	819	319.0	1264	449	444	16	819	351.9
B3	–	–	–	–	–	–	–	–	–	–	–
B4	736	736	108	2175	931.3	2913	740	736	108	2175	1040.2
B5	–	–	–	–	–	–	–	–	–	–	–
C1	–	–	–	–	–	–	–	–	–	–	–
C2	–	–	–	–	–	–	–	–	–	–	–
C3	–	–	–	–	–	–	–	–	–	–	–
C4	–	–	–	–	–	–	–	–	–	–	–
C5	–	–	–	–	–	–	–	–	–	–	–

Table D.1: Search results per image for tree search with $\varepsilon = 0.1$

image name	# nodes inv.	exp.	# trafo	max. stack	time [s]	# nodes inv.	exp.	node sol.	# trafo	max. stack	time [s]
A1	415	415	98	296	316.7	706	421	415	97	298	324.8
A2	20	20	2	29	11.5	70	44	20	4	29	25.0
A3	299	299	72	264	188.5	6696	6598	384	2288	1372	5596.8
A4	1796	1796	168	2607	1155.5	5180	2286	2009	300	2998	1598.9
A5	119	119	12	161	93.4	332	214	104	36	141	180.2
B1	883	883	76	742	304.5	1909	1092	1120	142	784	446.3
B2	44	44	5	93	54.1	152	67	44	11	93	76.2
B3	4111	4111	300	9557	8325.0	14633	4931	5030	436	9557	10531.0
B4	79	79	16	180	79.3	268	93	79	18	180	101.2
B5	219	219	25	326	190.7	546	223	219	25	326	205.1
C1	138	138	24	482	215.6	627	158	138	36	482	251.6
C2	–	–	–	–	–	–	–	–	–	–	–
C3	–	–	–	–	–	–	–	–	–	–	–
C4	3226	3226	546	6849	7780.0	10264	3542	3226	638	6849	8755.5
C5	1918	1918	168	4331	4554.0	7231	3071	1918	574	4331	4554.0

Table D.2: Search results per image for tree search with $\varepsilon = 0.2$

image name	# nodes inv.	exp.	# trafo	max. stack	time [s]	# nodes inv.	exp.	node sol.	# trafo	max. stack	time [s]
A1	319	319	74	196	257.1	522	371	319	82	196	274.2
A2	20	20	2	29	12.2	70	44	20	4	29	24.1
A3	116	116	28	87	60.2	726	627	134	212	158	461.3
A4	127	127	4	239	67.4	882	687	118	160	220	406.5
A5	110	110	10	141	69.3	354	233	140	36	142	184.6
B1	457	457	28	291	144.7	1082	709	948	99	346	269.7
B2	46	46	5	92	58.8	154	69	46	10	92	77.1
B3	62	62	14	111	70.1	1204	1132	432	269	122	880.1
B4	79	79	14	184	72.1	278	99	79	18	185	100.1
B5	141	117	13	74	85.0	211	140	149	27	74	101.3
C1	62	62	16	231	118.5	323	101	62	36	232	178.6
C2	123	123	15	257	172.5	923	747	120	205	243	1072.5
C3	90	90	21	143	90.4	226	123	63	41	112	138.7
C4	95	95	14	188	116.7	1177	871	247	159	383	1179.7
C5	451	451	11	1218	362.4	3179	1899	522	500	1334	2512.9

Table D.3: Search results per image for tree search with $\varepsilon = 0.3$

image name	# nodes inv.	exp.	# trafo	max. stack	time [s]	# nodes inv.	exp.	node sol.	# trafo	max. stack	time [s]
A1	203	203	49	118	169.3	448	370	203	81	118	266.1
A2	30	30	6	35	22.6	86	55	30	8	35	35.2
A3	42	42	13	41	25.4	628	590	73	205	106	450.5
A4	41	41	2	64	25.4	5080	5045	24	1356	667	3187.3
A5	143	143	18	167	82.3	413	268	172	44	167	198.2
B1	916	916	54	372	229.0	1604	1192	1581	139	401	366.6
B2	58	58	6	114	74.4	187	80	58	11	114	93.3
B3	67	67	18	127	85.4	1226	1138	263	270	128	883.3
B4	141	141	23	411	171.5	425	134	111	22	297	148.1
B5	47	47	8	65	39.5	213	151	167	19	65	107.8
C1	116	116	31	300	243.7	381	129	93	44	261	263.6
C2	271	246	34	292	341.0	1000	796	205	200	215	1047.4
C3	91	91	24	149	99.3	547	307	309	80	230	349.0
C4	352	352	51	755	623.9	2729	1271	646	186	1509	1912.9
C5	306	299	40	510	358.5	2377	1735	547	498	634	2349.8

Table D.4: Search results per image for tree search with $\varepsilon = 0.4$

image name	# nodes inv.	exp.	# trafo	max. stack	time [s]	# nodes inv.	exp.	node sol.	# trafo	max. stack	time [s]
A1	103	103	29	48	101.6	368	343	75	81	55	264.5
A2	38	38	8	35	33.2	121	81	59	16	43	65.2
A3	60	60	19	48	41.1	674	618	98	212	95	469.6
A4	69	69	16	85	89.2	5070	5045	20	1356	540	3170.9
A5	245	245	25	264	181.5	607	362	294	48	267	290.2
B1	2226	2226	489	676	646.9	2555	2102	2102	342	466	593.4
B2	96	96	9	218	117.7	329	118	96	14	218	140.4
B3	109	109	25	208	145.6	1340	1171	275	277	208	948.5
B4	180	180	18	479	198.5	680	202	187	23	482	233.9
B5	48	48	9	77	43.5	218	153	172	20	67	110.9
C1	692	651	38	234	512.7	1120	741	747	73	359	675.4
C2	1032	997	61	321	721.4	3790	3370	1130	667	433	4361.8
C3	649	633	41	95	466.9	667	350	299	107	326	419.0
C4	4071	4007	149	4115	5043.8	6398	3596	2975	205	2800	4341.0
C5	1492	1271	97	1101	1233.2	18184	16769	1126	5571	2094	31800.5

Table D.5: Search results per image for tree search with $\varepsilon = 0.5$

Printing: Druckhaus Beltz, Hemsbach
Binding: Buchbinderei Schäffer, Grünstadt

Lecture Notes in Computer Science

For information about Vols. 1–544
please contact your bookseller or Springer-Verlag

Vol. 587: R. Dale, E. Hovy, D. Rösner, O. Stock (Eds.), Aspects of Automated Natural Language Generation. Proceedings, 1992. VIII, 311 pages. 1992. (Subseries LNAI).

Vol. 588: G. Sandini (Ed.), Computer Vision – ECCV '92. Proceedings. XV, 909 pages. 1992.

Vol. 589: U. Banerjee, D. Gelernter, A. Nicolau, D. Padua (Eds.), Languages and Compilers for Parallel Computing. Proceedings, 1991. IX, 419 pages. 1992.

Vol. 590: B. Fronhöfer, G. Wrightson (Eds.), Parallelization in Inference Systems. Proceedings, 1990. VIII, 372 pages. 1992. (Subseries LNAI).

Vol. 591: H. P. Zima (Ed.), Parallel Computation. Proceedings, 1991. IX, 451 pages. 1992.

Vol. 592: A. Voronkov (Ed.), Logic Programming. Proceedings, 1991. IX, 514 pages. 1992. (Subseries LNAI).

Vol. 593: P. Loucopoulos (Ed.), Advanced Information Systems Engineering. Proceedings. XI, 650 pages. 1992.

Vol. 594: B. Monien, Th. Ottmann (Eds.), Data Structures and Efficient Algorithms. VIII, 389 pages. 1992.

Vol. 595: M. Levene, The Nested Universal Relation Database Model. X, 177 pages. 1992.

Vol. 596: L.-H. Eriksson, L. Hallnäs, P. Schroeder-Heister (Eds.), Extensions of Logic Programming. Proceedings, 1991. VII, 369 pages. 1992. (Subseries LNAI).

Vol. 597: H. W. Guesgen, J. Hertzberg, A Perspective of Constraint-Based Reasoning. VIII, 123 pages. 1992. (Subseries LNAI).

Vol. 598: S. Brookes, M. Main, A. Melton, M. Mislove, D. Schmidt (Eds.), Mathematical Foundations of Programming Semantics. Proceedings, 1991. VIII, 506 pages. 1992.

Vol. 599: Th. Wetter, K.-D. Althoff, J. Boose, B. R. Gaines, M. Linster, F. Schmalhofer (Eds.), Current Developments in Knowledge Acquisition - EKAW '92. Proceedings. XIII, 444 pages. 1992. (Subseries LNAI).

Vol. 600: J. W. de Bakker, C. Huizing, W. P. de Roever, G. Rozenberg (Eds.), Real-Time: Theory in Practice. Proceedings, 1991. VIII, 723 pages. 1992.

Vol. 601: D. Dolev, Z. Galil, M. Rodeh (Eds.), Theory of Computing and Systems. Proceedings, 1992. VIII, 220 pages. 1992.

Vol. 602: I. Tomek (Ed.), Computer Assisted Learning. Proceedings, 1992. X, 615 pages. 1992.

Vol. 603: J. van Katwijk (Ed.), Ada: Moving Towards 2000. Proceedings, 1992. VIII, 324 pages. 1992.

Vol. 604: F. Belli, F.-J. Radermacher (Eds.), Industrial and Engineering Applications of Artificial Intelligence and Expert Systems. Proceedings, 1992. XV, 702 pages. 1992. (Subseries LNAI).

Vol. 605: D. Etiemble, J.-C. Syre (Eds.), PARLE '92. Parallel Architectures and Languages Europe. Proceedings, 1992. XVII, 984 pages. 1992.

Vol. 606: D. E. Knuth, Axioms and Hulls. IX, 109 pages. 1992.

Vol. 607: D. Kapur (Ed.), Automated Deduction – CADE-11. Proceedings, 1992. XV, 793 pages. 1992. (Subseries LNAI).

Vol. 608: C. Frasson, G. Gauthier, G. I. McCalla (Eds.), Intelligent Tutoring Systems. Proceedings, 1992. XIV, 686 pages. 1992.

Vol. 609: G. Rozenberg (Ed.), Advances in Petri Nets 1992. VIII, 472 pages. 1992.

Vol. 610: F. von Martial, Coordinating Plans of Autonomous Agents. XII, 246 pages. 1992. (Subseries LNAI).

Vol. 611: M. P. Papazoglou, J. Zeleznikow (Eds.), The Next Generation of Information Systems: From Data to Knowledge. VIII, 310 pages. 1992. (Subseries LNAI).

Vol. 612: M. Tokoro, O. Nierstrasz, P. Wegner (Eds.), Object-Based Concurrent Computing. Proceedings, 1991. X, 265 pages. 1992.

Vol. 613: J. P. Myers, Jr., M. J. O'Donnell (Eds.), Constructivity in Computer Science. Proceedings, 1991. X, 247 pages. 1992.

Vol. 614: R. G. Herrtwich (Ed.), Network and Operating System Support for Digital Audio and Video. Proceedings, 1991. XII, 403 pages. 1992.

Vol. 615: O. Lehrmann Madsen (Ed.), ECOOP '92. European Conference on Object Oriented Programming. Proceedings. X, 426 pages. 1992.

Vol. 616: K. Jensen (Ed.), Application and Theory of Petri Nets 1992. Proceedings, 1992. VIII, 398 pages. 1992.

Vol. 617: V. Mařík, O. Štěpánková, R. Trappl (Eds.), Advanced Topics in Artificial Intelligence. Proceedings, 1992. IX, 484 pages. 1992. (Subseries LNAI).

Vol. 618: P. M. D. Gray, R. J. Lucas (Eds.), Advanced Database Systems. Proceedings, 1992. X, 260 pages. 1992.

Vol. 619: D. Pearce, H. Wansing (Eds.), Nonclassical Logics and Information Proceedings. Proceedings, 1990. VII, 171 pages. 1992. (Subseries LNAI).

Vol. 620: A. Nerode, M. Taitslin (Eds.), Logical Foundations of Computer Science – Tver '92. Proceedings. IX, 514 pages. 1992.

Vol. 621: O. Nurmi, E. Ukkonen (Eds.), Algorithm Theory – SWAT '92. Proceedings. VIII, 434 pages. 1992.

Vol. 622: F. Schmalhofer, G. Strube, Th. Wetter (Eds.), Contemporary Knowledge Engineering and Cognition. Proceedings, 1991. XII, 258 pages. 1992. (Subseries LNAI).

Vol. 623: W. Kuich (Ed.), Automata, Languages and Programming. Proceedings, 1992. XII, 721 pages. 1992.

Vol. 624: A. Voronkov (Ed.), Logic Programming and Automated Reasoning. Proceedings, 1992. XIV, 509 pages. 1992. (Subseries LNAI).

Vol. 625: W. Vogler, Modular Construction and Partial Order Semantics of Petri Nets. IX, 252 pages. 1992.

Vol. 626: E. Börger, G. Jäger, H. Kleine Büning, M. M. Richter (Eds.), Computer Science Logic. Proceedings, 1991. VIII, 428 pages. 1992.

Vol. 628: G. Vosselman, Relational Matching. IX, 190 pages. 1992.